Environmental Education

Environmental Education

Babita Verma

KUNAL BOOKS
New Delhi-110 002

KUNAL BOOKS
4648/21, First Floor,
Ansari Road, Daryaganj,
New Delhi-110002
Phones: 011-23275069, 9811043697
E-mail: kunalbooks@gmail.com
Website: www.kunalbooks.in

Environmental Education

First Published 2009
Reprint 2018
ISBN: 978-81-907129-9-6

Published in India by Prem Singh Bisht for Kunal Books, and Printed at Milan Enterprises, Delhi.

Contents

Preface

Environmental education aims for a democratic society in which effective, environmentally literate citizens participate with creativity and responsibility. Eco- education/ environmental education is not a new concept. It has been in existence since the origin of humankind, as all human knowledge is derived out of interaction with nature and learning from nature. As human society evolved and progressed, human being involved themselves in pursuit that made our living more and more conducive and comfortable. During the process, history also witnessed the emergence of various problems, both from the natural and social environments.

Environmental education refers to organized efforts to teach about how natural environments function and, particularly, how human beings can manage their behavior and ecosystems in order to live sustainably. The term is often used to imply education within the school system, from primary to post-secondary. However, it is sometimes used more broadly to include all efforts to educate the public and other audiences, including print materials, websites, media campaigns, etc. Related disciplines include outdoor education and experiential education.

Environmental education has been considered an additional or elective subject in much of traditional K-12 curriculum. At the elementary school level, environmental education can take the form of science enrichment curriculum, natural history field trips, community service projects, and participation in outdoor science schools. In secondary school, environmental curriculum can be a focused subject within the sciences or is a part of student interest groups or clubs. At the undergraduate and graduate level, it can be considered its own field within education, environmental studies, environmental science and policy, ecology, or human/cultural ecology programmes.

Environmental education has crossover with the disciplines of outdoor education and experiential education. Both disciplines complement environmental education yet have unique philosophies. The goal of environmental education is to develop a world population that is aware of, and concerned about, the environmental and its associated problems, and which has the knowledge, skills, attitudes, motivations, and commitment to work individually and collectively toward solutions of current problems and the prevention of new ones. Environmental education has its roots among a cross-section of people in developed countries which witnessed the systematic destruction of its environment about 30-40 years ago.

Babita Verma

1

Introduction

Education is also undergoing review and change. Reorienting education as a whole towards sustainability involves the various levels of formal, non-formal and informal education at all levels of society. Environmental education has developed within the conceptual framework that emerged from the first international conference in Tbilisi (1977) and is now seen as education for sustainability. This allowed environmental education to address the broad range of issues and concerns included in Agenda 21 and others which evolved through the meetings of the Commission on Sustainable Development (UNESCO 1997).

The key international conventions on environment place a high value on public awareness, education and training and obtaining information through monitoring as essential elements for the success of the conventions. For example, the Convention on Biological Diversity emphasizes the importance of public education and awareness through promoting and encouraging measures required for the conservation of biological diversity. Since the convention came into force in December 1995, the contracting parties (countries) have been motivated to address issues related to education and awareness on biodiversity.

In addition countries in the region recognize the

immensity of the challenges they face, and of the vital role that environmental education can play in meeting these challenges. There is a growing perception by governments of the need to integrate environmental education information and communication into the country's on-going programmes. As a result of the Agenda 21, the level of cooperation and collaboration between environmental and the educational institutions has increased. In some countries, governmental environmental agencies have statutory requirements to engage in activities related to environmental education and awareness. For example, the Malaysian Department of Environment has established an educational division under the Environmental Quality Act, which is actively engaged in promoting and implementing a variety of activities in many countries of the Asia.

The pursuit of sustainable development and environmental conservation policies, objectives and targets requires the public to be sufficiently sensitized about the multiple dimensions of environment and development. Awareness and understanding of environmental issues provide the basis and rationale for commitment and meaningful action towards environmentally sound and sustainable development. This chapter provides an overview of developments in environmental education, information, awareness and training in the Asian and Pacific region during the 1990s. The trends and patterns in environmental education in formal and non- formal sectors, and initiatives and programmes that have been undertaken by governments, non-governmental organizations, communities and by regional and international organizations are also identified. The underlying needs for environmental education, information and communication are also discussed with a particular emphasis on the constraints and key issues that need attention.

Environmental Education

Main Trends and Conditions Education has been identified as a critical driving force for change in the Asian and Pacific Region, and countries and regional organizations have adopted a range of strategies for implementing programmes in environmental education. The overall trends in environmental education information and communication in the region reflect the concerns of people and societies in transition. Environmental education is now being seen as an instrument and a process that enables participation and learning by people of all ages, based on two-way communication rather than the old paradigm of a one-way flow of information, from teachers co pupils. The content and substance of environmental Sedan and the Pacific Region environmental topics have been included in education courses, through integrating environmental concerns in other subjects and through specific courses for the environment.

Government, NGOs, educational institutions and media have undertaken some serious efforts to meet the growing environmental challenges by promoting environmental education, information and communication in their respective countries. Activities such as green bank, green press, eco-lubs, eco-polies, eco-farming and eco-harvesting; are emerging in the region. Special economic incentives (such as subsidy, tax-exemption and other incentives) are provided to schools in some countries where environmental education courses are offered. There is greater recognition of the role of NGOs and civil society organizations, and the need for meaningful community participation in debates and action programmes aimed at education and training for sustainable development. NGOs and governments are increasingly working together, reinforcing each other's strengths and outreach. Linkages between governmental institutions and NGOs are improving in most countries of the region, and in some cases, governments are actually depending on mature and experienced NGOs to promote environmental awareness, communication, and training activities.

Formal Environmental Education

Environmental education is increasingly a prominent part of primary, secondary and tertiary education in Asia and the Pacific. The formal education sector plays a vital role in environmental education and awareness by exposing the younger generation to the information, issues, analyses and interpretations on environment and development. A number of factors have influenced the development of environmental education in the region. The two over-arching factors are national education policy and national environment and population policy. These policies are a reflection of national cultural values, priorities and socio-economic goals in most countries. The national environmental education policy is usually the result of decisions made in these broader fields. For example, environmental education in Australia has seen two major shifts since 1970s. First, there has been a distinct move away from nature and science-based environmental education to a concern with the social, economic and political aspects of sustainable development.

There has also been a major shift from schools to adult and community environmental education. Rather than establishing a new subject, most countries have opted to infuse environmental education objectives and strategies into the existing curricula, while some other countries practice both options. In addition, the focus on practical learning in the real world in environmental education helps schools to address important general educational objectives related to values and to skills development. Nationally determined syllabi often provide for a coordinated programme of environmental topics in both primary and secondary schools in countries of the region. However, there is some lack of coordination at different levels of education in the national framework, which prevents the development of a comprehensive environmental education programme.

Primary and Secondary Levels

The diversity of approaches in primary and secondary

education seen across the Asian and Pacific Region are based on each country's major and threatened resources, and issues of concern. For example, in the Maldives, environmental education and awareness programmes highlight issues of the marine environment emerging from the National Environment Action Plan of 1989 whereas in Nepal, the national goals of education are to teach thoughtful protection and wise use of the natural environment and national heritage. In Nepal, the general need of environmental protection from specific problems resulting from population pressure on natural resources, and the links between environment, population and natural resources, were addressed in the environmental education plan.

In Republic of Korea, during the 1990s, "Environment" and "Environmental Science" were included in the middle school curriculum as separate courses, attributing to the common understanding that environmental education for young children was the most important means to solve persistent environmental pollution. In order to raise young people's awareness of environmental preservation, and to cultivate environmental perspectives, the Republic of Korea designated 63 schools as demonstration environmental schools from 1985, and has disseminated their best practices to an additional 26 schools in 1999. These schools are now eligible for subsidies and environment- related educational materials.

In People's Republic of China, environmental education is coupled with the working schedule of public agencies and educational institutions. This was formalized by a regulation issued by the National Bureau in the Conference of National Environmental Education in 1992. At pre-school and primary levels, environmental education is carried out through games, audiovisual means and the study of natural systems. In secondary schools, environmental concepts are infused into the courses of physics, chemistry, biology and geography.

At the same time, the teachers use local examples to help develop environmental understanding among the students. In small island countries of the South Pacific sub region, considerable effort is directed towards infusion of environmental education into various subjects within the primary and secondary school systems. The syllabus for the secondary level has a strong emphasis on environmental studies, developed either independently, as in the Solomon Islands and Papua New Guinea, or in collaboration with the South Pacific Regional Environmental Programme, SPREP.

Tertiary Level

Tertiary level education has responded to the increasing demand for environmental managers and experts in the 1990s. Key trends have been observed across the region in relation to environmental education at tertiary level these include:

- basic environmental concepts and elements added to existing courses at undergraduate and postgraduate levels, for all students irrespective of their courses;
- new environmental units or modules introduced into a large number of courses at undergraduate and post-graduate levels, thus increasing the depth and detail of environmental study;
- new non-degree programmes and courses (at foundation, certificate or diploma levels) introduced by tertiary education institutions to cater to the demand for in-service training and upgrading of knowledge and understanding on environmental issues and practices;
- an increase in the publication of relevant textbooks and audio visual material;
- greater emphasis on training the trainers, and in streng-thening the tertiary education system and research capabilities;
- more research on environmental education policies and practices;
- a greater dialogue and information exchange between the users of environmental skills and talent, in government, private and NGO sectors etc., and the

institutions of tertiary education, ensuring, education and training address prevailing practical needs; and

- increasing emphasis placed on adult and community education, using both formal and non-formal methods to raise the overall environmental literacy levels.

Increase in environmental studies has been a response to the market realities, and also to the growing recognition of the environmental crisis and the management options available. Countries have adopted different mechanisms to cater to their specific needs in tertiary education. For example, in Viet Nam in 1995, the Ministry of Teaching and Education made it compulsory for a course in Environment and Man to be taught in all aspects of natural sciences, social sciences, humanities, agriculture etc., with more specialized environmental science and technical courses in other university courses. Since the early 1990s, short, medium and long-term postgraduate courses for environmental managers and researchers have been conducted in various specialized centres.

Specialized degree courses have been introduced in Thailand, at graduate level, with compulsory course introduced and targeted to first year undergraduates. The courses raise awareness and understanding of topical environmental issues and are integrated with other courses, especially science and social science. In People's Republic of China and Pakistan, many colleges and universities have introduced environmental courses for undergraduates and postgraduates, and have also directed then towards training professionals and officials. In Mongolia, the government has prepared a master plan for environmental education and awareness, which will cover both formal and non- formal education and communication. However, constraints that prevent countries in Asia and the Pacific from achieving their environmental education and training needs are evident.

At a UNESCO sponsored regional seminar on

environmental education in 1996, it was noted: "Each country has already initiated a number of education and training programmes at the tertiary or higher level of education that are related to aspects of the environment. In various ways and to varying degrees, each of the countries has responded to the problems of the environment with environmental laws and regulations, and with associated political and institutional initiatives. However, in all countries, the development of persons with the conceptual understandings and skills that these regulatory intentions require for implementation and management lags well behind what is needed".

Materials and Study Aids

In line with the growing interest and activity in environmental education, awareness and training, the demand for educational materials and study aids has also increased. However, the limited availability of materials may not meet individual country requirements in terms of local language and in coverage of the most relevant issues to the country. Many government and non-government institutions have risen to this challenge. For example, in Malaysia, the Academy of Writers was enlisted to produce storybooks that will instil environmental values and attitudes amongst primary school children. A similar initiative has been made in the South Pacific sub region where there have been several efforts to produce locally relevant environmental education material at the primary and secondary school levels. A widely felt constraint has been the lack of standardization in textbooks and other material on environmental issues and a failure to provide the full information base.

While the subject of environment can be interpreted and presented in many ways, and it can be looked at through a scientific or cultural angle, there is a basic need to present facts accurately and discuss issues in a balanced manner. If this is lacking, the wider goals of environmental education cannot be met. An extensive review of environmental textbooks, supplementary readers and other material is required in many countries of the region as part of a process to improve their quality. Establishment of environmental study centres has helped a great deal in developing materials and study aids for both formal and non-formal environmental education. Such centres also provide students with information, insights and practical activities, and adult visitors gain information and advice. In Indonesia, the Ministries of Environment and Education have been collaborating since 1979 in establishing Environmental Study Centres (PSLs) in all public universities.

By 1997, there were more than 72 PSLs covering all 27 provinces of Indonesia. These centres perform three functions: education and training pertaining to environmental management; extension services, fostering public education and awareness; and research and surveys in support of environmental management. The Department of Environmental Quality Promotion (DEQP) in Thailand has supported the establishment of Provincial Environmental Education Centres (PEEC) in selected schools since 1995 and are expected to expand these to every province by 2001. The main objectives are to develop environmental education materials and tools in relation to local environmental problems, and to strengthen the capability of environmental educators in all parts of the country.

Issues and Constraints

There are many constraints and barriers to the widespread adoption and practice of environmental education in the region. In the formal education sector, class sizes are often large and teachers lack resources and experience in interactive pupil-centred teaching strategies. School curricula are also dominated by a competitive academic curriculum which prioritizes end-of-course examinations and discourages the development of locally and personally relevant intellectual skills. Outside the formal education sector, environmental education is often poorly organized and resourced. Another common constraint is the lack of clear integration of environmental education objectives and programmes with national education and environmental policies. In some countries, the absence of national policies or guidelines for environmental education has resulted in a lack of coherent strategies and long term planning.

Even in those countries which do have such policies, the educational systems are often insufficiently dynamic to accommodate the evolving social, economic, political and conservation aspects of sustainable development. The important pre-requisites for the successful introduction of environmental education in schools include: the existence of clear and well communicated policies; the political will and availability of sufficient resources for implementation; curricula revision; proper preparation of teachers through in-service training; the availability of relevant materials in local languages; networks for exchange of expertise between teachers; and adequate assessment and incentives for teachers development. It is encouraging to note that in spite of many constraints, practitioners and promoters of environmental education have found innovative ways of teaching throughout the region.

Non-formal Education

Non-formal environmental educational activities exist alongside the formal educational systems, at curricular and extra curricular levels, in occupational training, and through wide public awareness activities through non-formal channels such as mass media, and voluntary organizations. Different communities, institutions and individuals choose methods and practices that best suit their local needs and capacities.

Learning by Doing

In several countries, there are efforts to get students to relate to local problems, while understanding their global implications. In Bangladesh, an environmental education programme called Muktangan Siksha, or open-air education, encourages field programmes related to the surroundings and communities. In Myanmar, an imaginative pre-school and lower primary environmental programme bases its teaching on a study of the surroundings, or patwinkyin, without formal textbooks. In Sri Lanka, a WWF-supported innovative environmental education programme involving over 750 schools has been implementing an approach called 'greening of learning'. In this, students are encouraged to beautify the school garden, start a plant nursery or engage in other 'green' activities within the school premises.

Due to its success the WWF has started introducing the same concepts and approaches in other countries, such as Viet Nam. Research and advocacy organizations are increasingly involved in developing non-formal environmental activities. For example, Development Alternatives (DA) located in India, has launched the Community Led Environmental Action Network (CLEAN) which promotes among school children and communities activities based on the "four r" concept: refuse, reduce, recycle and reuse. In several countries, government agencies or NGOs support nature clubs or environmental societies in schools as a means of encouraging and inspiring students to undertake non-formal environmental activities.

Outdoor Activities

Government agencies as well as NGOs have developed a wide array of outdoor activities that expose youth and adults to different aspects of environmental awareness, action and understanding. For example in Nepal, Environmental Camps for Conservation Awareness (ECCA), a local NGO, has been active for over a decade in organising outdoor environmental activities aimed at children, both able and disabled. These camps are held at places of environmental significance and aim to raise awareness about conservation issues, and to potential careers in conservation. Similar environmental camps have become a regular feature in many countries. For example, in Malaysia, environmental awareness camps are regularly organized by the Department of Environment. Tine camps are for children between 14 and 16 years of age, at the Nature Education Centre (NEC) established in 1992 by the Malaysian Nature Society.

In Singapore, the Ministry of Environment allocates small portions of the beach to volunteering schools under an 'Adopt a Beach' programme. Students are then responsible for keeping that stretch of the beach clean, and in that process learn aspects of the coastal and marine environment. The China Association for Science and Technology (CAST) is engaged in the promotion of non- formal science education for children and youth. CAST has 165 natural science societies and is established at county level all over the country. CAST relies on its member scientists and technologists to provide the knowledge base and necessary human resources for various activities organized to promote better understanding of science, technology and environmental issues.

Also in People's Republic of China, the State Environmental Protection Administration (SEPA) is playing a lead role in non-formal activities, and has introduced the Global Learning and Observations to Benefit the Environment (GLOBE) Programme, a worldwide network focusing on science and education, which brings together students, teachers and scientists in order to share information on monitoring the global environment. In Australia, Water-watch was established in the early 1990s as a national level, community-based water quality monitoring programme under the National Landcare Programme. Monitoring water quality on a regular basis gives communities a greater understanding of the natural environment, and may lead to action which will have local, regional or even national benefits. Both school children and adults participate in water monitoring activities, and government funding is provided through facilitators who have been appointed in each state attached to a lead state government agency.

Innovative Approaches

New strategies and innovations for environmental education have been developed and applied throughout the region. For example, in Singapore, the Ministry of Environment in 1996 published the 'Fun and Discovery Through Environmental Clubs', outlining environmental activities and clubs. Similar publications have been developed in Japan, India and Bangladesh. The observation of National Environment Days and Weeks across the region, provide a focal point for environmental activities, including seminars and exhibitions. In New Zealand, school education kits on sustainable agriculture are also provided to educate young people about agriculture and to survey changes in land management and planning. Japan, has various examples of innovative education, public awareness and training activities including, Environmental Counselor Registration System, the Environmental Activities Evaluation Programme and various campaigns for conservation of natural resources and energy.

In addition to these programmes, the "Junior Eco Club programme" supported by the Environment Agency has been a very effective programme at the elementary and junior high school age children level. Club activities are supported by local governments, and a nationwide festival for the Club is organized at the end of each school year. There are about 4 000 clubs with 70 000 children in Japan and its popularity is increasing (ITO 1999). Rising to the challenge of going beyond mere awareness raising, the Centre for Environment Education (CEE) in India has produced an exhibition package called 'Act Now'. It focuses on some actions that people can take in their everyday lives to help improve the environment. Another environmental education package produced by CEE consists of a one-hour video story in Hindi called Dhraki, which discusses some concepts of drought, conservation of water, land and vegetation, and the management of exotic plant species.

The accompanying booklet suggests ways of developing activities that will involve children or other viewers on these issues and themes and has been used widely in classrooms, environmental camps and workshops. In response to the lack of material the CEE has also developed the Environmental Education Bank, providing situation specific material for use in both formal and non-formal instructional situations. Such materials include physical resources like posters, kites, booklets, films, publications and a computerized database of over 800 environmental concepts, 2 500 activities and 600 case studies.

The Bank is usually accessed through a five-day workshop, organized by the Centre at the request of small groups. In Thailand, an example of innovative education and public awareness activities related to sustainable development is a Management of Science and Environment course in Hard Amra Aksornluckvittaya School, in Samutprakan Province. This project used local problems, such as a degraded mangrove, to let the student groups analyse problems systematically, searching for options and solutions and preparing work plans for action. As a result, teachers and students replanted the mangroves in the Asokaram Temple and used the area as a study site.

Environmental Training

Agenda 21 states that training is one of the most important means to develop human resources and facilitate the transition to a more sustainable world. "It should have a job-specific focus, aimed at filling gaps in knowledge and skill, and would help individuals find employment and be involved in environmental and developmental work. At the same time, training programmes should promote a greater awareness of the environment and development issues as a two-way learning process".

Types of Training

Teachers in Formal Education

In a large number of countries in the region, teacher-training programmes at both pre-service and in-service levels have incorporated elements of environmental education. In general, governments of most the Asian and Pacific Region are responsible for training teachers in formal environmental education.

In Malaysia, the establishment of National Institute for Environmental Skill and Training (IKLAS) is an important step forward for the Department of Environment to equip its own personnel, as well as staff of other related government agencies and private sector, with the knowledge and skills for pollution control and sound environmental management. The IKLAS is expected to be operational by the year 2001. Similarly, in Thailand, the Ministry of Education has trained teachers, administrators, educational planners, and non-formal educators. In Sri Lanka, March for Conservation, a university-based NGO, has designed modules for introducing environmental concepts to primary and secondary teachers, and conducts short-term training programmes for teachers.

Regionally, initiatives for training teachers focus mainly on material development and training of trainers. Learning for a Sustainable Environment: Innovation in Teacher Education through Environmental Education Project is a joint undertaking of UNESCO's Asia Pacific Centre for Educational Innovation for Development (ACEID) and Australia's Griffith University. This long-term project seeks to expand the range of innovative practices used in teaching education programmes by introducing teachers and teachers-in-training to the curriculum planning skills and teaching methodologies of environmental education. In the South Pacific sub region, teacher training in formal education is seen to be the key to the success of environmental education in schools. A teacher's guide to environmental education has been produced for adaptation by all countries. Several teacher- training workshops have been held at national and sub regional level, where the teachers are encouraged to use outdoor education and investigative learning approaches.

Practitioners of Non-formal Education

Training for the practitioners of non-formal education is less systematic in most countries, and on the whole fewer opportunities exist. This is partly due to the enormous diversity of professional backgrounds of the individuals engaged in non-formal environmental education activities. Most non-formal education activities are designed and carried out by NGOs or community organizations, whose large numbers and wide geographical spread makes it difficult to expose them to centralized and long-term training programmes. More effective in their case are short-term refresher courses and skills development seminars and workshops. The Indian Centre for Environmental Education, offers a training Programme in Environmental Education for Indian and overseas participants and introduces various approaches and methods in communicating environmental messages to different target groups.

The CEE in cooperation with IUCN and WWF also offers a Certificate Course in Environment Education (CCEE) as a means of in-service training for professionals already engaged in environmental education work. The Centre for Environmental Concerns (CEC) in the Philippines, offer a course that includes elements of community- based rehabilitation technology, community-based environmental monitoring, and participatory approaches to environmental education. In Bangladesh, the Environment and Social Development Organization (ESDO) has conducted, with the support of the Advocacy Institute in the US, several national workshops to train local activists, with examples of strategies and practices of the US counterparts. In the South Pacific sub region, organizations like SPREP and the SPC (Secretariat of the Pacific Community) have concentrated on providing communication skills for extension workers in specific fields such as fisheries, coral reef monitoring and conservation area management.

Training Media Professionals

Training and sensitizing journalists on different aspects of the environment remain urgent needs in most countries of the region where the standards of environmental reporting are low. Even journalists and broadcast producers who are well trained in their craft face new challenges in reporting on issues related to environment and sustainable development. The technical nature of most environmental issues requires the ability to grasp these technicalities and then to interpret these in layman's terms.

Many environmental stories involve the assessment of risks and the weighing of costs and benefits, all of which require experience, skill and a strong sense of balance in journalists. In spite of a decade of heightened interest in environmental journalism in the region, the formal training courses and curricular for journalists in many countries do not as yet pay sufficient attention to the specialized needs of environmental journalism. However, some national forums of environmental journalists regularly organize short training activities, including workshops, seminars conferences etc., for the benefit of their members and other environmental journalists.

The national forums in Bangladesh, People's Republic of China, Japan, Malaysia, Nepal, Pakistan, Philippines and Sri Lanka have been particularly active in this respect. For example, from 1995 the Japanese Forum of Environmental Journalists (JFEJ) has organized an annual environmental study tour of Japan for selected journalists from both print and electronic media in the region. Journalists and producers are exposed to Japanese environmental policy and practice through a series of lectures, discussions. At a regional level, several initiatives are noteworthy. UNEP has conducted several workshops, seminars and training programmes under its Environmental, Communication and Information Strategy for Asia and the Pacific.

A high-level meeting was held in Beijing, People's Republic of China, in 1996 that brought together editors and managers from leading publications in the region to discuss how to boost environment related coverage in the media. Parallel to this, training workshops were organized for environmental journalists drawn from several countries in the region. In the Pacific Island countries, SPREP and UNESCO have cooperated on a series of national 'Environment and Media' workshops to train television, radio and print journalists in incorporating environmental issues in their reporting. Five training workshops were held in 1999 (Samoa, Tonga, Marshall Islands, Cook Islands and Fiji) and an additional 4 are proposed for 2000.

One weakness in short-term training activities available for journalists is that most programmes are targeted only at the print media, with relatively few opportunities for journalists and producers working in radio and television. With this in mind, regional organizations have started supporting training for broadcast journalists. Panos South Asia office, based in Kathmandu, is placing particular emphasis on training radio journalists to improved coverage of environment and development. Panos has also organized several field study tours for environmental journalists from South Asia to better understand the complex issues of trans-boundary water resource sharing and management. The training of audio-visual communications is another widely felt training need and several organizations are now engaged in offering such training.

The Worldview International Foundation regularly conducts training courses for NGO activists and media professionals in the use of video for documenting environmental abuses, issues and problems. Meanwhile, the Television Trust for the Environment (TVE) annually organizes a technical skills development workshop for NGO professionals on using television and video for awareness and advocacy work. It has also conducted national level training programmes on environmental video programme making for producers in People's Republic of China, Bangladesh and Sri Lanka, each tied up to an actual production that was later broadcast. In mid 1999, Panos and TVE collaborated in organising a South Asian level workshop that exposed mainstream print and broadcast journalists to the effective ways of using the Internet for researching environmental stories, and also disseminating them through the World Wide Web.

Specialized and Technical Training

The number of specialized training programmes at country and regional levels has increased since the 1990s, a reflection of the greater market demand for specialized environmental skills and environmental managers. Traditional areas of environment related specialized training includes protected area management, environmental quality monitoring and environmental information systems. Relatively new areas of training include, environmental economics, environmental impact assessment (EIA) and in the adoption and implementation of environmental standards, especially the ISO 14000 series. In Malaysia, for instance, universities have worked with experts from the SIRIM Industry Standards Committee on the Environment to produce both training materials and training modules for ISO 14000 implementation.

Training activities are also conducted by some of the larger and well-established NGOs working nationally or regionally. For example, the Society for Participatory Research in Asia (PRIA), based in New Delhi, India, regularly organizes national and regional level training courses and programmes on occupational and environmental health. The UNEP International Environmental Technology Centre (IETC), based in Osaka, Japan, organizes specialized training programmes at regional and sub regional level under its capacity building initiative. Professional target groups for its post-graduate training interventions are decision-makers in central and local governments, civil society and industry, academia, NGOs and senior trainers attached to regional or national environmental training centres. Other specialized training includes the Regional Community Forestry Training Centre (RCFTC), Thailand, which runs several courses on areas such as community-based ecotourism for forest conservation and rural development, offered in collaboration with the Institute of Forestry in Nepal.

The United States-Asia Environmental Partnership (US-AEP) is a regional initiative that provides technical assistance and training to Asian governments, business and industry, and NGOs in relation to environmental management and technologies. Training focuses on five critical environmental areas: addressing global climate change; providing safe drinking water and wastewater management; reducing urban air pollution; promoting solid waste management (including medical waste and landfill methane recovery); and participating in regional policy projects on performance matrix, environmental management systems, and public disclosure. The Pacific Islands Climate Change Assistance Programme (PICCAP) at SPREP, undertakes Greenhouse Gas Inventory and Vulnerability and Adaptation Assessment (V&A) training for countries who have insufficient capacity to undertake these tasks, in order to fulfil their obligations under the United Nations Framework Convention on Climate Change.

Case Study

A Training Success in the South Pacific

The Pacific Island Climate Change Assistance Programme (PICCAP) is a GEF funded regional climate change project. It involves 10 Pacific Island countries (Cook Islands, Federated States of Micronesia, Fiji, Kiribati, Marshall Islands, Nauru, Samoa, Solomon Islands, Tuvalu, Vanuatu) and is coordinated and executed by the South Pacific Regional Environment Programme (SPREP). PICCAP has been designed in such a way as to strengthen the capacities of participating countries, in terms of training, institutional strengthening and planning activities, to enable them to meet their reporting obligations under the United Nations Framework Convention on Climate Change (UNFCCC). In less than three years, PICCAP has achieved excellent results.

Through its sub regional approach, PICCAP has fostered greater sharing of information, built up a qualified pool of climate change experts from within the South Pacific sub region, instituted cross-sectoral climate change country teams with technical and policy-related functions, established a database of climate change information, and assisted with the development of national climate change action plans which have formed the basis for initial national communications and the implementation of the UNFCCC at national level. Much effort has gone into the training and related activities needed to the build in-country capacity that has allowed these countries to prepare and report on their national greenhouse gas (GHG) inventories, GHG mitigation strategies, assessments of vulnerability to climate change impacts and of adaptation options, national climate change action plans, and enabled their initial national communications to the UNFCCC.

One notable achievement under PICCAP has been the design, development, and delivery of a comprehensive university-based vulnerability and adaptation certificate programme for the region. This was done in conjunction with the Climate Change Training Programme implemented by UNITAR and with co-funding from the Government of New Zealand, and included the transfer of entire training course from the originating institution (the International Global Change Institute IGCI, University of Waikato, New Zealand) to a regional institution, the University of the South Pacific in Fiji. PICCAP is an example of a sub regional training and technical and policy-related cooperation activity that has enhanced national capacities to address an environmental issue of critical importance to the small island developing states of the Pacific.

Main Trends and Conditions

As countries in the Asian and Pacific Region address environmental management problems and create institutional mechanisms in response, the training needs in environmental related sectors continue to expand rapidly. A variety of training and skills development activities are being pursued at local, national, sub regional and regional levels by governments, NGOs as well as by international and inter-governmental organizations in the region. In terms of content, duration, methodology, instruction mechanisms, types of participants and other factors, there is great diversity, but the end result is an overall strengthening of skills and capacity to better manage the environment and natural resources.

The need for greater numbers of trained personnel in a wider range of environment related disciplines and skills are required for:

- the implementation of National Environmental Management Plans (NEMPs) or action plans (NEAPs);
- servicing of international environmental conventions and treaties that many countries have become parties or signatories to, each of which places specialized demands and requirements on the participating countries;
- the adoption of international environmental standards, such as ISO 14000, as well as environmental policy and management tools including environmental impact assessment, environmental audits and eco-labelling, which require well-trained and highly skilled personnel in sufficient numbers within government, industry and other sectors, and
- the provision of environmental procedures, systems and checks, demanded by the increased environmental awareness of the public.

Market forces are also demanding greater commitment to, and professionalism in, environmental management and compliance. A question often arises as to who should be trained given the limited available resources. While environment related training is needed across the board in a large number of sectors, professions and pursuits, some prioritization is required to identify areas for immediate support and intervention. In this regard, UNEP's Environmental Education and Training Unit identified the following categories for priority environmental training: teachers, teacher trainers and teachers' curricula developers; students at all levels; policy makers; decision makers; media professionals; and other opinion leaders and multipliers.

In addition, foreign service personnel who negotiate environmental conventions on behalf of their countries; government officials who negotiate donor funding support for development projects; managers and administrators in educational and media institutions, who often act as gatekeepers, deciding what training and exposure trainees will receive, have all been identified as target groups for environmental training.

National Networks for Environmental Training

National level networks of tertiary level institutions have been formed in several countries of the region to share resources and efforts in providing environmental training. One such network is the Philippine Association of Tertiary level Educational Institutions in Environmental Protection and Management, PATLEPAM, which by mid 1999 had linked over 300 higher educational institutions. It has conducted training programmes in environmental impact assessment, and a large number of seminars and workshops on environment and education. UNEP/NETITAP has catalysed the formation of two country level networks in Thailand and Malaysia for environmental training and research.

These networks, known by their acronyms THAITREM and MATREM respectively, have brought together dozens of tertiary level institutions in each country for undertaking collaborative research and training activities. The Australian Environmental Education Network (AEEN) is a national network of environmental education and information programmes, materials and publications. The Network includes access to materials and programmes produced within the Federal Environment Portfolio, States/Territories Environmental Education Resources, a number of current school and community environmental programmes, and links with tertiary resources and a bulletin board for the exchange of ideas. Education Network Australia (EdNA) aims to facilitate the provision of cost effective education to all parts of the education community in Australia.

EdNA is founded on cooperation and consultation between representatives of all sectors of the education community including Commonwealth, State and Territory governments, non government schools, the vocational education and training sector, the higher education sector and the adult and community education sectors. The aim is to maximize the benefits of information technology for all sectors in education and to avoid overlap and duplication between the various sectors and systems.

Cooperation for Environmental Education and Training

Recognition is growing that many environmental issues and challenges are common to more than one country in the region and that countries and communities can learn from each other in their responses to similar situations and problems. In some cases, the transboundary nature of environmental problems and their impact make it an imperative for countries in the same geographical vicinity to work together to address and cope with environmental trends and conditions. Regional networking is one of the most cost-effective ways of promoting active cooperation among those engaged in environmental education and training. The Asia Pacific Network for Tertiary Level Environmental Training (NETTLAP) contributes to human resource development and the strengthening of tertiary institutions in the Asian and Pacific Region.

Staffs of tertiary institutions are key targets for environmental training for the multiplier effect they can generate; they often act as advisors to government and industry; and because of the high standing university staff members enjoy in many communities as opinion leaders. Another example of regional network is the South and Southeast Asia Network for Environmental Education (SASEANEE). It was initiated in 1993, coordinated by the CEE in India and the Commission on Education and Communication of IUCN. SASEANEE membership includes governmental and non-governmental organizations, academic institutions, as well as agencies and individuals involved in or interested in networking, initiating or supporting environmental education activities in the South and Southeast Asian countries. Activities include: a directory of persons and institutions involved in environmental education; a newsletter called SASEANEE Circular; and short training courses in environmental education.

In 1995, the South Asia Cooperative Environment Programme (SACEP) initiated a project to assess environment related training needs in its member countries, with a view to developing a Regional Plan of Action. Country studies were carried out in Bangladesh, Bhutan, India, Maldives, Nepal, Pakistan and Sri Lanka, which were coordinated by CEE, India. Based on the country level assessments, SACEP and CEE prepared a Regional Plan of action that sought to help synergize environmental capacity building within the sub region. It found that courses were well developed and that some institutions had also developed considerable expertise and experience in their areas of specialization and provide appropriate training. However, the assessments underlined the fact that the available training opportunities were inadequate to cater to the growing needs, and in some cases, the quality of training required improvement.

Monitoring Assessment and Reporting

Environmental monitoring by government agencies and institutions in many countries has focused on certain environmental concerns, such as the quality of air, water and other natural resources. Monitored data are transformed into information that show environmental trends and effectiveness of past mitigation measure which are vital for environmental management. This information is also utilized in the state of environment reports; for example, of Australia; New Zealand; Malaysia; India; Fiji; Japan; Hong Kong, China; Turkmenistan; Azerbaijan; Uzbekistan; and Palau. NGOs and community-based organizations also play a significant role in collecting and disseminating information to the community and to all spheres of government. 1. National level Air pollution is a concern for which extensive monitoring systems have been put in place in many countries of the region. In the Republic of Korea, for example an automatic air pollution monitoring network measures seven atmospheric pollutants which include TSP, $S0_2$, $N0_2$, CO, O_3, etc.

Other countries in the region may not have such a sophisticated system but nonetheless have established monitoring systems to cover sites across the country. Indonesia now has 31 air quality monitoring stations nationwide to help check increasing air pollution arising from motor vehicles in large cities. People's Republic of China illustrates a wide array of monitoring stations and also implements a quantitative examination system for urban environmental control. The central and provincial governments have already performed quantitative checks in over 37 major cities and 330 smaller cities. In the Russian Federation, special attention is given to the development and support of a system for monitoring the condition of the ozone layer as well as a system for monitoring ultraviolet radiation over the whole country and adjoining territories. Information is processed and presented in the form of daily maps showing deviations in the volumes of total ozone content from norms established over many years.

Case Study

Building Regional Capacity through Environmental Research, Training and Education

In 1993, UNEP's Regional Office for Asia and the Pacific (ROAP) established an ongoing programme to enhance the region's capacity to manage the environment in a sound and sustainable manner. This initiative, called the Network for Environmental Training at Tertiary Level in Asia and the Pacific (NETTLAP), has evolved into a major contribution in helping to achieve both national and regional goals of sustainable development. It has explicitly recognized that tertiary institutions such as universities, technical and training institutes and teacher training colleges, play a major role in building capacity for sustainable development. Staffs of these institutions were identified as "agents of change" for two reasons. Firstly, a large multiplier effect is associated with actions that strengthen tertiary institutions and enhance the abilities of staff to transfer, to their colleagues and students, state of the art understanding and international best practices.

The improvements involve many people in a short period of time-graduates are soon improving the environmental management policies and practices in industry, government and the community. Secondly, governments and industry keenly seek the advice and guidance of staff from universities and technical institutes. Industry in particular recognizes the ability of such people to bring innovative solutions to current environmental problems and creative approaches to preventing the occurrence of new problems. Initially NETTLAP focussed on strengthening key tertiary institutions in 35 developing countries in the region. The early efforts of NETTLAP did more to recognize the enormity of the need and, in relative terms, little to address it. But incrementally NETTLAP made a difference throughout the region. The benefits of the multiplier effect have begun to be seen. This was particularly so in the case of the design, preparation and dissemination of environmental curricula and the suppor-ting instructional methods, materials and tools for use in tertiary and other relevant institutions in the region.

These efforts resulted in sets of curriculum guidelines and associated training methods, resource materials and tools cover such topics as environmental economics, hazardous waste management, toxic chemicals management and coastal zone management. These outputs are still widely sought, and extensively used in the region. By the late 1990s, NETTLAP had matured in several ways. Significantly, it has shifted its target from institutional strengthening and human resources development in the tertiary sector itself to assist developing countries to plan and implement their own activities to build the capacity to achieve effective environmental management, and sustainable development. Countries can take a comprehensive approach that targets other important "agents of change" - politicians, government officials, and leaders from the private sector and NGOs.

Therefore, in recent years NETTLAP has focussed on building national networks that can facilitate the linking of policy makers, development planners, and environmental managers from industry and key staff from tertiary institutions. In addition to sharing expertise, experiences and best practices, the networks are also designed to help identify current and emerging needs that can best be addressed through a symbiotic relationship between these key players. Through these national partnerships, NETTLAP is linking research, training and education in order to improve the capacity to prevent or minimize adverse impacts on the environment. This involves identifying and implementing responses that are sustainable, assured of achieving the desired results and identified needs, supportive of related policies (e.g. appropriate economic and social development), innovative but consistent with traditional indigenous practices, add value to other initiatives and encourage complementary activities.

NETTLAP has played a key role by facilitating nationally "owned and driven" environmental capacity building networks in the Philippines, Malaysia and Thailand. The major achievements of the latter two networks for training and research in environmental management have resulted, in part, from significant funding from DANCED, an initiative of the Government of Denmark. Given the success of its current approach of "Regional Cooperation with National Implementation", NETTLAP is in advanced discussions to help develop similar networks in People's Republic of China, Viet Nam, India and the Mekong countries. Key players in NETTLAP's strategy - "Regional Cooperation with National Implementation" - are such sub regional organizations as SACEP, ASEAN and SPREP. NETTLAP is working with these, and similar organizations, to ensure that its actions are supportive of their strategies and action plans related to environmental research, education and training.

NETTLAP has evolved as new needs are identified and past needs are addressed. But despite its efforts, and its significant successes, much more needs to be done. NETTLAP has shown that the most effective approach is one that builds synergies between key international, regional, sub-regional and national players. In Australia, a number of strategies and plans provide a focus for particular resource issues, including Agriculture Land Cover Change project and the revised National Overview for the Decade of Landcare Plan (the main strategic plan for the National Land- care Programme. The government, through its Commonwealth and State agencies, funded a programme to monitor changes in Land cover from 1990-1995, through the use of Satellite data. Information from the project provides as base-line for future monitoring which is vital to land clearing and agriculture development that have major impacts on wide impacts on wide range of country's natural processes.

Wastewater is also intensively monitored in some countries across the region. Databases in Australia (Australian Waste Database) and New Zealand (Waste Analysis Protocol; WAP) are used for collating national baseline and update information, so as to monitor waste management services and ensure national objectives are met. These data will also eventually form the basis for developing national waste reduction targets. Environmental quality monitoring has also been focused on natural resources, such as coastal and marine resources. In Thailand, the Fisheries Department of the Ministry of Agriculture monitors coastal zones and estuaries for toxic chemicals, heavy metals and oil pollution. India has a programme on Coastal Ocean Monitoring and Prediction System that is engaged in a systematic monitoring of marine pollution in the country and conducts studies relating to waste assimilation capacity of coastal waters.

The Russian Federation monitors and evaluates the environmental impact of activities affecting coastal and marine regions such as in the Caspian Sea where a system is being developed to forecast its fluctuating level over various time spans to predict possible future changes. Forest resources and biodiversity are extensively monitored throughout the region. For example, National Biodiversity Surveys are carried out approximately every five years in Japan. Indonesia conducted a project with GEF support to establish a Biological Diversity Inventory and develop a User Advisory Group Information System. In Australia, a National Forest Inventory and Wilderness Inventory are carried out to produce a national State of the Forests report every five years. The Republic of Korea has a 10-year periodic forest inventory with site surveys to produce a geographic map that is computerized into digital databases.

Monitoring for forest pests and diseases has also been developed in the Russian Federation and the Republic of

Korea for early warning systems related to pest and disease outbreak. Other monitoring techniques include the use of Geographical Information Systems (GIS), which are used to establish nationwide conservation and protected areas (Australia); identification of environmentally sensitive areas (Malaysia, Fiji); forest resource mapping (Indonesia, the Philippines, Myanmar, Solomon Islands); flood action planning (Bangladesh); studying ecosystem changes, river pollution and marine environmental surveys (Republic of Korea); analysis of river change, water logging and salinity, desertification, and agro-ecological zonal maps for water research (Pakistan); and industrial pollution control (Thailand). The significance of disaster prevention and mitigation has also prompted many countries to take initiatives in the areas of disaster forecasting, early warning, risk assessment and mapping of climate and water related hazards.

Regional and Global Monitoring

Environmental quality monitoring goes beyond country activities and programmes when environmental concerns take on transboundary characteristics. An example is the Mekong GIS project (of the Interim Committee for Coordination of Investigations of the Lower Mekong Basin), which was initiated to evolve a network of data centres in Lao People's Democratic Republic, Thailand and Viet Nam. Regional cooperation in Central Asia has also been initiated on questions relating to radiation safety. Remote Sensing and GIS are also being applied as a tool for monitoring at regional level. The value of remote sensing in monitoring transboundary pollution was demonstrated recently when ASOEN (ASEAN Officials for the Environment) used the data developed from these for planning inter-country cooperation regarding haze caused by forest fires in Indonesia. 3. Issues and Problems in Monitoring and Assessment The most often cited constraints in relation to environmental quality monitoring in developing countries relate to inadequacy of funds and the lack of manpower and/or training, which leads to low coverage and low frequency of monitoring, particularly in the rural areas.

This is especially so when the monitoring cover a wide area, for example, in Mongolia there is a need to monitor about 20 000 bored wells and a similar number of dug wells as it is believed that 70-80 per cent of these are contaminated. However, present capacity only allows chemical analyses for 14 per cent of the bored wells and none of the dug wells. Lack of training and technical capacity has also reduced the capacity of developing countries to actively participate in global monitoring efforts. Environmental monitoring and assessment in the developing countries of the region still requires strengthening in terms of standardization of, monitoring network system design; sampling and analytical methodologies; quality control in data collection and laboratory analysis; national procedures for harmonizing data collection; and improving the access to data of researchers and interested citizens. There is also a need to establish systems for collecting new benchmark data to assess the sustainability of resources, as well to environment with health, population, and economics.

Information Dissemination

Dissemination of environmental information is extremely important in integrated environmental management, since it plays a vital role in sensitising individuals to environmental issues. In the past, dissemination has been done through campaigning using mass media and scientific publications, however, advanced technology, especially the electric media, is now playing an increasing role. However, access to environmental information is not easy in most countries in the Asian and Pacific region. Some region-wide efforts such as the UNDP funded Asia Pacific 2000 initiation has concentrated on promoting such efforts.

National Level

In some countries, there is no legal policy to disseminate

environmental information to the public or private sector. Lack of effective coordination makes information exchange more difficult. For example, in the Russian Federation, though environmental information distribution policy does exist by law, there is no legal administrative mechanism available to put it into practice. As a result, the information cannot be obtained easily, even among coordinating agencies. In Australia, environmental information can easily be accessed from a diverse range of institutions. There are numerous projects being undertaken by government agencies at the Federal and State level and in research and teaching institutions, which are aimed at developing methods of integrating economic, social and environmental information. These include state of environment reporting, the development of indicators of sustainable development, methods for resource valuation and systems of environmental and natural resources accounting. The Environmental Resources Information Network (ERIN), located in Environment Australia provides environmental information for policy development and decision-makers.

Case Study

Awareness Raising Campaigns

The UNDP-funded Asia Pacific 2000 initiative (AP2000) seeks to support and strengthen the role of civil society in meeting the challenges of urban environment and poverty. Established in the early 1990s, it works closely with governments, NGOs, researchers and all other stakeholders in the region's unfolding urban drama. Studying how AP2000's partners are mobilizing themselves sheds light on the use of different campaign methods for environmental awareness, advocacy and activism. Environmental Campaigns in urban areas of Asia and the Pacific have taken various forms. Some have been as simple as making and putting up posters, or conducting slide presentations and exhibits, for example as the Penang Organic Farm (PAF) does to promote the concept of Eco-cities. Eco-cities are designed to revitalize nature in over-exploited areas, while bringing new prosperity to its inhabitants.

The Asia Pacific 2000 initiative has involved PAF to become the core of an Asia-wide Eco-cities network that will create awareness of alternative ways of building cities and to create sensitivity toward the environment. There are many other ways of carrying out campaigns. For example, in March 1995, AP2000's partner Waste Wise in Bangalore organized a three-day 'Festival of Recycling'. This event brought together the community, local authorities and private enterprise to promote the concept of reducing, reusing and recycling as a way of life. Now, the organization is spreading its advocacy work beyond Bangalore to the region with Waste Wise Asia Pacific. Some campaigns target specific audiences. Magic Eye, a Thai community development organization, for example, aimed its 'Do Not Litter' campaign at school children. The programme, which made children aware of the need for proper waste disposal - for instance through separation and recycling - was a success.

But Magic Eye's ultimate target was the parents, who are in a better position to put into practice the waste management schemes advocated through the programme. Sometimes campaigns involve protest and agitation against policies or practices that are felt to be harmful to the environment. Across the region, NGOs and other citizens' groups regularly organize such campaigns which employ a variety of means, ranging from letter writing, marches or rallies, to the more active forms such as ***satyagraha*** or sit-in protests that are often adopted in parts of South Asia. In India, sustained campaign efforts have also used the method *oiyatras* or long marches by groups of people - sometimes stretching across hundreds of kilometres - which attract news media interest, and expose thousands of people in communities along the way to the messages of the campaign. Government agencies also use campaigns to rally public support for specific environmental issues. Singapore has a well established practice of environmental campaigns like the Clean and Green Week, and it's calls to Save Energy and Save Water. In Japan, October of each year is observed as the Recycling Promotion Month, during which all government ministries and agencies concerned with the environment conduct an extensive campaign to persuade the people to recycle resources. Hopefully these and other campaigns in the cities of Asia and the Pacific will go a long way in improving the urban environment.

Information is drawn from many sources including maps, species distributions, documents and satellite imagery and the information is easily accessible through the internet. Similarly in Japan, public access to data on air and water pollution and natural environment is provided to government agencies, laboratories and outside users under pollution control laws. The Government of India and the State Governments, through several of their organizations have taken various steps to develop information network capabilities of both the public and private sectors. The Environment Information System (ENVIS) has the joint objectives of building a repository and dissemination centre for environmental science and engineering, and providing national environmental information services to originators, processors, and disseminators of environmental information.

International Level

Internationally, INFOTERRA of UNEP is an important source of information. Additionally, United Nations system-wide Earthwatch programme initiated in 1994 by UNEP has emphasized environmental education. It aims at coordinating, harmonising and integrating observation, assessment and reporting activities across the United Nations system in order to provide environmental and socio-economic information to interested parties. Some countries also promote dissemination of environmental information for users around the world. The National Resource Information Centre (NRIC) of Australia develops advanced computing systems designed to service policy and community needs for information, for example, on sustainable development. Its information resources consist of more than 50 national and 100 regional spatially maintained datasets, and FINDAR, a software package for interrogating metadata on more than 6 500 databases that it maintains as a directory linked to all other major international directories. In March 1996, the NIES, Japan, began to provide environmental information from its research activities to the world via the Internet.

At the same time, the Centre established a computer communication system for the general public called the "Environmental Information & Communication Network (ElCnet)" in order to promote national activities for conservation of the environment, including "El-Guide" a survey of environmental information including explanations of laws, treaties, and environment-related terms.

Issues and Constraints in Information Dissemination

Effective communication plays an important bridging role between information and target groups. The first stage of communication, however, w'hich is listening to what people know, think, believe and do, has often been weak. In the formal education sector, timely access to credible information is one of the major constraints for environmental education in the region. Furthermore, in some countries, although data and information are often collected by different agencies, a lack of effective coordination and communication among related agencies make information sharing ineffective. NGOs have been effectively involved in dissemination of environmental information to promote environmental awareness, although there is still a need for improved promotion at the regional level.

2

Media and Environmental Communication

Environmental Communication

Environmental communication has now emerged as strong complementary practice to environmental education. A broad definition of environmental communication would be, "the sharing of information, insights and opinions on environmental issues, trends, conditions and solutions using any means of communications, ranging from inter-personal methods to means of mass communication using the modern as well as traditional media". In this sense, environmental educators constantly engage in environmental communication. However, an important distinction is that, while all environmental educators are communicators, not all environmental communicators are necessarily educators. Across the Asian and Pacific Region, individuals and institutions engage in a very wide range of environmental communication activities with varying degrees of sophistication, outreach and impact.

Communication Trends

In the mid to late 1990s, the main focus in environmental communication was to inspire positive behaviour, on the part of individuals, communities, corporate and industrial bodies and others, to help conserve the environment and achieve sustainable development. A key issue for many countries in the region is to integrate environment into development policy, and to use communication and education in an integrated way as an instrument of policy. There is, however, a tendency to focus on formal school education target groups, both by governments and NGOs, rather than addressing other groups who can make a difference in a policy issue, or in an immediate practical sense (IUCN 1998).

One of the major channels through which environmental communication is practised is the mass media, which includes both print and electronic sections. The communication media in Asia and the Pacific underwent rapid change during the 1990s, with liberalization of media policies allowing private sector involvement, spread of global media networks owned by trans-national companies and the proliferation of new communication technologies which have removed the barrier of large investments required to enter the media field. Transnational television is the most prominent example of the changes taking place in the region's communications scenes. More than 386 million households in the region (more than 55 per cent) are now equipped with television sets. Estimates indicate that by the year 2005, more than 447 million households will have television sets (UNESCO 1997b).

The last few years has also seen the rapid expansion in the use of the Internet, with most countries in the region already connected to the global information superhighway. Cellular phones, faxes, email, electronic networks and cable are also expanding countries' outreach, often at unprecedented growth rates. The Asian and Pacific Region are experiencing a trend where the public service component on television is declining while the number of broadcast hours and channels continues to increase. The medium's potential for non-formal education and for raising public awareness remains largely untapped. While advertisers and sponsors compete to support entertainment, news or sports programmes, the more educational programmes, documentaries, investigative current affairs programmes or in-depth interviews, have to contend with budget cuts, intense competition for prime-time slots, and an overall decline in the public service spirit in broadcasting.

Media's role in environmental communication remains effective only to the extent that the environmental experts, researchers and activists engage and use the media to influence and shape the accuracy, balance and scope of environmental coverage. In response, throughout the region, governments and NGOs are adopting strategies to mobilize communications and cooperate with the media, and in some cases, to strengthen the media's capacity to cover environmental issues more effectively. In 1996, Malaysia's Department of Environment (DOE) launched two major programmes with the cooperation of the electronic media. One was a TV serial called 'Bicara Alam' that discussed environmental issues of current interest; the other was a radio environmental awareness quiz. B. Print Media Environmental reporting is now well-established within the region's print media, newspapers and magazines.

Investigative journalism on environmental issues has resulted in exposing environmentally damaging plans, polices or practices. Newspaper exposures and subsequent public pressure have forced governments, local authorities, industries and others to change their plans, to tighten laws and regulations, and to abandon certain development projects whose environmental and social costs outweighed any benefits. This is illustrated by Thailand's two leading English language newspapers, the Bangkok Post and The Nation, both of which have been honoured by UNEP with its Global 500 awards for excellence in environmental coverage and for their commitment to the environmental cause. The Nation newspaper has a recognized tradition of covering groundbreaking environmental stories, and the production of a weekly environmental page, Earth Focus.

In Malaysia, a leading newspaper group, the New Straits Times, has supported and managed a national environmental education programme for students since 1992, which aims to enhance the awareness of the environment, culture and social values, whilst encouraging problem solving, motivation and participation in environmental programmes. Producing special publications for children is another important strategy. Many conservation organizations produce material meant for children and young adults. The Centre for Science and Environment (CSE) in India, for instance, has published the science and environment fortnightly Down to Earth since 1992 and launched a children's supplement in 1998, called Gobar Times. It aims to stimulate young minds to question prevailing development patterns, lifestyles and governance systems.

The supplement carries news and views on the environment, science and technology, stories from various traditions including environmental movements and inventions, and highlights of social implications of the issues. It uses comic strips, cartoons, quizzes, essay competitions and interactive pages to engage children's minds.

Case Study

New Environmentalism in People's Republic of China

In the 1990s, the environmental movement in People's Republic of China gained considerable momentum at all levels: in the media, among academics and professionals, and at different levels of government. At the official level, the National Environmental Protection Administration (NEPA) has a Centre for Environmental Education and Communication (CEEC) based at the Sino-Japanese Friendship Centre for Environmental Protection in Beijing, a modern facility opened in 1996. The CEEC's main functions include organising and undertaking national communications activities on environmental protection; managing a public inquiry system for information of environmental communications and education; compiling teaching materials on environmental protection; producing TV programmes on environmental issues; conducting training; and providing professional advice to local level CEECs.

Under CEEC's leadership, a vast network of environmental communicators has been mobilized across People's Republic of China, to provide information, clarifications and interpretations on a wide range of environmental issues and concerns. Meanwhile, a growing number of citizens' groups and .media professionals are also actively participating in strengthening environmental awareness and advocacy work. A pioneering role is played by Friends of Nature, a citizens' group formed in 1993 whose membership comprises several hundred academics and journalists concerned about the environment. In 1996, Friends of Nature initiated a campaign that prompted the government to ban logging in Deqing country in the south-western province of Yunnan, home to the endangered golden monkey (due to excessive deforestation).

Similar campaigns have been launched on saving the natural habitats of other endangered species, and to stop the caging of wild birds. Campaigns are carried out using persuasion as well as pressurizing tactics (media exposure) rather than using directly confrontational approaches. A concerned and sympathetic media has become one of the biggest forces for change in People's Republic of China. For many years, People's Republic of China has had substantial coverage of environmental issues in its media: by the early 1990s, the country's environmental protection institutions at various levels had founded 16 specialized newspapers and 87 special magazines on environment, and there were eight newspapers and magazines with a national readership devoted solely to this subject. A major trend observed in the mid 1990s was the emergence of television as a powerful medium for raising awareness and advocating policy reforms on environment. The Global Village Environmental Culture Institute of Beijing (GECIB) has been at the forefront in using television for environmental communication.

In 1996, it created two successful television series. The first series, called Green Civilization and People's Republic of China, is aired on China Educational Television (CETV). It aims to cultivate the people's environmental consciousness through spreading basic knowledge on sustainable development encouraged by the response to this series, GECIB created a second series of weekly programmes called Time for Environment, which runs on China Central Television (CCTV), the country's national television network. This programme deals mainly with the latest international and domestic environmental events. GECIB's work symbolizes the commitment of the new environmental movement in People's Republic of China. It is run by professionally skilled volunteers; the actual costs are covered by donations and grants.

Encouraged by GECIB's successful television ventures, several television stations have launched their own programmes looking at different aspects of environment and development. While some deal with the traditional aspects of natural history, other programmes adopt a more investigative approach, probing and exposing environmental degradation, violation of existing laws and regulations, and instances of corruption and negligence leading to environmental disasters. Expansion of operations to engage in book publishing and multi-media ventures that disseminate environmental information in a variety of ways is also on the agenda. Other bodies are already exploiting the Internet for this purpose: for example, the China Green Students Forum, a network of 20 university- based environmental groups, are linked through the Internet. As People's Republic of China expands its presence in the Internet, more groups and organizations are poised to take advantage of the new medium.

Broadcast Media

The broadcast media, radio and television, in all their variations, have established themselves as the most pervasive and powerful forms of mass media in Asia and the Pacific today. They represent a major channel through which information on environment can be conveyed to the people. Recognising the need for programmes in the regional language and context, major international media groups have associated with regional and national companies. A wide range of activist groups and media organizations also produce television and radio programmes on environmental issues, using the media as a means to raise awareness. For instance, since 1996, the Nepal Forum of Environmental Journalists (NEFEJ) has been producing a weekly radio programme for Radio Nepal on community forestry. Called "Samudayik Ban", it is produced on behalf of the Federation of Community Forest Users in Nepal, and is designed to support community forest user groups through sharing experiences on

Case Study

Moving Pictures to Save the Environment

As the audio visual media become the dominant source of information and entertainment in the Asian and Pacific Region, more environmental activists and organizations are moving to take advantage of these powerful media for environmental education and awareness. Using low cost video production equipment spawned by the digital revolution, and responding to the growing demand for programming in most countries, NGOs and small media organizations are carving out their own niche in the region's media landscape. While many use video as a medium to raise public awareness and understanding of environmental issues, some are using it to document instances of environmental crimes and degradation; to lobby for specific policy reforms; or to raise funds for specific campaigns.

Recognizing that their effectiveness depends on having access to skills, information and programming, a number of the region's organizations have come together to form the Asia and Pacific Video Resource Centre (VRC) Network.

A 'VRC' is an existing environmental or media organization that commits itself to using television and video for environmental communication. By mid 1999, 18 such VRCs were active in 15 countries in the region, engaged in a range of activities such as: producing new video programmes; versioning or adapting foreign programmes into local languages; and distributing the programmes using means such as public screenings, seminars, and film festivals. The network is affiliated with the Television Trust for the Environment (TVE) which provides them with high quality programmes and technical assistance. VRCs also receive support from UNEP and other agencies. Members of the VRC network have found innovative means of using the audio visual media to promote environmental awareness.

For example: WWF Pakistan has made arrangements to screen environmental videos at departure lounges of key international airports in the country; Nepal Forum of Environmental Journalists is producing its own weekly magazine programme for local television where environmental issues are regularly covered; Environmental Broadcast Circle in the Philippines has integrated video film viewing into the course work at some universities; Women's Media Centre in Cambodia produces short duration television 'spots' that convey concise messages on topics such as women and the environment; Centre for Environment Education in India uses videos in awareness programmes organized for children. Several members of the network regularly organize environmental film festivals. Earth Vision has emerged as a leading environmental film festival in the Asian and Pacific Region.

Conducted every year since 1992 by the Earth Vision

Organization in Japan, it is open to film makers in the region, and offers prestigious awards and cash prizes. Film South Asia is another documentary festival that was started in 1997 by the Kathmandu-based Himal magazine. According to the organizers, the festival is an attempt to counter the domination of satellite television. Sometimes, individual television programmes can capture the attention of viewers across boundaries and catalyze change. In 1995, TVE Japan produced a 30-minute documentary titled Japan's Lessons on the Economy and the Environment: Our Pollution Experience. It traced Japan's industrial pollution problems and effects on public health and the environment, and documented how the Japanese industry was forced to adopt pollution control measures.

Because of its clear lessons for the currently industrializing countries in the region, this programme has been versioned into several main Asian languages - such as Mandarin, Hindi, Urdu, Tagalog and Bengali - by members of the VRC network to promote the key message in the film. Similarly, a UNEP/TVE video called Saving the Ozone Layer: Every Action Counts, produced in 1995, has been versioned into several key Asian languages and is used widely for education and awareness purposes. This forms part of the audio-visual material available to organizations marking the World Ozone Day on September 16 each year.

Similar community radio broadcasts are also taking place from a number of radio stations in the region. Other private sector organizations are also engaged in producing environmental material for broadcast. For example, a private television production company named Miditech, based in New Delhi, India, has been producing a weekly television series called Living on the Edge which combines news and views on environment with clever visuals and interactive segments, and making the programme both educational and entertaining. D. Major Constraints and Responses Even though the quantity of environmental coverage in the region's media has continued to increase since the mid-1990s, several constraints and drawbacks remain. A major difficulty faced by journalists and producers covering the environment is access to.

Case Study

Community Radio: A Growing Cacophony of Local Voices

Community radio stations are designed to encourage participation by a large representative sample of the various socio- economic levels, organizations and minority groups within a community. The stations facilitate the free flow of information and opinions, encouraging freedom of speech and enhancing dialogue. In recent years, there has been an increase in the number of local or community radio stations usually characterized by their low transmission power and restricted audience. This could be a university campus, a specific district in a large city, or small stations in rural areas servicing distinct communities. Since the late 1970s, when the technology and expertise for starting community radio stations became widely available, a whole range of community radio experiments has taken place, and today community radio initiatives are found in all regions of the world. Some have been used effectively to promote environmental awareness and to generate community level discussion and debate on sustainable development issues. Community radio is found in many countries of the Asian and Pacific Region.

In the Philippines, parallel to the conventional radio stations (of which there are more than 500), there are some 35 local radio stations headed by community groups, denominational associations and educational organizations. Among the best known is the Network of Tambule Community Radio, comprising eight small community stations located in isolated regions. Set up and managed by local volunteers, the network receives support from UNESCO and the Danish International Development Agency

(DANIDA). With basic technical training in radio broadcasting, villagers prepare news bulletins as well as programmes focusing on local issues. Open debates on these stations maintain pressure on the local authorities to find viable solutions to environmental, social and other community problems. In Thailand, the community radio station in Chiang Mai has been broadcasting programmes on substitution crops as part of a government programme to reduce the poppy crop.

This Hill Tribes Radio also seeks to improve the socio-economic conditions of the mountain tribal people living in the northern region of Thailand. In Australia, the 'Public Radio' community network was given legal status in 1974, and now has more than 130 community radio stations. In Sri Lanka, Mahaweli Community Radio (MCR) was started in 1980 to support the new settlers in the Mahaweli River diversion programme, one of the largest development projects in Asia at the time. Radio has been used to motivate people in the Mahaweli settlements to take on the responsibility of bringing about change in them and in their communities. MCR has adopted many concepts of community-based radio programming and production, and has demonstrated that the medium of community radio can influence the thinking and attitudes of rural populations. MCR programmers have incorporated concepts of sustainability and conservation into their programmes over the years.

In 1997, Radio Sagarmatha in Nepal became the first privately owned and managed community radio service in South Asia. The station is run on a non-profit basis by the Nepal Forum of Environmental Journalists (NEFEJ) in collaboration with Himal South Asia magazine, Nepal Press Institute and the Worldview International Foundation. Initially starting with two hours of transmissions every day to the Kathmandu valley, the new station quickly increased its number of broadcast hours as well as its audience share. The core programming covers social, cultural, environment and developmental issues, while the rest of the air time is used to broadcast Nepalese classical music and folk songs, etc. The growing developments in community radio throughout Asia and the Pacific are facilitating the dissemination of cultural and community specific information and awareness raising with respect to local environmental concerns.

Although identified some time ago, the response to this constraint has been slow. The restriction of access to information by the public and media still prevails in some countries and inhibits open coverage, discussion and debate of issues that are of public interest. In other cases where information is available, journalists lack credible means of interpreting technical issues and explaining them in layman's terms. In some countries, such as the Philippines, the scientific community has set up media referral services which offer free advice and information to journalists working on a science or environment related story, directing them to relevant experts and institutions. In the few instances where such collaboration has been established between the environmental community and the media, impressive results have been recorded.

In Pakistan, for example, the IUCN has involved the media as a key target group and stakeholder in the implementation of the National Conservation Strategy, resulting in a strengthened capacity of the media to cover the complex issues of sustainable development. However, in many countries, environmental activists and government agencies handling the subject of environment have not developed fruitful media relations and use the media only to generate publicity for events and individual actions. While such publicity campaigns are useful, the greater interests of communities and sustainable development are better served by permitting investigative, balanced and accurate reporting. Environmental journalism encounters other problems that are not easily overcome.

For example, bottlenecks sometimes exist, where editors and programme managers may not appreciate, and thus pay limited attention to, environmental news. These bottlenecks remain partly because the sensitization that has occurred among reporters and producers has not been extended sufficiently well to cover the media gatekeepers. Another limiting factor is legitimacy of environmental issues and where such legitimacy is derived from. For instance, sometimes major environmental stories are under-reported in the country of origin until the foreign media picks it up and gives international coverage. In other cases, owing to prevailing restrictions on media freedom or due to problems of accessing reliable information, local journalists are unable to cover certain environmental stories. Foreign correspondents, operating at a different level are usually not as restricted by domestic information policies, and are better positioned to cover such stories. However, coverage by global news networks or international features services are tailor-made for a global audience, and as a result only highlights of a complex situation may be covered.

The anomalies of global media are such that sometimes the international media organizations enjoy a disproportionately high degree of influence. A case in point is the mass-scale arsenic poisoning in Bangladesh and West Bengal in India due to naturally occurring arsenic levels in the groundwater. Some fifteen million people in Bangladesh are forced to use the groundwater contaminated by arsenic, and it has become one of the largest cases of poisoning in history. This major environmental story has been reported and covered in the Bangladeshi media for several years since the mid 1990s. But worldwide attention increased only after the influential global media started reporting on it. The BBC and the New York Times, between them, covered the story and raised the issue to a new level of recognition among donors, the development community and the public than had been achieved by the previous media coverage in Bangladesh and in the region.

The Internet and World Wide Web

Recent years have seen the extremely rapid growth and development of the Internet as an information provider. According to the International Data Corporation, the number of Internet Web users in the Asian and Pacific Region will rise from 6.5 million in March 1998 to 29.3 million by the year 2001. However, large disparities in access and use of the Internet exist across the region and in individual nations. Major constraints remain that hinder the rapid expansion in Internet access in developing countries such as: poor telecommunications (lack of working phone lines); an inability to afford computers; and the higher cost of providing Internet services. However it is predicted that the Internet will move from a minority to a mass medium, with wide accessibility in a short period of time. The earliest users and disseminators of Internet use and technology were academic and research organizations, belonging to the Association of Progressive Communications (APC).

These have actively supported or established networks in regions around the world for several years, and often provided countries with their only link to the Internet until commercial Internet Service Providers (ISPs) became operational. Partly because of these initiatives, analysts say the Internet may have a greater social impact in developing countries than anywhere else, as the academic organizations are some of the best-informed and are often campaigning for greater democracy, social equality and protection of the environment. During the past few years, an increasing number of environmental organizations in the region have recognized the potential of the Internet and started using it for exchanging information; for advocacy and activism; for public awareness and education; as well as for publicity and promotional purposes. Although the number of websites with a strong environmental content originating from the region is still numerically low, the quality and scope of some of the currently available sites are impressive.

Traditional Media

For many years, environmental communicators have recognized the value and power of using folklore and traditional media, such as, dance, songs, drama, puppetry and miming, to take environment and development messages to the public. Historically, traditional or folk media have often played a role in the communication and promotion of new ideas, apart from its traditional role of preserving and teaching established values. Today, in spite of advances in the modern forms of mass media, many people still relate more readily and easily to traditional media, which are closer to their local cultures, and are often more interactive and participatory than the regular forms of mass media. Various forms of traditional media are being used or adapted to convey environmental messages to children, communities and specific target groups in different countries of the Asian and Pacific Region.

For example, the wayang kulit or puppet's shadow play is one popular folk art form among Javanese communities in Indonesia. These plays tell stories containing important values relevant and useful to people's lives, both physically and spiritually. The original way an stories are rich in ethical messages regarding the close relationship between people and nature, appreciation of other living beings, warnings on probable natural hazards due to human actions, etc. In recent years, wayan plays have been used to communicate messages supporting Indonesia's national family planning programme, reaching vast audiences.

Environmental Communication beyond Media

Environmental communication and awareness rising is also taking place through citizen volunteers, through the efforts of the corporate sector, and through law and faith-based approaches. Each of these approaches has wide ranging applications across the region.

Citizen Volunteers

Mobilising volunteer action is a time-tested tradition

in environmental management and activism. Volunteers may be drawn from different sections of society; some will bring in specialized skills and knowledge; others will provide a donation of labour and time. For example, in 1987 the Regional Environmental Management Offices in the Republic of Korea launched the Environmental Watchdog System to raise public awareness of the need for environmental conservation and to encourage citizens to monitor environmental pollution. The system has contributed greatly to increasing public awareness of environmental issues through public relations, monitoring, reporting, and by accommodating public views and opinions. While the vast number of people involved was a positive development, it also posed management difficulties. To address this concern, the Ministry of Environment set up the Honorary Guard System for the Natural Environment as a watchdog in accordance with the Natural Environmental Preservation Act. In 1995, there were more than 11 000 honorary environmental watchdogs, representing every walk of life in society.

Working with the Corporate Sector

Today, environmental communication initiatives often work closely with the corporate sector. Recognising that business, commerce and industry are key players in achieving sustainable development and equitable growth, environmental educators have started to form partnerships with socially and environmentally responsible corporations. Increasingly, the corporate sector is initiating environmental awareness, communications and education activities on its own, as part of their community outreach or service programmes. In some cases, large corporations underwrite the cost of environmental communications activities initiated by inter-governmental organizations.

A prominent example is how the Canon Corporation of Japan has consistently supported the United Nations Environment Programme (UNEP) to organize a worldwide photographic competition entitled "Focus on Your World" in 1992, 1995-96 and again in 1999. The Environmental Conservation Committee of Sony has been actively involved in environmental work for many years, monitoring regional committees set up in North America, Europe and Asia. These committees identify environmental problems in their regions, and devise responses that can be implemented easily and efficiently. In October 1998, Sony Group in Singapore, in association with the Tertiary Institutions Council for the Environment (TICE) and the Ministry of Environment, established the Sony Environmental Conservation Prize to stress the importance of environmental issues.

Open to university and polytechnic students, the competition solicits innovative ideas for environmental conservation. Other Sony companies across the region are working with environmental initiatives and activities, such as protecting mountains and rivers in the Republic of Korea, and assisting with the provision of forestry education at Muhak Mountain in the Masan region. In a growing number of countries, business and industry are coming together to form alliances or common fronts for taking corporate environmental responsibility to greater professional levels. Such business councils for sustainable development have already been formed in several countries, such as Japan, the Philippines and Sri Lanka, and the chambers of commerce in these countries are actively involved in enabling companies to become more environmentally responsible corporate citizens.

Faith and Law based Approaches

Public interest environmental litigation is increasingly popular in the region. In this, a group of lawyers or an NGO would initiate legal action for and on behalf of a local community directly affected by a specific instance of environmental degradation. The strengthening of environmental legislation in most countries during the 1990s, and the increased awareness on environmental rights, has fuelled this process. Beyond mere litigation, most.

Environmental law groups also engage in raising awareness on the legal provisions and rights related to the environment. The Bangladesh Environmental Law Association (BELA) has been at the forefront in using the law as an instrument of environmental education and awareness raising. It works with both the victims of environmental degradation, helping them to assert their rights, and also with law enforcement and judicial officers, assisting them in their official functions.

In Sri Lanka, the Environmental Foundation and the Mihikatha Institute are both engaged in similar tasks of advocacy and education. Both organizations operate environmental legal aid clinics which not only offer free legal advice to those affected by environmental problems, but also engage in awareness raising related to legal provisions and rights. The Mihikatha Institute carried out a country-wide training programme that exposed over 2,000 practising lawyers on the aspects of environmental law, mediation and rights. Environmental education and the promotion of environmentally friendly life-styles can also be carried out through faith groups. In the mid 1980s, the WWF brought senior representatives of the world's major religious iaiths together in Italy to discuss each faith's teachings and principles on man and the environment.

Having found a considerable amount of common ground among all religions on this subject, it was adopted as a strategy to enlist the support of religious leaders and groups to promote environmental awareness and, in particular, environmentally friendly lifestyles. In the Asian and Pacific Region, a number of initiatives have also been started with support from the UK-based Alliance of Religions and Conservation. Some countries are actively supporting the development of sustainable lifestyles through religious teachings. For example, Bhutan is actively promoting the

Buddhist way of life to ensure that its citizens are sensitive to the conservation of environment and natural resources.

The Royal Government of Bhutan made a national commitment in 1995 to uphold its obligations to the future generations by charting a path of development called the Middle Path. This development upholds both environmental and cultural preservation as an integral part of the development process. To ensure that the modern development pressures will not lead to negative impacts on the environment, the Bhutan government is invoking Buddhist teachings to impress upon the people the value of environmental conservation and sustainable lifestyles (Royal Government of Bhutan 1999).

As the Asian and Pacific Region enter the new millennium, it is clear that a new surge of interest, enthusiasm and activity is underway on many fronts to place environmental education, training and communication higher on the public agenda in countries of the region/ Although a considerable amount of work has been done and achievements made in the 1990s, many challenges remain. As many countries of the region struggle to overcome the social, economic and cultural barriers placed on them by poverty and underdevelopment, and at the same time face up to the new challenges of economic globalization the priority assigned to environmental issues and conservation is at risk of being overlooked or traded off for more immediate benefits,, and for survival needs. The environmental educators and communicators of the region need, therefore, to be vigilant and active to ensure that governments, industry and other key players in the sustainable development arena remain mindful of their international arid national commitments to environmental conservation, in addition to ensuring that sufficient investments of resources, time and attention are made to consolidate the achievements of the 1990s.

3

Environment and Tank Waste Retrieval

The effectiveness of waste retrieval technology is central to the committee's task because it drives the cost, worker risk, and secondary waste production associated with the removal of waste from the tanks. These are key factors in deciding how much waste should be left behind in tanks for on-site disposal. The status, effectiveness, and challenges of waste retrieval technologies are the focus of this chapter. DOE has developed and deployed a number of technologies for retrieving tank wastes. Because the three sites use similar technologies, this section begins with a generic description of the technologies and approaches used in various stages of the waste retrieval process. Most of this chapter addresses retrieval from the large underground storage tanks at the three DOE sites.

However, the Idaho National Laboratory also has six sets of large stainless steel bins containing reprocessing waste that was converted to a fine granular powder by a process called calcinations. The calcined material is very different from the wastes stored in the tanks, and factors affecting its retrieval are discussed in the section concerning waste characterization. The chapter ends with the committee's findings and recommendations related to tank waste retrieval.

Waste Retrieval Technologies

The waste that is to be retrieved from DOE's large underground storage tanks can contain three distinct phases: (1) supernatant liquid, (2) precipitated saltcake containing mostly non radioactive sodium compounds and soluble radionuclides such as cesium-137, and (3) viscous sludge. The phases usually occur in this order from top to bottom although the sludge and saltcake may be layered to some extent and both contain interstitial liquids having a composition typical of the supernatant liquid. Other materials may be present in the tank, such as debris and abandoned equipment. The objective of DOE's tank cleanup program is to retrieve waste to the maximum practical extent for subsequent processing.

However, waste retrieval technologies suitable for removing large amounts of bulk waste are generally not suitable for removing small amounts of residual waste in a tank. Thus, tank waste retrieval technology is discussed in two parts, which address: (1) bulk waste retrieval (including supernatant liquid, saltcake, and sludge retrieval) and (2) retrieval of the residual remaining after bulk waste retrieval.

Bulk Waste Retrieval

Retrieval of the bulk of the tank waste necessarily begins with the supernatant liquid at the top and works down through the saltcake and sludge. The following sections describe the mobilization, collection, and removal of the bulk of these wastes.

Supernatant Liquid

Retrieving the bulk of the supernatant liquid is straight forward because liquid waste is inherently mobile and can be removed readily by a "transfer" pump, much like a sump pump in a basement. The transfer pump is lowered into the tank to remove the liquid through a pipe or hose into a doubly contained underground pipe. The pumps used for this purpose need relatively low power compared to the mixing pumps used to mobilize waste forms such as saltcake and sludge, as discussed below. The technology for retrieving supernatant liquid is efficient and well established, although minor improvements continue to be made as a result of field experience.

Saltcake

Saltcake is composed mostly of readily soluble salts that precipitated because the saturation limit in the supernatant liquid was exceeded due to evaporation. The saltcake is dissolved to prepare it for removal by adding "fresh" water to the tank. Although it would be preferable to avoid adding fresh water to the tanks by using already contaminated recycled fluids, these fluids, such as supernatant liquid, are less efficient in dissolving the saltcake because they already contain high concentrations of salts or solids. Both the Savannah River and the Hanford Sites use "inhibited water" or "raw water" to dissolve saltcake.

At Hanford Tank S-112, approximately 95 percent of the tank waste inventory was retrieved using saltcake dissolution; additional retrieval using high-pressure (>5000 pounds per square inch [psi]) jets of water is being performed to break up and mobilize the remaining hard heel. The resulting solution is circulated through the tank until the desired specific gravity (usually 1.3 to 1.4) is achieved. Tank S-102 is also currently undergoing saltcake dissolution. Once the saltcake is dissolved, the resulting solution is then retrieved in the same manner as the supernatant liquid as with supernatant liquid retrieval, this technology is efficient and well established with only minor improvements continuing to be made.

Sludge

Bulk retrieval of the sludge and other solid materials is considerably more challenging than supernatant liquid and saltcake retrieval because the sludge cannot readily be dissolved in water and pumped from the tank; it first has to be mobilized, suspended in the liquid, and collected near a transfer pump. At the Savannah River Site, the sludge is mobilized using large mixer pumps (also called "sluicing pumps" or "slurry pumps") that mix it into slurry by directing a jet of water into the waste layer. At the Hanford Site, mixer pumps are planned for retrieval of waste from the newer double-shell tanks.

However, the sludge waste in Hanford single-shell tanks is mobilized using different equipment. For structurally sound single-shell tanks, high-pressure jets of water and mixer pumps and transfer pumps, similar to the equipment used for saltcake retrieval, will be used to retrieve sludge. For single-shell tanks with questionable integrity, a vacuum retrieval system in combination with a mobile retrieval system (except for smaller-diameter 200-series single-shell tanks) will be used to retrieve sludge. The Savannah River and Hanford Sites recognize that using recycled fluids, such as supernatant liquid from the same or surrounding tanks, to mobilize the sludge is better than using so-called fresh water because there is no net increase of waste volume and no subsequent need for evaporation.

Moreover, the supernatant liquid has a viscosity 10 to 20 times higher than that of raw water because of its high salt content. The supernatant liquid has self-sealing properties (i.e., it will plug small leaks) and keeps the slurry better suspended. However, if only a small addition of fluid is needed to suspend solids, raw water is used to minimize equipment contamination, worker exposure, and risk of leaks. The jets from the mixer pumps can be directed to impact various parts of the sludge layer and steer it toward the transfer pump intake. As with the supernatant liquid and dissolved saltcake, a transfer pump is then used to pump the slurry to a double- shell tank or compliant ("new-type") tank.

Eventually, the sludge from different tanks will be sent to processing facilities at the Hanford Site to separate the high-activity fraction from the low-activity fraction of the waste before vitrification, or washed then vitrified at the Savannah River Site. The primary challenge in sludge retrieval is creating a slurring jet that has sufficient energy to mobilize and mix the sludge across distances on the order of half a tank diameter (10.7 to 12.2 m or 35 to 40 feet) amidst the internal structures and debris. The Savannah River Site approach has been to build a steel superstructure atop each tank that is sufficient to mount four large (200 to 300 horsepower [hp]) electric motors.

Each motor rotates a 12-meter- (40-foot-) long drive shaft having a directional pump attached at the bottom to mobilize sludge into slurry that can be removed from the tank with a transfer pump. At Hanford, single-shell tank retrieval from tanks with questionable integrity is performed using installed sluicing jets, the Hydrolaser, the vacuum retrieval system, or a crawler system described later. The approach to bulk sludge retrieval described above suffers from two significant shortcomings, the first of which is cost.

The typical cost to retrieve the bulk of the waste from a single large tank is about $16 million to $24 million depending on whether there is a need to build a massive superstructure to support the mixer pumps. The second shortcoming is the occupational dose to workers during mixer pump removal and insertion and during maintenance to repair problems caused by the bearings along the pump shaft.

Calcine

DOE has not yet begun retrieval of the 4,411 m^3 of calcine from the bins at Idaho National Laboratory.

Technology Advances in Bulk Waste Retrieval

Advancements in technology for retrieval of bulk wastes are directed primarily at making engineering improvements in the large mixer pumps used to mobilize sludge to reduce cost and worker dose through incremental improvements in pump reliability. A notable recent technology at the Savannah River Site that may represent a step improvement in bulk waste retrieval is the "waste on wheels" (WOW) concept for bulk sludge removal. The WOW concept is centered on a specially designed submersible mixer (slurry) pump. This pump is similar to a conventional mixer pump except that a 305 hp drive motor is coupled to the pump and submerged, instead of being attached with a long shaft. The submersible mixer pumps are designed to be "self-supporting," with some tanks requiring "limited" structural steel supports, while others require a more robust structural steel supporting system similar to standard slurry pumps. The amount of structural steel required will depend on a technical evaluation of each tank.

Submersible mixer pumps are designed to be retractable, portable, and reusable. The infrastructure (power, instrumentation) that supports each of these is also designed to be movable; hence, the name WOW. These pumps address the shortcomings of traditional mixer pumps: They eliminate the troublesome 12-meter shaft, have sufficient power and directional control so that the number of pumps used in each tank can be reduced from four to two, and allow bulk waste retrieval in some tanks without having to build a costly steel support structure over the tank. These pumps have been successfully demonstrated in the cold test facility at the Savannah River Site and installed to retrieve waste in Savannah River Site Tank 5 as this report was being written. As a consequence, information on the effectiveness and/or shortcomings of the submersible mixer pump is only just beginning to become available. Additional details are provided in a later section titled Retrieval Experience.

Residual Waste Retrieval

Residual waste is what remains after the application of

bulk retrieval technologies described above. Residual waste can be composed of any or all of the following:

- Liquid and sludge in the bottom of the tank that could not efficiently be recovered using bulk retrieval technology;
- Radioactive material on the internal surfaces (e.g., walls, cooling coils) of the tank above the level of waste in the bottom of the tank; and
- Wastes composed of agglomerated materials that resist physical removal techniques to varying degrees. One example of such a material is the zeolite in some of the tanks at the Savannah River Site.

Waste remaining in the tank after the residual waste has been removed to the maximum extent practical is referred to as the "heel." The heel is the fraction of the waste that cannot be further mobilized and removed by practical means and, therefore, will be grouted inside the tank. The heel is composed mostly of insoluble metal hydroxides, oxides, and (at Hanford) phosphates containing strontium 90 and transuranic isotopes that are often viscous or consolidated into solids that are difficult to remove or located in inaccessible locations. To limit the amount of waste left in the tanks, the mobilization and collection steps of residual waste (after bulk waste retrieval) are critical to the success of the tank cleanup process.

Physical Technologies

The primary objective of residual waste retrieval technology is to mobilize and collect the waste at a point where it can be removed from the tank while minimizing secondary waste production. A variety of physical mobilization and collection technologies have been developed and these have been implemented using a variety of deployment technologies. Physical technologies for mobilizing residual waste and collecting it at a point in the tank that is accessible by a transfer pump include using a combination of the following: hydraulic techniques involving the use of pressurized water; a vacuum; mechanical techniques to dislodge the waste for collection and mobilization.

All phgysical techniques for retrieving redidual wastes in tanks require some type of deployment technology. To date the dominant deployment technology for residual waste retrival has been mechanical arms. The most popular type of arm used at DOE sites is a relatively simple mast inserted through a riser from which an arm containing one or two joints projects and some type of retrieval device extends.

Chemical Technologies

When physical technologies for retrieving residual waste have not been deemed sufficient, DOE has employed chemical technologies to remove remaining tank wastes. Tests performed in the late 1970s and early 1980s proved oxalic acid solutions to be the most effective reagent for dissolving sludge while not corroding the carbon steel tank. One reason DOE has cited for not using oxalic acid is a concern that it may compromise nuclear criticality safety. Since its interim report, the committee has received additional information from the Savannah River Site staff on criticality concerns.

According to the Savannah River Site staff, sludge heels after bulk waste removal may contain enough fissile mass, on average, to cause a criticality event. As DOE recognizes, the available data are inconclusive with regard to the potential for criticality during oxalic acid dissolution because the bulk of the material, including the fissile material, may be romoved before the ratio of fissile to poison falls below safe storage limits. Savannah River Site staff told the committee that each tank heel needs to be evaluated before attempting dissolution with oxalic acid to determine whether any potential for criticality exists and if so how to mitigate that risk. The committee has not seen any additional calculation regarding the criticality issues and cannot determine whether the concern is well founded.

According to DOE, there are additional downstream complications when using oxalic acid due to the large amounts of acid needed to dissolve the residual sludge. If oxalic acid is added to the sludge before washing, it goes to the evaporator and may precipitate in the feed tank. If oxalic acid is added to the salt tank, it may precipitate and form a hard salt layer that would require additional water to remove. DOE has indicated that it is planning to use oxalic acid as a final cleaning step at the Savannah River Site on a tank-by-tank basis, taking into account the factors listed above. Hanford is not planning at this time to use oxalic acid to clean its tanks.

Technology Advances for Mechanical Residual Waste Retrieval

DOE is considering the use of the Power Fluidic Technology developed by AEA Technology and a similar Russian Pulsating Mixer Pump technique for residual waste retrieval at the Hanford and the Savannah River Sites. This technology involves using two or more nozzles in a tank to establish a "back-and-forth" motion of the sludge and a vacuum induced by fluid flow through a "jet pump system,". This technology does not have any mechanical devices inside the tank and is supposed to use water more efficiently than conventional mixer pumps. Fluidic technology is claimed to be useful for bulk waste as well as residual waste retrieval and for mixing the grout with waste residuals that cannot be removed further.

However, like other technologies, its effectiveness on waste in tanks with vertical cooling coils is uncertain. Hanford tested a prototype using fluidic technology in a full scale cold test facility, and determined that the complex air and fluid controls and air handling systems would require significant maintenance. Concerns were also raised about radiation exposures to workers and meeting ALARA (as low as reasonably achievable) requirements for operations in the single-shell tank farm system. To the committee's knowledge, no further deployment of fluidic technology for waste retrieval from single-shell tanks is planned. Use of fluid jets for mixing grout with waste residuals is still under consideration.

General Waste Retrieval Issues

The discussion above has alluded to future difficulties that can be expected when retrieving waste from DOE's "complicated" tanks. Some of the important complications are discussed below. In addition to general issues, a number of site-specific issues may limit the extent to which wastes can be retrieved, are to be deployed; debris may become a problem even if these systems are capable of removing or moving this debris around the tanks.

Evaluation of Retrieval Technology Status

The purpose of this section is to evaluate the status of retrieval technologies by drawing on the discussion in the foregoing sections.

Technology Availability

The waste retrieval tools are grouped in broad classes because each site has developed or is using modified versions of the techniques. The table also indicates if and where a device was deployed or tested.

Retrieval Experience

All three DOE sites have operational experience retrieving liquid wastes from many tanks as a result of years of moving waste among the tanks as a part of day-to-day operations in the tank farms. There is no estimate of the amount of liquid waste that has been retrieved but such operations are considered routine. Both Hanford and Savannah River Site staff have some experience retrieving saltcake wastes (Idaho tanks have no saltcake) although not nearly as much as with liquids. In some cases, higher-pressure liquid jets and higher dissolution temperatures have been needed to overcome endothermic reactions and some complex waste chemistry solid-liquid equilibrium issues.

However, DOE has substantial operating experience in dissolving saltcake and retrieving the resulting liquids. The Savannah River Site has some operational experience with sludge removal. Sludge removal operations began in 1969 at the Savannah River Site for tank space management, to test waste retrieval technologies, or to retrieve sludge for processing and immobilization in the Defense Waste Processing Facility. However, past sludge removal operations were not carried out with the purpose of removing waste from a tank "to the maximum extent practical."

That is, there is much more experience with bulk retrieval of sludge than with residual waste retrieval. Savannah River Site tank retrieval experience is summarized as follows:

- Tank 16 was taken out of service because of leaks and became the first case in which DOE attempted to completely remove the bulk of the waste from a tank at the Savannah River Site. In 1979 254 m^3 (67,000 gallons) were removed with hydraulic techniques, and 5.3 m^3 (1,400 gallons) were removed in 1980 with chemical cleaning. There was minimal saltcake in this tank. The slurry pumps were extremely effective in removing the sludge. Oxalic acid was used to remove the residual waste. This tank has cooling coils.
- Waste has been retrieved from Tanks 17 and 20, and these tanks have been filled with grout. Tank 20 contained very little sludge, while Tank 17 contained a minimal amount of sludge and no zeolites. Neither of these tanks has cooling coils.
- Waste has been retrieved from Tanks 18 and 19. DOE has submitted a draft waste determination necessary to allow these tanks to be closed. Tank 19 contained very **little** sludge and a substantial

amount (49.2 m3 [13,000 gallons]) of zeolites, while Tank 18 contained substantial amounts of sludge and minimal amounts (7.6 m^3 [2,000 gallons]) of zeolites. Neither of these tanks has cooling coils.

- Waste retrieval from Tank 5 began in October 2005 and is ongoing. Bulk waste retrieval ended mid-December 2005. The submersible mixer pump used on this tank is described above. The volume of wet solids remaining after the first phase of bulk waste retrieval in Tank 5 is between approximately 68 m^3 (18,000 gallons) as calculated and 93 m^3 (24,500 gallons) as estimated from mapping the sludge mound at the bottom of the tank. Most of the remaining solids were located in the northwest quadrant of the tank where an array of cooling coils partially obstructed the mixer discharge jets. This is the first tank with cooling coils that has undergone bulk retrieval operations since Tank 16. A second mixing campaign was initiated in late November 2005 using a new mixer orientation to focus on the remaining solids. An additional 7.6 m^3 (2,000 gallons) of sludge were removed in the second sludge retrieval campaign. The submersible mixer pumps have been taken out of Tank 5 and installed in Tank 6 for bulk waste removal. Waste removal activities in Tank 5 will resume following completion of waste removal from Tank 6. Heel removal and cleaning of Tank 5 will follow completion of the bulk waste removal phases.
- Tank 6 is also undergoing waste retrieval. As noted above, the submersible mixer pumps have been removed from Tank 5 and installed in this tank. Waste removal activities in Tank 6 are anticipated to occur through April 2006. This tank also has cooling coils.

After Tank 16, Savannah River Site staff chose to begin waste retrieval from relatively uncomplicated tanks to obtain experience and is now proceeding to work on the more complicated Tank 5. Removal operations in Tank 5 and Tank 6 are DOE's first attempt to retrieve substantial quantities of sludge from tanks containing vertical cooling coils. Tank 5 is a leaking tank, with 13 known leak sites, although there is no significant waste accumulation in the tank annulus. A new leak appeared within two weeks of initiating sludge removal operations but only as a wet spot on the tank's outer wall. Leaks are monitored with video cameras in the tank annulus; however, only 25 percent of the annulus surface is visible because of the location of the cameras and risers. Tank 4 is the next Savannah River Site tank to be cleaned; it also contains sludge and cooling coils. The order in which waste is retrieved from the tanks depends on the feed blending requirements for the Defense Waste Processing Facility.

The Flanford Site has somewhat less operational experience with sludge removal than Savannah River. Hanford experience is as follows:

- Tank C-106 had a significant amount of sludge removed (187,000 gallons) during the 1997-1998 campaign using sluicing techniques. Sludge removal was enhanced using modified sluicing and chemical dissolution (additional 32,500 gallons) in the 2003 campaign,
- Sludge removal using modified sluicing started in November 2005 and is in progress in Tank C-103 (75,000 gallons of sludge initially).
- Hanford gained experience removing hard deposits of saltcake in Tank S-112 by using water jets to break them up, facilitating dissolution.
- Waste retrieval using the vacuum retrieval system is deemed complete in Tanks C-202 and C-203 (both 208.2 m^3 [55,000-gallon] tanks).
- Waste retrieval using the vacuum retrieval system is under way for Tank C-201 (started in October 2005).
- Waste retrieval from Tank C-204 will begin in April 2006.

- Removal of 302 m^3 (80,000 gallons) of sludge from Tank C-108 has slated to start late in 2005 using the modified sluicing technique.
- Removal of 302 m^3 (80,000 gallons) of sludge from Tank C-101 using the Mobile Retrieval System is planned but a date has not been set.

Because of the number of tanks and waste types present at this site, the sludge removal experience gathered thus far is not necessarily representative of the type of waste retrieval challenges faced when cleaning the site's 18 tank farms. To date, all experience has been in a few tanks inside just two of these tank farms. The Idaho site has retrieved waste from 7 of the 11 1135.6 m^3 (300,000-gallon) tanks and from all 4 of the 113.6 m^3 (30,000-gallon) tanks. The other tanks are still being used to hold sodium-bearing waste awaiting immobilization. The site has successfully deployed the same retrieval techniques (pumping and water washing) for the tanks thus far and plans to use the same technology for all of the remaining four tanks.

Retrieval Effectiveness

The most important measure of retrieval effectiveness is the amount of radioactive material left in the tank for on- site disposal (i.e., increasing retrieval effectiveness leaves decreasing amounts of radioactive material). While bulk retrieval may remove most of the radionuclides, the effectiveness of bulk retrieval technologies is essentially irrelevant to determining the amount of radionuclides left in a tank. As a consequence, this section focuses on the effectiveness of residual waste retrieval technologies.

Based on the information, it is evident that waste retrieval has been very effective for certain tanks. For example, the heels in Savannah River Site Tanks 17 and 20 and all of the Idaho National Laboratory tanks cleaned to date each contain less than 3,000 Ci (l.xl.llxlO^{14} Bq). Indicators of more effective retrieval appear to be (1) the absence of solid materials such as sludges and (2) the use of chemical cleaning on deposits where the chemicals would be expected to be effective. Experience with cleaning tanks with oxalic acid indicates that it is not universally effective in reducing the amount of radionuclides remaining in the tank. For example, it appears to be effective on many sludges but not on zeolite deposits.

Indicators of less effective retrieval appear to be the presence of recalcitrant solid materials, especially zeolite deposits containing relatively high concentrations of cesium- 137. It is too soon to tell how the general and site-specific issues discussed above will affect retrieval effectiveness because retrieval from tanks having such materials is just beginning. In summary, each tank is essentially unique in terms of waste type, tank design, and history. DOE's bulk waste removal strategy is sensible and has thus far been successful.

DOE is learning from experience, improving its understanding of the unique conditions in each tank as it progresses with tank cleanup, and developing and adapting technology to accommodate these differences. DOE is to be commended for exchanging technical information among sites to allow lessons learned to be incorporated in the program. Activities such as the yearly Hanford and Savannah River Site technical exchange meetings, the workshop on lessons learned from the closure of Tanks 17 and 20 at the Savannah River Site in 1998, frequent conference calls, and activities previously undertaken by the Tanks Focus Area are helpful. The Savannah River Site is also planning a technical workshop in March 2006 to identify technologies, including commercially available ones that could be implemented for the heel removal and tank cleaning activities for Tanks 5, 6, and others, with emphasis on techniques that minimize secondary waste volume generation.

The Tanks Focus Area was a particularly helpful approach for centralizing information and lessons learned for all DOE tank sites. The Tanks Focus Area was a user-driven, needs-based program within DOE's Environmental Management Office of Science and Technology. This program performed research, development, and deployment activities on tank waste characterization, monitoring, safe waste storage, retrieval, closure, pretreatment, and immobilization. The Tanks Focus Area's reports and the Innovative Technologies Summary Reports (the latter was another initiative of DOE's Office of Science and Technology) are still available on the Internet and provide a valuable although somewhat dated centralized information database on DOE's tank waste sites, including lessons learned.

Operations at Other DOE Sites

DOE has two additional sites at which radioactive waste has been stored in underground tanks: (1) the West Valley Demonstration Project (WVDP), New York, and (2) Oak Ridge National Laboratory, Tennessee. Some of the information is based on data published in 2002. Since then, most of the waste at the two sites has been retrieved and the remaining out-of-service tanks at Oak Ridge have been closed. DOE reports that retrieval of high-level waste from the West Valley Demonstration Project tanks was completed in 2002 and the residual sodium-bearing wastewater was retrieved from the two largest underground tanks in 2003. The wastes at these sites have some characteristics in common with wastes at the Savannah River Site and Hanford, although the tanks in New York and Tennessee are not as large as the largest tanks at the Hanford and Savannah River Sites.

West Valley Demonstration Project

Between 1966 and 1972, the West Valley Demonstration Project plant generated approximately 2,317 m^3 (612,000 gallons) of high-level waste. This waste consisted of 2,271 m^3 (600,000 gallons) of alkaline plutonium- uranium extraction (PUREX) sludge and supernatant liquid and approximately 45 m^3 (12,000 gallons) of acidic thorium extraction (THOREX) waste. The site had two tanks for these waste streams, and two additional tanks were used for secondary waste streams during waste processing. The retrieved wastes were immobilized in a vitrification facility, which operated between 1996 and 2002. The vitrified high-level waste canisters are intended for disposal in a geologic repository.

Oak Ridge National Laboratory

The liquid low-level radioactive waste system at Oak Ridge National Laboratory (ORNL) dates back to the mid-19405 when ORNL was constructed as part of the Manhattan Project. ORNL was a pilot site for Hanford chemical processes and had approximately 390 m^3 (103,000 gallons) of sludge stored in a system consisting of nine large Gunite tanks and numerous smaller metal tank systems. In addition, the tanks contained small quantities of dried waste that had the consistency of chalk. The Gunite tank sludge (solids) contained approximately 85,000 Ci (3.1×10^{15} Bq). This radioactivity came from uranium, plutonium, thorium, and other long-lived isotopes, as well as from the high concentrations of cesium-137 and strontium-90, which have relatively short half-lives.

The tanks also contained organic materials in trace amounts and other heavy metals. Groundwater had leaked into the tanks, adding approximately 1300 m^3 (345,000 gallons) of water. This water accumulated on top of the sludge in an aqueous supernatant layer. The supernate and the tank walls contained an additional estimated 15,000 Ci (5.6×10^{14} Bq). In tank cleanup operations, ORNL constituted a test bed for a number of retrieval technologies considered for deployment at other sites.

The Savannah River Site, the Hanford Site, and Idaho National Laboratory, shows the similarities and the differences among the tank types and types of waste at Oak Ridge and West Valley. Given the differences in the physical and chemical properties of the waste and tank designs, not all the experience gathered at these other sites is relevant to the three sites addressed in this report. However, sharing lessons learned and communication among the sites may still be helpful as DOE continues its cleanup mission.

Cost of Bulk and Residual Waste Retrieval

The cost of waste retrieval includes costs for bulk waste retrieval and costs for residual waste retrieval. Despite the relatively limited number of waste retrievals that have been completed, the cost of waste retrieval has decreased substantially as a result of learning from experience. The best example of this occurred at Hanford where the combined cost of the first retrieval effort on a large tank (C-106) was about $140 million, whereas the comparable costs of more recent retrievals ranges from $20 million to $40 million. The projected cost for the next group of tanks (208.2 m^3 [55,000-gallon]) is around a few million dollars each and estimated to be about $15 million for a large tank and the use of temporary above-ground transfer lines that substantially reduce infrastructure costs.

The third (projected) cost decrease appears to be driven by a transition from existing hydraulic technologies (e.g., water jets) to the reusable Mobile Retrieval System, which further reduces water usage by employing a vacuum device combined with a mechanical vehicle to push waste. It should be noted that in all cases, most of the cost is attributable to moving equipment to a tank and installing it, not to retrieval operations per se. The estimated cost for retrieving waste from the larger 100-series tanks using the Mobile Retrieval System is about $20 million per tank. However, the cost savings realized so far do not necessarily reflect substantive cost savings in waste removal operations in the future, given the limited number of tanks that have been completely cleaned to date.

Retrieval at the Savannah River Site began with modified sluicing for bulk waste retrieval. As a consequence, combined retrieval costs are comparable to those at Hanford and range from \$23 to \$34 million per tank excluding costs for chemical cleaning. As previously mentioned, the Savannah River Site has just begun retrieving waste from Tank 5 using a submersible mixer pump. This technology is expected to reduce the retrieval cost to a range between \$6 and \$14 million. The cost reduction is attributable to the pump's added effectiveness compared to the long-shaft mixer pumps, so that the number of pumps required in each tank is reduced from four to two; also to the use of the submersible pumps in multiple tanks, which reduces the cost per tank.

The spread in cost range is attributable to the need for superstructure above the tanks: tanks with small amounts of sludge do not require a superstructure, whereas tanks with large amounts of sludge would require such a superstructure. The design safety analysis at the Savannah River Site requires an evaluation for hydrogen gas release from tanks containing sludge when mixing-removal operations are planned. Safety analyses assume that the quantity of sludge in the tank dictates the amount of hydrogen gas retained in the sludge (same number of grams of hydrogen per inch of depth). Mixing the sludge releases gas that is otherwise held up in the sludge. There is a limit to the allowable rate of hydrogen released.

The submersible mixer pumps mix everything above them and are assumed not to mix sludge 30-45 cm (12 to 18 inches) below. To reduce the gas release rate, submersible mixer pumps are suspended closer to the top of the sludge and work their way down. Suspending the submersible mixer pumps at different heights requires a superstructure. In the case of Tank 5, because of its gas release calculation, all of the sludge could be mixed simultaneously. Therefore, the Tank 5 submersible mixer pumps could be lowered to the tank bottom. In some of the other tanks (e.g., Tank 4), the gas release calculation from sludge mixing may dictate that submersible mixer pumps cannot be lowered to the tank bottom, and therefore some superstructure will be required to support them at different levels of mixing.

At the Idaho National Laboratory, waste has been retrieved from seven 1136 m^3 (300,000-gallon) tanks and four 114 m^3 (30,000-gallon) tanks from 2002 to 2005 at a total (development plus operations) of $35 million. This yields an average cost of $7 million per tank, although this number is likely to decrease slightly because some of the development costs will be allocated to the four remaining tanks where retrieval has not yet been completed. Although many of the Idaho tanks have cooling coils on their bottoms, the relatively low retrieval costs can be attributed to the favorable physical characteristics of the waste (i.e., absence of hard sludges, solid particles easily washed from walls and suspended in the tank liquids).

Cost of Additional Residual Waste Retrieval

One important factor in determining whether radionuclides have been removed to the maximum extent practical is the cost of retrieving additional residual waste from the tanks when the limit of the baseline technology has been reached. Savannah River Site staff has developed cost estimates for additional waste retrieval from Tanks 18 and 19 using three different approaches: (1) additional hydraulic sluicing using a closed loop similar to that in the Mobile Retrieval System now being deployed at Hanford, (2) an in-tank vehicle similar to the vacuum device now being deployed at Hanford as part of the Mobile Retrieval System, and (3) chemical cleaning with oxalic acid. The additional cost for such cleaning is estimated to range from $10 to $15 million per tank if a tank has been taken "out of service." This estimated cost for chemical cleaning can be compared to the estimated cost for chemical cleaning of Tank 16 ($250,000) and a 1999 estimate of about $1 million.

The significant increase in the recent estimate for Tanks

18 and 19 is due to the fact that these two tanks have been taken out of service, which means substantial efforts are required to reverse preparations made for closure (e.g., reconnecting support equipment and utilities) and additional safety and operational constraints. These same assumptions were used for the other two alternatives. Presumably, the cost of applying chemical cleaning to a tank that is still in service would be closer to \$1 million than to \$10 million given the additional safety requirements that were introduced since oxalic acid was applied to Tank 16. At the Hanford Site, costs for additional waste retrieval from Tank C-106 have been estimated to be \$1.24M to \$2.97M per m^3 (\$35,000 to \$84,000 per cubic foot), or a total of \$5.7M to \$13.5M, depending on the retrieval technology if it is assumed that approximately 4.5 m^3 (160 cubic feet) of waste would be removed. This assumption was made for purposes of analysis only and is by no means assured if the additional technology were to be actually deployed.

At the Idaho National Laboratory, development and deployment of a new technology for retrieval of additional residual waste is estimated to cost slightly more than development and deployment of the existing tank cleaning system. The cost of the new technology (mechanical, chemical, or arm based) was estimated by applying an escalation rate of 10 percent to the tank waste retrieval cost to date, yielding \$38.5 million per tank. Idaho National Laboratory believes the actual cost would likely be higher because the new technology may not be able to use much of the existing infrastructure at the site. A large fraction of the cost is independent of the technology used to retrieve waste because it involves the preparation of plans and other documentation, testing, readiness reviews, equipment mobilization, installation, demobilization, and leak detection and monitoring during waste retrieval.

Worker Dose Estimates During Retrieval

Cleaning up large underground tanks is a hazardous

operation even for tanks that do not contain radioactive waste. The additional cumulative worker doses resulting from further retrieval efforts is estimated to be 7,150 millirem (mrem or 71.5 millisieverts, mSv) for 11 1135.6 m^3 (300,000-gallon) tanks at the Idaho National Laboratory and ranges from 4,500 to 7,500 mrem (45 to 75 mSv) per tank at the Savannah River Site. The larger values at the Savannah River Site are presumably a result of the substantial effort that would be required to prepare a "ready-for-closure" tank for retrieval operations.

Site staff are still analyzing the information on worker dose risks gathered during waste retrieval (e.g., through radiation surveys and job task analysis). Hanford does not have worker dose estimates for waste retrieval. Information on worker doses during retrieval from Tank C-106 is not readily available because waste retrieval operations comprised many activities spread over a 7 to 10 years and the site did not keep track of cumulative worker dose at that time. It is possible to reconstruct the cumulative worker dose for the entire period, but the information has not yet been compiled.

Estimated Dose to the Public from Closed Tanks

The reduction in dose to the public from retrieving additional residual waste has been estimated by DOE for both the Savannah River Site and Idaho National Laboratory tank waste determinations and for Tank C-106 at Hanford. The estimates are based on the extent to which the dose rate to a hypothetical member of the public would be reduced by removing or reducing the radionuclide inventory in the tank and multiplying this by an assumed 50 years of exposure to yield the dose avoided by an individual. If 100 percent of the residual waste were to be removed by additional retrieval, a situation that is not actually possible because of limitations on the efficiency of separations, the avoided all-pathways dose to an adult residing in proximity to the F Area Tank Farm at the Savannah River Site is 2 mrem for Tank 18 and 0.45 mrem (4.5 mSv) for Tank 19.

The Idaho Section 3116 waste determination for its tank farm estimates that the remaining radioactivity in the tank farm poses a potential radiation all-pathways dose to a member of the public on the order of 0.5 mrem (5 mSv) per year, with approximately half of the dose due to tank heels. Removing all tank residuals would achieve a dose reduction of approximately 0.25 mrem (2.5 mSv) per year, or 12.5 mrem (125mSv) over 50 years, regardless of cost.

The Hanford Site estimates that removing an additional 4.5 m^3 (160 cubic feet) of residual waste from Tank C-106 would reduce the all-pathways doses from the current residual volume (10.5 m^3 [370 cubic feet]) from 2.5 x 10^{-3} to 1.39 x 10^{-3} mrem per year (2.5 x 10^{-5} to 1.39 x 10^{-5} mSv per year) calculated at the fence line of Area C. Therefore, the avoided dose over 50 years would be 0.05 mrem (or 1.11 x 10^{-3} mrem [1.11 x 10^{-5} mSv] per year over 50 years) for Tank C-106. Hanford estimates that this further waste reduction entails an incremental lifetime cancer risk reduction of 8 x 10^{-9} at a cost of $5.7 million to $13.5 million. The avoided dose over 50 years at each site is significantly different because of differing natural settings (e.g., different hydrogeology) and assumptions used in the underlying performance assessments.

Adequacy of In-Tank Waste Characterization

Waste retrieval requires knowledge of physical data about the waste (e.g., density, particle size, viscosity, fraction of solids) to facilitate pumping and to avoid plugging the pipelines. Such knowledge is gathered relatively easily by grab sampling. DOE's approach has been thus far to begin waste retrieval with the knowledge available on the waste and adapt retrieval technologies to the conditions encountered in the tanks. One case that may prove to be more complicated than anticipated is retrieval of calcine waste at the Idaho National Laboratory. DOE plans to retrieve this granular powder from the stainless steel silos (bin sets) by reversing the process bv which it was emplaced:

vacuuming it from the bins through the risers at the tops. DOE conducted a successful test with simulated waste: caked calcine was readily dislodged by physical contact with the vacuum head, and the calcine could be transported pneumatically.

However, whether the actual calcine will behave like the stimulant after residing in the bins for several decades is uncertain. Retrieval of a different calcine from a silo at DOE's Fernald site proved challenging because of compaction. A previous National Research Council report states that, given the little characterization information about the Idaho calcine, it would be difficult to conclude that there would be no problem with pneumatic retrieval. Indeed the committee believes that there will be problems but that they can probably be handled. However, this eventually might require mechanical operations to aid particle flow and more elaborate retrieval methods (e.g., a manipulator arm) than simple pneumatic transfer.

The committee agrees with this assessment. Previous studies have concluded that the calcine in the bins can be safely stored for hundreds of years because of the absence of water in the bins, the stability of the calcine, and the dry environment. As a consequence, addressing the disposition of the wastes contained therein has justifiably been accorded a lower priority in the face of more pressing issues at the Idaho National Laboratory and other DOE sites. The committee identifies the calcine retrieval and bin disposition as issues for further examination.

Support Operations and Disposal of Retrieved Wastes and Heels

Characterization of heels is necessary to determine their chemical and radionuclide composition (actinide content, alpha, gamma, and beta emitters) to calculate the "source term" in the performance assessment of the tank once closed. Tank heels left in the tanks must also be characterized to demonstrate that the waste has been adequately removed and that the residues can be left in the tanks. Heel characterization is performed by visual inspection through cameras, sampling, special analysis, and predictions based on knowledge of wastes that were sent to the tank (process knowledge). Obtaining, packaging, shipping, and analysis of each sample resulted in personnel radiation exposure. Tank 19 sample dose rates were as high as 8,000 mrem (80 mSv) per hour dose to the hands and 4,000 mrem (40 mSv) per hour dose to the whole-body.

The total whole-body worker dose received from the three solid samples was approximately 200 mrem (2 mSv). Tank 18 sample dose rates were as high as 150 mrem (1.5 mSv) per hour dose to the whole body. The total whole-body worker dose received from the six solid samples and the one liquid sample was approximately 120 mrem (1.2 mSv). Detailed discussion of tank heel sampling can be found in the performance objective demonstration document for Tanks 18 and 19. The heel sampling campaign at the Savannah River Site showed that the heel contains less radioactive material than the bulk of the waste because it was thoroughly rinsed by waste slurring and tank washing.

Those rinses removed some of the soluble radionuclides, which decreased the radioactive inventory and leachability of the heel compared to the bulk waste. The time that water would be in contact with the waste in post- closure degradation scenarios is, however, much greater than the duration of tank cleaning operations; thus, even low leach rates for long-lived radionuclides, such as technetium-99 and neptunium-237, can result in groundwater contamination. Both the reduced release rates and the duration of contact with water are important factors in determining residual risks to a member of the public and hence how clean is clean enough.

Evaluation

Up to this point the sites have used similar information to decide when to cease retrieving waste. All three sites use the amount of solids removed from the tanks per cycle of mixing and pumping as the main criterion for determining that waste has been removed "to the maximum extent practical." The solids removal rate is usually high at the beginning of waste retrieval, regardless of the technique used, but as retrieval proceeds and there are fewer solids to recover, it decreases and eventually becomes constant at a low value. At some point, considerations such as the amount of secondary waste generated versus the amount of solids removed, cost, worker dose, and tank space limitations justify a decision to stop waste removal.

At the Savannah River Site, 46 cycles of sluicing and pumping were applied to remove the zeolite from Tank 19 and six cycles for Tank 18. Once the removal rate decreased significantly and went below 200 gallons of solids per cycle and 5,000 gallons of solids per cycle for Tank 19 and Tank 18, respectively, waste removal was deemed complete. The Draft Section 3116 Waste Determination reads:

a number of obstacles prevented further residual waste removal. The obstacles fell into three categories: (1) fast-settling zeolite resins, (2) general tank access limitations and obstructions, and (3) mounds of insoluble. In addition to those obstacles, FFA [Federal Facility Agreement] requirements [i.e., tank closure milestones] for closure of Tank 19 and Tank 18, as well as tank space constraints were additional factors that prevented further residual waste removal."

However, the committee observes that if one retrieval method shows diminishing effectiveness, other methods may still prove effective. Simply repeating a procedure 46 times does not demonstrate that all practical efforts have been made. Also, constraints imposed by closure schedules should not be an important consideration in selecting retrieval methods if scheduling interferes with effective waste removal. At the Hanford Site, before DOE can make a waste determination concerning classification of the residual waste, it must meet the waste retrieval requirements specified in the Tri-Party Agreement (TPA).

The TPA directs DOE to "remove as much tank waste as technically possible, with tank waste residues not to exceed ..." 30 cubic feet (.85 m^3) in the small 200-series tanks and 360 cubic feet in the large 100-series tanks. Then, to make a determination that the waste is not high-level waste under DOE Order 435.1, DOE must, among other things, demonstrate that the residues remaining in the tank "have been processed, or will be processed, to remove key radionuclides to the maximum extent that is technically and economically practical."

To meet this criterion, DOE must remove *waste* from the tanks to the maximum extent that is technically and economically practical because radionuclides generally cannot be removed from the tanks without removing other wastes as well. The metric that Hanford uses to decide when to cease retrieving residual waste is the volume of waste being retrieved versus the amount of new waste being created. At Idaho National Laboratory, the waste retrieved from the tank was monitored for its radioactivity until it reached an asymptotic value. Visual examination (comparison of waste levels in the bottom of the tank to the thickness of known benchmarks) and waste sampling are also used at the three sites to assess the progress of waste retrieval.

In the two recent tank waste determinations at the Savannah River Site and Idaho, DOE presented (although in a somewhat qualitative way) its trade-offs among some of the key technical factors that lead it to conclude that enough waste has been retrieved from Tanks 18 and 19 at the Savannah River Site and will be retrieved from the entire tank farm in Idaho. DOE also made similar trade-offs in the documents recently submitted to the U.S. Nuclear Regulatory Commission (USNRC) showing how waste removal from Tank C-106 at Hanford has reached the technology limit, as required by the Tri-Party Agreement. In essence, DOE separately compares the estimated cost (dollars) and worker dose (millirem) from additional retrieval for each tank to the estimated dose to a hypothetical member of the public over 50 years (millirem) that would be avoided by the additional retrieval.

This comparison (a ratio) is used as the primary justification in the Savannah River tank waste determination for waste having already been retrieved to the maximum extent practical. As stated previously, the 50-year avoided all-pathways dose to a member of the public residing in the proximity of the tanks ranges from 0.45 to 2 mrem (4.5 to 20 mSv) for the Savannah River Site, and 12.5 to 23 mrem (125 to 230 mSv) for Idaho National Laboratory, and is 0.05 mrem ($5 * 10^{4}$ mSv) for the Hanford Site. The cost per avoided unit of dose ranges from about $5 million per mrem to more than $30 million per millirem at the Savannah River Site, from $1.7 to $3.08 million per millirem at Idaho National Laboratory, and from $100 to $240 million per millirem to further remove waste from Tank C-106 at Hanford.

The Idaho waste determination reports that the average worker dose for cleaning and closing the 11 1135.6 m^3 (300,000-gallon) tanks is expected to total about 7,100 mrem (71 mSv) for all occupational exposure. The ratio of increased worker dose to avoided 50-year dose to the public ranges from about 2,000 mrem (20 mSv) to more than 16,000 mrem (160 mSv) at the Savannah River Site and between 309 and 568 mrem (3.1 to 5.7 mSv) at Idaho. Both ratios assume that all of the residual waste is recovered. Similar information is not available for the Hanford Site because worker doses received during cleanup of Tank C- 106 are still not available. On this basis, DOE determined that the risk reduction does not justify further waste removal from Savannah River Site Tanks 18 and 19.

The committee notes that the risk-benefit assessment used as a rationale for the waste determination at the Savannah River Site did not discuss the assumptions about the "dollar value" of a dose or provide any framework to compare the doses and costs calculated for additional waste retrieval to doses and costs in different scenarios (e.g., doses to the public after only the waste that is easy to retrieve is removed). The Idaho waste determination reaches the conclusion that further waste retrieval is not necessary in a different way:

> With typical average doses to the public from natural sources and medical treatment in the range of 300-400 mrem per year, it is not judged practical or cost effective to reduce the estimated dose from [the tanks] by such a small amount.

The Hanford Site compares the additional waste retrieval costs for Tank C-106 to human health risk reduction (expressed as incremental lifetime cancer risk) based on residual waste volume in the tank. The cost ratios for the Savannah River Site were based on what DOE considers conservative assumptions but could be considerably lowered with foresight — for example, by undertaking additional residual waste retrieval before preparing the tank for closure. Additional discussion of doses to the public from the tank heels and assumptions used in the tanks performance assessments is provided in.

For completeness, at Oak Ridge National Laboratory the criteria for stopping waste retrieval were to leave (1) no visible sludge; and (2) residual dirty water in bottom of tank roughly equivalent to the water that would be added during decontamination of retrieval equipment during retraction. At the West Valley Demonstration Project site, flushing effectiveness was monitored using sampling, radiological dose rate changes, and visual inspection. The heels in the tanks were then characterized as described above to determine whether they meet the Class C criteria. Three important operational criteria that determined whether residuals were removed to the maximum extent practical were (1) the chances for melter or major equipment failure during waste retrieval; (2) loss of qualification of vitrified high-level waste form; and (3) significant increases of glass volume.

The committee observes that the question, how clean is clean enough? Has both policy and technical dimensions because it involves trade-offs among risks to workers, the public, and the environment and cost. In theory, some combination of residual waste retrieval technologies could continue to be applied until the radionuclides in the waste residuals are reduced to negligible levels. In practice, the possibility of removing radionuclides to this extent is counterbalanced by diminishing returns; reduced leachability of residual radionuclides, limits on funds; the dose to workers that occurs during retrieval efforts; the potential for or reality of leaks to the environment during retrieval; and the generation of increasing amounts of secondary waste. There are also non technical factors to be considered such as stakeholder values.

Data on the costs and worker doses associated with each tank cleaning option were scant. Input to decisions about the maximum extent practical and ALARA would be improved if DOE kept careful records of costs and worker doses as progress is made on these first tank cleanings and closures. Part of the answer to the question, how clean is clean enough is provided by performance assessments to evaluate whether waste left in the tanks meets the performance objecti ves set forth in the legislation, DOE orders, and federal facility agreements governing waste removal. Results in the performance assessment are based on assumptions and scenarios that take place over long periods of time and involve great uncertainties. Assumptions about the duration of institutional controls are a particular case in point. If DOE's assumptions about institutional controls are not correct, members of the public could reside near the closed tanks or low-activity disposal site within a few hundred years, and doses to the public could be sufficiently large enough that the cost and worker risk associated with additional retrieval might be justified.

The issue of how long institutional controls are assumed

to keep people away from the closed tanks is a matter of policy that cannot be resolved scientifically. Another part of the answer to the question, how clean is clean enough is provided by DOE and its contractors through a discussion of technology limitations. Waste retrieval from DOE tanks is a one-of-a-kind and first-of-a-kind endeavor. There is no other activity that can serve as a benchmark for estimating radiation exposure to workers, technology possibilities and limitations, cost estimates, time lines, and so forth. The regulators and stakeholders have to rely on DOE for such inputs to the decision about whether waste has been retrieved to the maximum extent practical.

Deciding the appropriate balance among these competing factors is the essence of deciding whether radionuclides have been removed to the maximum extent practical and, thus, that the tank is "clean enough" to proceed to closure. Therefore, the debate often revolves around what "retrieval to the maximum extent practical" means and whether further decreasing the estimated risks to the public by retrieving additional waste from the tanks justifies additional worker exposure and retrieval costs. Because of the variability of the physical, chemical, and radiological characteristics of the residual waste in each tank, such decisions must be made on a tank-by-tank basis.

4

Paradigm Shift in Environmental Education in India

Since environmental sciences have now been introduced as a compulsory subject, at various levels in the formal education system, it has assumed greater importance. How should the subject be taught? The curriculum developed seems to be exhaustive, but do we have the basic infrastructure for its effective delivery? Such questions are being raised, and environmental sciences educators have begun to prepare to shoulder the responsibility of teaching the subject. Various training sessions and refresher training programs are being organized for the educators. The difficulties faced in teaching the subject have already started filtering in for discussions in the academic circle and will begin to surface sooner or later. Why is it difficult to teach environmental science? Why is it that earlier efforts have only partially reached the level of awareness they should have?

The answer lies in the complex nature of the subject and the interpretations of its various aspects. No single one of its aspects can be given greater importance. Nor can any one of them be ignored. It is a multidisciplinary area, where the overlaps and inter-linkages are intricate. Dexterity is required for handling the subject. For an in-depth understanding of environmental science at the graduate level, the students must be prepared right from their school days. For effective delivery of the subject, especially at the primary and high school levels, three important things have to be taken into consideration.

The Focus of Science Education

The first is that science plays an important role in developing and nurturing interest in our environment. A keen look at the science curriculum suggests that along with the basics in chemistry, physics and biology (NCERT), a child learns that all known sciences have various applications, primarily, for the benefit of mankind. Many eminent scientists have devoted their lives to research in the field of science and awesome scientific and technological progress has been achieved. This must be communicated to the children, and no doubt, formal education is an excellent medium for it. It is now clear that technological progress, and the way it progressed, had a disastrously negative impact on our environment.

This is something our children should know as well. Imagine a chapter from a science textbook devoted to basic science; the next devoted to technology or applied science; the third devoted to the positive and negative impacts of the development of science and technology; the fourth to the conservation of the environment; the fifth to biodiversity; and the sixth to agriculture and the use of fertilizers and bio-magnification. The learner might end up being utterly confused. But this is virtually what students go through in a single academic year. The student learns to appreciate his curriculum thus: what he learns has to be reproduced during the academic evaluation, for which, he is expected to know everything that is taught, whether relevant or not..He has to score in a test that tells him how much he knows. Secondly the student learns that everything that is developed for the good, has a bad outcome as well, which is noticed a little or much later than the positive outcome, so one has to take care while planning.

So how the information should be presented? What should be the focus of science education? At this juncture, it is appropriate to quote that debates were raised several times in the early 20th century on how science should be taught. The world (people) was just overcoming the belief that God was the creator and that God had made man differently—probably in his own image. From the year 1900 to 1970, crucial decisions have been taken by leading nations through discussions and debates among scientists and the Christian religious leaders about the science curriculum. The theory of evolution proposed by Sir Charles Darwin and his two important books The Origin of the Species and The Descent of Man provoked these debates. Could man be just another animal or is he meant to rule the world as Genesis suggests? Does our ancestry lie among the apes? Such crucial questions profoundly influenced the formation and development of the science curriculum at the school level.

Creationism or the creationist approach got the better of evolution or the naturalistic approach in the decision-making process and the human race became the focus of the school science curriculum. If students learn science with such notions of superiority, will effective EE for Sustainable Development (SD) be achieved? The concept of superiority can be dealt with later. If a natural system is to be sacrificed for technological or industrial development it will be sacrificed by our future generations, as they too will be doing it for good or valid reasons. Unless it is taught that man is not special and is only as important as other biological specimens, and that if he is special it is only so that he can care for the well being of the wide range of other organisms like plants and animals, and that coexistence with them is the only thing that is going to brighten up his future, his earth—only then can the pupil be motivated to do so and learn to do so.

Yes, all this is a part of the present curriculum as well, but in the end, what the student learns is that the human race is superior and that it must make progress, and progress means technological and industrial growth. Without using the exact words, this is what is impressed upon the learner's mind repeatedly through his entire schooling. Can this be termed a fallacy of curriculum design? Probably not, but the concept underlying science education must be rethought.

The Absence of Learner Centered Education

Another concern is how should the learner appreciate environmental sciences? Recently a debate ensued on whether geography, history and the natural sciences should be taught as a part of environmental sciences. What needs to be understood is should the student appreciate environmental science as it is in India, Pakistan, UK, US, etc? The geography of the world differs from country to country and so does the climate, and so arises the diversity in the biological world. The student also learns that country x is rich in such and such minerals and so such industries are in large numbers in that country. The nature of pollutants is so and so and that the pollutants have affected agriculture in that country in such and such a manner. Also, such are the effects of pollution on the population, the forests and the rivers and the soil. So it is appreciated as a problem of 'that' country.

This is what a child learns, wordlessly again. The recent event in which the US refused to agree with the post Kyoto commitments is a very good example of how the concept of country, and thinking only of the citizens of that country, dictates the decision-making process. On the other hand, the cleaning of the Rhine sets an example as to how the river's natural beauty and cleanliness were restored by Holland, through an international program. When it becomes everyone's concern, things happen. Is it possible for the student to learn about his environment as 'his home; his earth'? This will make it easier for the learner to realize why he needs to know all this. If the boundaries of various countries are laid down in the geography curriculum, and if through history the child is going to understand that people from so and so country have come and plundered our country in the past, will he be able to appreciate that the environmental concerns of any other country have a direct bearing on his life and are his concerns as well?

The seeds of distinction once sown at a tender age are difficult to remove. How can global environmental issues filter down to a graduate student, if he repeatedly learns such distinctions during the ten-twelve years of schooling? Instead of generalizing and speaking about the various distinctions, if the learner is put at the center, and if the education imparted respects his identity not as an Indian or American, but him as a part of the environment, as a part of this world, the appreciation of environmental sciences will be much better. What the student needs to learn is his role as a part of the environment and the best way to act without harming his environment. The complex notions of boundaries of various countries and the economy must come later, when the mind becomes mature enough to understand that such distinctions are only man-made. The present adult population does not have this maturity, as they are loyal to their country, but not to the Earth (Our Earth!), because this is what they have learnt from their childhood.

Role of the Environmental Science Educator

To compound the problem, environmental sciences are linked to our daily existence and our private life and habits. EE was earlier introduced as one of the values in value education. This is the third most important concern that needs to be addressed right from the early days of schooling. Schoolteachers play a vital role in developing habits by setting an example. If a schoolteacher advocates the rejection of plastics but daily brings her meal to school in a plastic bag, her teaching, however well taught, becomes meaningless. To the pupil it might mean that this is only to be learnt and not practiced. In addition, if parents use and throw plastic bags, learning cannot take place.

Everything only remains in print, which is exactly what is happening presently. It is true not only of plastic bags but also of all consumables and even about the use of natural fuels for transport and communication so environmental science is not about industrialization alone, or deforestation and pollution, but our daily habits as well. How can environmentally friendly habits be developed?

The *gurukul* system once practiced in ancient India is a very good example of how habits and practices were inculcated, which were in tune with the local environment. The habits developed dexterity for living as a part of nature. Natural systems were not taxed and the guru achieved this through the *gurukul* system, which was the then existing formal system of education. A guru had several disciples of various ages living with his family. They were taught rituals and the disciples copied the manner in which the guru behaved. The guru's behaviour had a profound impact on the disciples' minds. Habits were handed down religiously and a harmonious balance with nature was maintained. The guru was the role model and was responsible for educating a batch of students who went back to their own worlds and raised a family and taught these habits to their children. A person undergoing such training spent several years with the guru. He was given sufficient time to develop the maturity required for performing the very acts his guru taught.

This was a balanced, time-tested approach and not the firefighter's approach that is now being used for teaching environmental sciences. Habits have to be handed down from the earlier generation to the next; it is only then and thus, that the deep-rooted meanings of these actions are also conveyed. It is seen in several schools and also appreciated by the educators that the learner is told to break his bad habits and, in case the parents suffer from the same condition, to break theirs as well. Children are told to tell their parents to repair leaking taps and segregate waste among other things. This might impress upon the child that his parents do not behave in a manner that his educator expects of them and as a result, he will lose respect for his parents and his educators as well, which goes against moral science and value education (also taught in schools) which are also compulsory subjects.

Educators are role models to the students until they are 10-12 years old. Since pre-school, interaction between parents and educators through parent-teacher meetings must be directed towards bridging this gap. Environ-mentalists can be invited for such meetings and policies must be developed for sustainable EE. Parents must be made aware of the things that will be taught in school and also should realize the need for their participation and cooperation. What is taught in school is not a part of scholastic education but is also meant to be an integral part of their lives and that of the future generation's. Children need appreciation, from their parents as well as from teachers. If they feel that they will not be appreciated by their teachers because their parents do not segregate waste or for any other issue discussed in class that is expected to be taken home, they might be driven to lie, or attempt to hide, or ignore what is being taught. These mental conflicts are not healthy.

It is known that children are aware of what goes on in their homes, and therefore, they are asked to teach their parents about what must be done about waste segregation, leaking taps and such other things. The real climax comes when it all ends with a question paper, which they answer either by rote learning, or by recalling the information given during lessons. In 1956, Benjamin Bloom headed a group of educational psychologists who developed a classification of levels of intellectual behaviour important in learning. Bloom found that over 95 per cent of the test questions that students encounter require them to think only at the lowest possible level...that of the recall of information...

Besides this, students are expected to carry out some projects on the environment such as collecting information and pasting pictures cut from magazines, or something along these lines. These projects are expected to fuel their creative abilities, which might be the case, but most of the time children turn towards their parents for assistance and often, it is the parent who plays a leading role in doing the project. What then, is achieved? The completion of such projects is mandatory as they are academically evaluated. Where and what is the value of the child's creativity? This is true of other subjects as well. But this is surely not education.

Why have we come to such a stage? Where do the roots of such a disastrous change lie and how did it go unnoticed? This is clearly evident from the history of our country: having lost several generations to battles with the invaders who looted the country and rendered the population insecure, followed by the last 57 and a half years for establishing as an independent nation. India does not have a generation that assumes the responsibility of becoming role models for teaching environment as a science, ethics and culture. The complexity arises because it is everyday science, with links to the past and the future.

Everything in this subject has a deep underlying meaning that speaks through actions, not words. Every significant environmental action has a cultural significance and a scientific base. It takes great skill to balance the two —the understanding and the action that follows. Each action has to be weighed as its roots lie in the past and its results will affect the future. Therefore the role of an environmental science educator is very important. Students follow/imitate an educator and consequently magnify through their actions whatever mistakes an educator makes. If an educator of environmental sciences is unable to practice what s/he preaches nothing can be achieved.

Therefore, to sum up, for achieving holistic EE, changes will have to be made in three important aspects that are the focus of science education, which is very fundamental to the process of learning environmental sciences. Superiority of the human race must not be employed to destroy the natural world. Secondly the approach should be cultivated with a student centered idea of the subject delivered. And thirdly, environmental science educators must become role models and must put into practice what is preached. Educators must give due respect and do the needful before they teach, only then will the learners be enabled to bridge the gap between walking the walk and talking the talk. Only then can the objectives of EE be achieved.

Environmental Protection as a Transnational Problem

Insufficient control of the exploitation of natural resources leads to their volume and quality decrease. People therefore have to modify nature only to the extent to which they would not endanger the living environment quality. The relationship of people and nature is the closest in performing agricultural activities. In the conditions of climate alterations, which are happening today and which will aggravate the regeneration of vegetation in future, farmers as the actors of the environment policy should not additionally endanger the biodiversity. Yugoslavia is one of over 150 signatory countries of the Convention on Climate Change, aimed at the stabilization of greenhouse gas concentrations in the atmosphere.

The usage of mechanical and chemical technology aimed at the agricultural productivity increase and at achieving self-sufficiency leads to the degradation of soil, water body and agricultural products themselves. Such conditions limit successful satisfaction of human needs for high-quality food, as farmers have transformed into polluters. The next stage of agricultural development in the Balkan countries requires a transformation of the farmers' behaviour, so that they can become the element of the integral environmental protection. The environment fulfills three major functions: to provide raw materials and energy inputs to the economy, to absorb losses, and to provide a number of services and ecological functions.

The World Commission on Environment and Development (WCED) and the International Union for the Conservation of Nature (IUCN) support the protection of natural resources and preservation of genetic diversity. Over 200 regulations in the European Union deal with the problems' of air, water and soil pollution, waste disposal, conservation of species and genetic resources, product standardization, assessment of impacts on the living environment, and protection of nature. The European Environment Agency (EEA) was established in 1993 in the European Union. In Serbia, the Law on Environmental Protection was enacted in 1991.

Unified standards in the Balkan countries may, for example, refer to the permissible presence of pathogens in bathing water, or nitrates in swimming pool and drinking water (measured in milligrams per liter). In order to achieve the desired results in practice, the environmental policy requires the assistance and cooperative action of ecology, biology, economics and other, particularly engineering sciences. The efficiency in reducing the consumption of natural resources is usually estimated with regard to the number of population in a specific region or state and generated GDP. Thus, the consumption of water, wood and energy is recorded per capita, while waste generation and energy usage are calculated per capita and per GDP unit.

It is also necessary to comprehend population density, the share of reproducible energy resources (substitutes) in the total energy consumption, the share of chemically active substances that are recycled, the part of new. non-conventional forms of non-reproducible resources, and similar. The databases that should be used here are related to the population, growth trends of main economic sectors, the condition of the environment and natural resources, and so on. A problem may occur therein, regarding the actual degradation estimate of the natural capital, which, although having a real value, cannot have a fixed price. The elements of nature are not products, and the consequences of diminishing their quantity and quality cannot be foreseen with certainty, particularly in case of exhaustible resources. For this reason, the market is not able to determine the rate of replacement of the natural capital by a human-made capital.

It is necessary to establish which of the environment qualities in the Balkan countries should be preserved for future generations. The ecosystem monitoring by the method of tele-detection enables identification, control and quantification of the factors affecting the environment, evaluation of the actual status of the environment and prediction of its future situation. The principles set by the Rio Declaration on Environment and Development (adopted at the United Nations Conference on Environment and Development in 1992) has to be followed. According to these principles, for example, states are liable to adverse trans-boundary environmental effects (destruction of the animal and plant life in the interstate waters, pollution of air and soil due to nuclear disasters, and similar), but they also have the obligation of protecting the environment as an integral part of their development, be- cause of the interactive relations of the economy and environment.

The Balkan countries should enter adequate agreements aimed at the improvement of environmental protection, applying the experiences of the most developed European countries. The protection of soil as "the skin of the planet" from erosion may include compensations to farmers for accepting not to use the land endangered by erosion. Compared to other continents, Europe has the biggest participation of degraded areas in its total arable land, with about 23%. It is followed by Africa, which has 22% of such areas. The South European countries face immense problems of soil erosion. More than 80% of the land in Serbia is affected by erosion, too. However, the medium-erosion processes are prevailing, as about 50% of the land is affected by light erosion, and some 22% by medium erosion.

The average erosion coefficient (Zsr) is 0.44. All ecologically vulnerable areas should get financial support for the agricultural production system reorientation, in order to foster interest of farmers in the environmental protection. The stability of agricultural production can be maintained together with the soil and water conservation. The European Un- ion allocates ca 3% of the agriculture budget for the purpose of transferring from the conventional to the organic agriculture. Alongside with the protection of the land from erosion, the already damaged areas should also be re-cultivated. The soil erosion problem is solved by lifting the land level and shaping it, as well as by planting quickset hedges and trees around the sown surfaces.

The reduction of cattle-breeding intensity decelerates the process of soil degradation. In France, for instance, the preservation program of extensive cattle-breeding system encompassed about 5.5 million hectares. In addition, the degradation reduction is stimulated by the reduction of the scope of mechanical work per the unit of arable land, as the technical capital often consumes the natural capital. Modern farming methods should be economically capable, socially acceptable and biophysically sustainable. Taking into account the significant impact of water on ecosystems, the fact that must not be neglected is that the world quantities of water have been reduced by 35 times during the last three centuries, thus thwarting the possibilities of satisfying the needs of all the consumers of water.

The increase of irrigation efficiency (which has been disregarded for a long period in Yugoslavia) may be achieved by the implementation of new irrigation methods, such as the drop-by-drop method of irrigation. The combat against the pollution of surface waters and groundwater has to start urgently, as the climate changes are announcing reduction in precipitation. On the other side, torrent control is required for diminishing the effects of water erosion. Construction of micro-reservoirs (which protect the crops from floods, among their other functions) is much more present as the activity in Bulgaria, for instance, than in Yugoslavia. The agricultural land in river basins should be fully encompassed by the hydrologic land reclamation projects.

Adequate waste water purification should also be implemented. Apart from this, the urban waste water and urban organic refuse treatment may be directed towards acquiring organic fertilizers needed in agriculture. Moreover, continuous activities in searching for new water streams is also one of the priority tasks related to a better usage of water resources. In the case of Yugoslavia, economic conditions have not allowed for appropriate investments into the environmental protection and improvement. For instance, there is a significant sulfur-dioxide pollution of the air, caused by the insufficient protection level, although industrial plants are not employed with full capacities. The factor of a forestation induces generation of milder climate in certain areas, while forest fires exert multiple negative effects. Another negative trend is the decrease in meadow surfaces by 12% and pasture surfaces by 15% per capita during the period from 1990 to 2000.

The Balkan countries should develop a joint strategy of mitigating the "greenhouse" effects. In the period from 1990 to 2010, the greenhouse gas emission shall increase by 25% in Greece and by 27% in Portugal. The biggest decrease of this emission in the EU shall be achieved in Denmark and Germany (for 21%), while Finland and France shall retain the same level of the gas emission as in 1990. Trying to reduce his dependence on the nature, by polluting the land, man has violated the biological balance that should exist in the nature. Degradation of natural habitats of plant and animal species influences the changes within the species and population. However, about 27% of the genetic material that should maintain and increase the agricultural productivity is kept in the USA, while European gene banks contain some 35% of the global genetic diversity of feed crops and animal feeds? The environment can be protected by the application of bio-stimulators and crop rotation (aimed at the prevention of plant diseases, pest control and weed control) instead of mineral fertilizers and pesticides.

The consumption of pesticides per hectare is double lesser, and the consumption of mineral fertilizers several times lesser in Yugoslavia than in the European Union countries. Biotechnology plays a substantial role in the changing of biodiversity. The FAO applies the term "agro-ecological diversity". In Yugoslavia, the conservation of genetic resources for agriculture has been insufficient. The implementation of biotechnology enables getting of yields even on marginal soil and in unfavorable climatic conditions. The transportation of hazardous substances bears risks and represents additional threat to the environmental quality preservation, especially in case of damages. Laws regulating these problems have to be enacted and their strict obedience is required in order to avoid ecological catastrophes. We should also mention the specific attack on the environment in Yugoslavia during the 1999 bombardment.

Several research institutions in Serbia are engaged in measuring the presence of harmful substances in the air, soil, drinking water, milk and other human foodstuffs and animal feeds. External radiation is investigated in the institutes in Subotica, Zajeear, Nis, Vranje, Krusevac, Kraljevo and Uzice, while aerosoles and air are checked in Subotica, Belgrade, Zajeear, Nis and Pristina. Daily and monthly precipitation are monitored in Belgrade and Pristina, only daily in Subotica and Nis, and only monthly precipitation in Prizren, Novi Sad, Kragujevac and Zlatibor. Drinking w'ater is monitored in Subotica, Belgrade, Pristina, Novi Sad, Krusevac, Kragujevac and Kraljevo. The institutes in Subotica, Belgrade, Zajeear, Nis, Pristina and Novi Sad check milk and other human foodstuffs for harmful substances, and checking of animal feeds is performed in all these institutes except in Zajeear.

The reduction in the effects of key polluters may be

achieved through the implementation of concrete programs that will mobilize great numbers of people. In the European Union, the number of farmers who have concluded territorial environmental-protection-program-based contracts with their respective states is growing. In France in 1995, only 3% of the total support allocated to the farmers was related to the environmental protection measures, but it covered 20% of the agricultural land. Premium rates are about .300 francs per hectare for the agricultural estates measuring up to 100 ha. Today, the protection of agricultural environment participates with less than 1% in the expenditures related to the support of European agriculture.

The participation of agricultural environment protection credits was 8% of the total environment protection credits in 1996. Although certain collision of interests may appear among the Balkan countries, their common interest is undoubtedly the avoidance of ecological risks. Tax levying on the environment pollution would enable reductions in some other taxation burdens in the Balkan countries. The taxes in the form of lump sums may also be introduced, for example, in the consumption of non-reproducible sources of energy. The efficiency of the ecological taxation system will depend on the tax rates.

Agreement on the methods of compensation for pollution-caused damages is of substantial importance. In case of interstate water resources (the rivers Danube, Sava, Tisza, Tamish, Drina, the Adriatic Sea), the upstream states compensate the damages to the downstream states. Special incentive earnings may be determined to protect the farmers with low income or living in mountain areas, if they voluntarily join the projects of environmental protection. As the possibilities of replacing the natural capital with the human-made capital are limited, the Balkan countries should strengthen their orientation to the usage of self-reproducible resources. The environment is affected by demographic, technological, economic, legal, cultural and other factors.

A timely detection of the factors that endanger the environment is necessary in order to provide a successful reaction. Better equipment of the laboratories measuring the pollution would also contribute to this goal. A uniform information system providing reliable data on the living environment status in the region of Balkan countries would be in function of rational joint environmental policy realization. The growth rate of GDP per capita in the Balkan countries is although much lower than in the European Union, shall provide a slow increase in environmental protection investments. Also, the funds of the European Bank for Reconstruction and Development may be taken into account regarding the costs of the environment protection and quality restoration.

In some parts, significance should be given to joint (bilateral or regional) investments into the environmental protection related to inseparable problems. The amount of assets needed for repairing the consequences of pollution depends on the level of pollution. It is necessary to establish cooperation in the sphere of eco-technology application (followed by the embargo laid on the "dirty technology" imports and by customs alleviation for the imports of eco-technologies) and the implementation of quality standards, alongside with the integration of regional interests. The measures that should contribute to the stability of the environment may be legal, economic, technological, educational, etc. It is of substantial interest for Yugoslavia to take an active part in the regional - Balkan strategy of environmental protection.

Decision-making for the Environment

The natural sciences provide an essential knowledge base for wise choices when human activities may have significant environmental consequences. Only through these sciences can decision makers understand the dynamics of environmental systems and the ways in which human actions reverberate through these systems to affect environmental quality. The social and behavioural sciences also provide an essential knowledge base, although their roles are not as commonly recognized or as fully institutionalized in environmental policy. Only through these sciences can decision makers understand which policies will induce the desired human actions in relation to the environment and what ultimate effects environmentally important decisions are likely to have on human well-being. Moreover, environmentally important decisions may themselves be improved with better application of behavioural and social scientific knowledge.

Recognizing the need to develop these kinds of knowledge, the U.S. Environmental Protection Agency (EPA) and the National Science Foundation (NSF) asked the National Academies to identify a few science priorities that could contribute to improved environmental decision making and also advance the social and behavioural sciences. The National Academies were given a broad purview for this study. The study was to consider all relevant social and behavioural scientific perspectives and approaches, both on their own and as they relate to and integrate with perspectives from the natural sciences, engineering, and mathematical sciences. It was to consider research on decision processes in government organizations and elsewhere, as well as research on human-environment relationships that might have practical value for decision making. It was to consider areas of research that could improve environmentally important decisions regardless of whether the decision makers are government agencies, private companies, other organizations, or individuals.

It was to focus, however, on the social and behavioural sciences other than economics because they have not received much attention from decision-making organizations, and to define research areas that would build on strengths in these sciences and link them with each other, with economics, and with the natural sciences so as to produce a deeper understanding of environmental issues. We understood the relevant social and behavioural sciences to include the traditional disciplines of anthropology, geography, political science, psychology, and sociology as well as various associated interdisciplinary fields, such as decision science, communications research, policy sciences, human ecology, and science and technology studies. Thus, we did not consider recommending priority research areas that we judged to fall primarily in economics, regardless of how well those areas might score against the decision criteria we used. This report has two main audiences: potential researchers and potential research sponsors.

The National Academies were asked to recommend research areas that score well as measured against three criteria: the likelihood of achieving significant scientific advances, the potential value of the expected knowledge for improving decisions having important environmental implications, and the likelihood that the research would be used to improve those decisions. They were also asked to consider recommending ways to overcome barriers to the use of research that would have high priority if such barriers could be overcome and invited to make general recommendations for infrastructure that could increase the likelihood that the recommended knowledge across several fields will be used.

The National Academies organized the study under the auspices of its Committee on the Human Dimensions of Global Change, which has since 1989 advised federal agencies on research issues in the area of human-environment interactions and has produced several previous reports identifying promising research directions. The committee participated in selecting the membership of the panel and in reviewing this report. Panel members were selected to include expertise from across the social and behavioural sciences, w7ith strong representation of researchers grounded in these disciplines who are engaged in studying environmental issues. Members also include individuals with backgrounds in the environmental natural sciences and engineering, experience in governmental and private organizations whose decisions have significant environmental impact, and expertise in the use of science in policy and organizational decision making.

Identifying Science Priorities

From the outset, we decided to look widely for ideas about research areas that might meet the three decision criteria. Before our first meeting, we sent a message to e-mail lists of all the relevant research groups and networks that we could identify in which we explained the panel's task, listed our decision criteria, solicited suggestions of research areas from the recipients, and invited them to pass the request along to anyone they thought might have worthy ideas for us to consider.

We considered all the suggestions that were submitted, along with suggestions from panel members and sponsors at our initial meeting in June 2003, and identified about a dozen broad research fields in which priority areas might lie. We then invited a scientist working in each broad field to write a short memorandum identifying research areas in that field that he or she thought met our decision criteria and to explain this judgment. We invited these individuals to discuss their memoranda with us at our second meeting. After that meeting, we invited some of them to expand these into papers that appear as appendices to this report. At our third meeting, we refined our focus to the five recommended research priorities.

Applying the Decision Criteria

The three decision criteria the panel was given entailed making predictive judgments about the consequences for science and decision- making of differential investments in research. Historical examples of important ad vances in the social and behavioural sciences suggest the difficulty of predicting the path, impacts, costs, and benefits from innovations in the social sciences. If would have been exceedingly difficult, if not impossible, to predict how Garrett Hardin's famous paper on the "tragedy of the commons" would have affected researchers in many different fields or stimulated the search for management regimes that do not result in degradation of common property.

Although we still do not have definitive answers in this search, much has been learned about what kinds of arrangements tend to work in certain contexts and why they work. Certainly the full body of research on problems of managing the commons has had a notable impact, but it would have been very difficult if not impossible to anticipate the nature of the impact or who would use the knowledge. Similarly, it would have been difficult to predict how the development of the field of applied welfare economics from the 1920s to the 1950s, including the evolution of its many analytic tools in the 1960s and 1970s that together comprise social benefit-cost analysis, would affect environmental decision making today.

These examples suggest that despite the admirable logic of the decision criteria, they are better suited to considering information that is provided for a narrowly defined application than for assessing the potential of basic research or research with a broad range of potential intellectual implications and practical applications. The panel sought nevertheless to discipline the study by repeated reference to the decision criteria, to develop collective judgments in relation to the criteria as conscientiously and consistently as possible, and to seek guidance from past experience and empirical research on the use of knowledge from the social and behavioural sciences in environmental and other practical decision making.

We consulted panel members with expertise in decision processes for advice on what procedure to use to judge potential science priority areas against the criteria. With their advice, we decided that the criteria as given to us were sufficiently vague (and the topics sufficiently unformed) as to make it highly likely that if we used a procedure of voting or subjective weighting of topics against criteria, the results might not be meaningful because different panel members would have interpreted the criteria differently. Consequently, we decided to specify the criteria further by identifying a number of factors that are likely to act as means to the ends outlined in the criteria (described below). Each panel member agreed to consider how each of these contributing factors applied to each research area and to judge that area accordingly against the relevant decision criterion.

At the third meeting, we engaged in a discussion of each of the previously identified topics (now accompanied by draft text that ensured a common understanding of what the topic covered) in light of the criteria and the contributing factors in the hope of reaching consensus on which topics deserved inclusion among the science priorities and which, for whatever reasons, did not. The chair held in reserve the option of using a subjective weighting scheme if discussion failed to reach consensus. That option turned out to be unnecessary, as we readily reached consensus. Once it was agreed which topics deserved inclusion, we worked to frame a set of no more than five science priorities that would coherently include the topics that met the criteria. The overall process of selecting topics and applying the decision criteria involved winnowing, combining, and reformulating the topics that had initially been proposed to arrive at the final list.

Likelihood of Achieving Significant Scientific Advances

We rated potential science priorities highly on this criterion when we judged the following factors to be applicable:

- The research community is ready and able to conduct the research (e.g., concepts, methods, and data are available but not yet adequately applied in this area).

- Successful research would provide new frameworks for thinking or sources of understanding (e.g., data, methods) that could lead to advances in environmental decision making over time.
- Successful research would overcome or reduce gaps in knowledge or skill that now inhibit opportunities for improved environmental decisions in a given context.

Potential Value of the Expected Knowledge

We rated potential science priorities highly on this criterion when we judged the following factors to be applicable:

- The research findings are relevant for decisions with important environmental consequences and social or economic implications that are significant to affected parties or governments.
- The research findings are relevant for a diverse range of environmental decisions.
- The research results have significant potential to create, compare, and implement more attractive policy alternatives.

Likelihood that the Research Would be Used

We informed our judgments of proposed science priorities in relation to this criterion by examining empirical research on the use of scientific findings by various kinds of decision makers. Much of this research focuses on the use of information from the social sciences in government and private-sector organizations. We also considered the results of research on the factors affecting individuals' use of information in making environmentally relevant decisions. The research suggests that the likelihood of use of social science research is affected by attributes of the decision-making organizations, the researchers' activities, and the links between researchers and users. Studies suggest that decision-making organizations are more likely to use science that they have expressly requested, particularly from internal sources; when unfamiliar problems arise; when there are incentives for seeking information; and when they believe the research can provide authoritative support for their decisions.

Information users' acquisition efforts are also important in getting research used. The pattern of scientific challenge, in which research results are more likely to be challenged if they threaten well-organized interests, affects the likelihood that scientific findings will be accepted by public policy makers. Characteristics of the research itself, including technical quality and the extent to which the research directly focuses on user needs rather than on advancing scientific knowledge, are not consistently related to utilization. However, researchers' efforts to disseminate results and to adapt their reporting to users' needs are strongly associated with increased use of the information in some studies. In addition, research use is facilitated by formal or informal links between researchers and research users. Because of the small number of empirical studies on these issues, however, the generality of the findings is uncertain.

We rated potential science priorities highly on the criterion of likely use of research results if we judged the following factors to apply:

- Decision makers, such as those in organizations that make environmentally important decisions or among groups affected by such decisions, would be likely to request the research or the information it can yield.
- Decision makers, including parties affected by decisions, have incentives to seek and use the information, for example, to help them achieve personal, group, or organizational objectives.
- Researchers have incentives to disseminate their findings in ways that usually reach potential users and not only to academic publication outlets.

- Good organizational links or intermediaries exist that provide lines of communication or "translation" services between the likely producers and the likely users of the research results.

The above factors favoring the use of research results are not external to the decision-making process. Organizations that support or use research can act to create favorable conditions for using research when those conditions do not already exist. In some of the recommended science priority areas, we have recommended such actions.

Science Priorities

The panel recommends five science priorities for improved environmental decision making that, in our judgment, strongly meet the selection criteria we have been given. We note the priorities briefly here.

1. *Environmental decision processes*-We recommend a program of research in the decision sciences addressed to improving the analytical tools and analytic-deliberative processes necessary for good environ-mental decision making. It would include three components: developing criteria of decision quality; developing and testing formal tools for structuring decision processes; and creating effective processes, often termed analytic-deliberative, in which a broad range of participants take important roles in environmental decisions, including framing and interpreting scientific analyses.
2. *Institutions for environmental governance*- We recommend a concerted effort to build scientific under-standing needed for designing and evaluating institutions for governing human activities that affect environmental resources. This science priority, which has been identified in several previous National Research Council reports and by the National Science Foundation, would bring together the research traditions of policy analysis and institutional analysis to elaborate science-based tools that participants in environmental decisions can use to improve resource

management institutions and to design more effective linkages among institutions at different levels of governance.

3. *Green business decision making- We* recommend substantially expanded support for research to understand the influence of environmental considerations in business decisions. The research would address such issues as when and under what conditions better environmental performance provides competitive advantages; how the demands of customers, suppliers, and investors affect environmental performance; how environmental outcomes may be affected by changes in business supply chains; and how environmental accounting procedures and sectoral standard-setting activities can affect environmental outcomes.
4. *Environmentally significant individual behaviour-We* recommend a concerted research effort to better understand and inform environmentally significant decisions by individuals. This priority includes research in four specific areas: indicators of environmentally significant consumption, fundamental research on consumer choice and constraint, transmission systems for decision-relevant information for individuals, and integration of information with other policy instruments.
5. *Decision-relevant science for evidence-based environmental policy-We* recommend that the federal government strengthen tine scientific infrastructure for evidence-based environmental policy by pursuing a research strategy that emphasizes decision relevance. It should do this by developing decision-relevant indicators for environmental policy, including pressures on the environment, environmental states, and human responses and consequences; by making concerted efforts to evaluate environmental policies; by developing better methods for identifying the trends that will determine environmental quality in the future; and by improving methods for determining the distributional impacts of environmental policies

and programs. These efforts will require integrating the social sciences and the natural sciences of the environment. Decisions about how to construct indicators, evaluate policies, and so forth will require the involvement of the full range of parties affected by environmental decisions because these choices are not purely technical. Measurement focuses attention on what has been measured, and affected parties often disagree about what is most worth measuring, which outcomes of policies are most important, and the like.

Cross-Cutting Issues

Because we were asked to identify a very small number of science priorities, we have not mentioned many other intriguing and meritorious topics. Here we highlight three topics that, although we have not identified them as separate science priorities, are so pervasive and so linked to several of the science priorities that they warrant attention across the science priority areas.

Innovation and Technological Change

Research on innovation has a long tradition and many different disciplinary sources, including psychology, history, anthropology, political science, economics, geography, and sociology. Many core concepts are shared broadly. For example, the ideas of "first movers" and "late adopters" one encounters in a corporate strategy or management journal have equivalents in each of the other disciplines just noted. Concepts of evolution and adaptation in innovations over time are also widespread, although interdisciplinary awareness of them is not. Early adopters typically pay a premium in economic and other terms compared with those who come later.

Innovations may work in some cultures but not in others for any number of empirical, researchable reasons. Issues of communication and education also appear routinely in studies of innovation across disciplines and fields of human endeavor. Innovation research offers a potentially fruitful approach for understanding and improving environmental decision making. Innovation is important for environmental policy both because of the role of technological innovation in creating and ameliorating environmental problems and because of the need for policy innovation at all levels and for its diffusion. Issues of innovation are particularly important to our science priorities in the areas of decision-making processes, environmental governance, green business decision making, and individual behaviour. Concepts from research on innovation and technological change can usefully be applied in all these priority areas.

System Complexity

Human-environment systems and the policy systems used to govern them are both highly complex? Researchers who study complex systems have developed a variety of concepts that can be useful for understanding these systems and improving their functioning. Consider, for example, the ways the highly capitalized and complex transportation systems upon which modern societies depend may resist the transformations required to sustain these societies into the future. The problem has been termed "technological lock-in" by systems theorists and is reflected in ongoing discussions about the future of a hydrogen-based economy.

One can readily build a hydrogen-powered car today, but the technology system required to get the hydrogen to it on a mass market basis does not exist. The gasoline engine is "locked in" by the fuel manufacture and distribution infrastructure. Change is still possible, but it will take much longer, is more complicated, and runs a great risk of generating unanticipated consequences as it ripples through the coupled technological, economic, and social systems. For comparatively less highly capitalized and simpler systems, in which enabling technologies are not tightly coupled, system changes may be easier to come by.

For example, one can usually change air scrubber technologies without affecting any of the underlying manufacturing technologies, since these are only loosely coupled. This is not the case with a core manufacturing technology such as the use of lead solder in electronics manufacturing, which is tightly coupled to other technologies. The resilience or brittleness of systems matters too. Resilient systems are capable of absorbing or otherwise dealing with external threats and opportunities. Brittle ones are usually less capable. Proposals to shift to "distributed generation" of energy and electricity arguably under-estimate the brittleness of existing and facilitating infrastructures in the face of change.

Brittleness need not preclude innovation, however, as the story of the cell phone and its winning battle with conventional telecommunications indicates so well. These observations suggest that research that provides environmental decision makers with better understanding of complex systems and their evolution may have widespread value. Organizational studies with a complex systems perspective, especially multi sectoral ones exploring the roles and relationships of private, public, not-for-profit, and nongovernmental institutional forms as these relate to environmental innovation and technological change, are likewise attractive. Thus, a complex systems perspective may be usefully applied in the recommended priority areas of improving decision processes, environmental governance, and business decision making.

Combining Social and Natural Science

Even though our task was to identify priorities that flowed out of the social and behavioural sciences, each of our recommended science priorities requires collaboration, and sometimes integration, across the social and natural sciences. Each one builds on measurement and analysis of both biophysical and human conditions and processes, as well as of human-environment interactions. Coupling the social and natural sciences is an increasingly important element of emerging research and development programs in the federal agencies. For example, the NSF's new cross-directorate program on environmental research and education (ERE) explicitly emphasizes the coupling of human and natural systems and of people and technology.

It emphasizes as principal research questions "how the environment functions, how people use the environment, how this use changes the environment and how the resultant environmental changes affect people". Efforts to implement our recommendations w^7ould therefore contribute to efforts at NSF, in federal environmental agencies, and elsewhere to develop the multidisciplinary science needed to inform environmental decisions. Considering the parallels between this study and forward-looking research planning efforts in federal agencies, it is not surprising to see numerous substantive overlaps in recommendations. For example, the NSF-ERE report identifies numerous recommended research areas, including:

- Identifying decision processes that effectively combine analytical, deliberative, and participatory approaches to environmental choices, which will guide scientists and engineers toward the generation of decision-relevant information.
- Understanding the patterns and driving forces of human consumption of resources, and identifying policies and practices that influence materials and energy use decisions, including incentives.
- Conceptualizing and assessing the role that institutions play in the use and management of global, national, and local common-pool resources and their associated environmental conditions.
- Developing decision-making strategies and institutional approaches to most effectively solve problems and deal with uncertainty.

Close parallels to each of these recommendations and

others recommendations from the ERE advisory group can be found in the present study. Our recommendations in turn are completely consistent with the recognition of the NSF-ERE group and others that an adequate decision-relevant understanding of the environment depends on better coordination across the sciences.

5

Environmental Decision Processes and its Improvement

The Research Need

The research effort would have three components: (a) developing useful criteria to characterize and evaluate the quality of environmental decisions, (b) developing and testing formal decision scie nce tools for structuring decision processes, and (c) building and testing concepts and practice for broadly based analytic-deliberative processes. Basic research on decision processes in individuals, groups, and organizations provides an essential foundation for this science priority. The National Science Foundation has supported such research in the past, sometimes in conjunction with the U.S. Environmental Protection Agency (EPA), and we expect support for basic decision research to continue. Our emphasis here is on research that would employ and advance basic understanding for the practical objective of improved environmental decision making.

Individuals, organizations, and ultimately societies, through their choices, have significant effects on the natural environment. The large human footprint on the Earth andthe potential for huge mistakes make it imperative that the major choices are well informed and adequately considered. Decisions affecting environmental processes, however, are among the most challenging facing humanity because of the following collection of attributes that environmental choices usually share:

- *Structural complexity-* choices affect phenomena that operate at multiple scales; decision-making entities also exist at multiple scales, not necessarily matched to those of the phenomena; and many different kinds of expertise are required to understand the issues.
- *Multiple, conflicting, and uncertain values*-people affected by the choices have deeply held values often tied to spiritual, cultural, stewardship, or equity concerns that they are unwilling to negotiate or trade off; people differ in their value priorities; and sometimes their values seem to shift unexpectedly.
- *Long time horizons-* the consequences of choices made now may extend for decades or longer.
- *Open-access structure-* it is often difficult to exclude people from using or polluting a resource, putting that resource at considerable risk of overuse and decline.
- *Incomplete and uncertain knowledge*-the consequences of choice options may be unknown or in dispute among scientists; they may also be dependent on ongoing processes of social or environmental changes that are also little understood.
- *High stakes-the long*-term implications of the wrong choice for environment and society may be profound.
- *Time pressure*-decisions must be made without waiting for scientific certainty or agreement on values.

These points are well recognized by observers of environmental decision processes. A further challenge is to address the linked nature of environmental processes and environmental decisions across time scales, physical scales, and institutional scales. Decisions made at one scale can be transformed or undermined by processes at other scales, which must therefore be taken into account. Researchers have only recently given serious consideration to this challenge to environmental decision making and management. In addition, environmental choices are affected by decision makers' attention to various environ-mental or other aspects of the choices. Individuals' apparent preferences shift depending on how choices are framed and on their interpretations of and affective reactions to information, and the apparent priorities of organizations and governments shift as a function of how interested parties shape decision agendas.

Decisions of such difficulty require a variety of inputs. Elected representatives, who are normally entrusted with making value choices, rarely have sufficient expertise to make well-informed decisions, but scientific and technical experts are not well suited or trusted to address the value issues. To meet the challenges, scientists have developed numerous analytical tools to inform decision makers about the functioning of environmental systems and the likely consequences of available choices. Mathematical models of complex systems represent the multiple layers and linkages that constitute environmental systems and forecast the consequences of interventions in them. Risk analysis techniques characterize undesired outcomes and the uncertainties that surround them and estimate their probabilities of occurrence. Various techniques based in economics quantify outcomes in terms of costs and benefits, compare outcomes occurring at different times in the future, and aggregate the outcomes facing individuals into measures of net societal outcome. Spatial analysis and mapping techniques combined with ground-based or remote observation represent environmental change and its effects.

Such analytical tools help address several of the challenges of environmental decision making, but not all. In particular, they often fail to meet the challenges of value conflict and uncertainty. Value choices are often hidden in the simplifying assumptions of analytic techniques, and the assumed values may not be universally shared. Over reliance on analytic tools without adequate consideration of their limiting assumptions can sometimes heighten mistrust of governments and their experts and make it difficult to get public acceptance of public policy decisions. Another problem that often arises with environmental analysis is a failure to address key decision-relevant questions. For example, a billion-dollar research program to assess the cancer risks of dioxin not only failed to resolve the scientific issues but also may not have been asking the right question, which, for many affected people, concerned the overall health risks to groups exposed to multiple hazardous chemicals, not just the cancer risks of dioxin exposure.

In all the likely decision contexts in which these risks matter, dioxin is only one among many hazardous chemicals involved and cancer is only part of the problem. Several billions were spent to characterize the risks of leakage of radioactive materials from proposed repository sites for high-level radioactive waste, but no comprehensive appraisal was done to compare these risks with the risks of continuing current practices of temporary waste disposal. Assessments of acid precipitation, including the U.S. National Acid Precipitation Action Program and similar assessments in several other countries have been criticized for overemphasizing the collection of new data and not doing enough to interpret existing data to understand their implications for societal decisions. In short, when science is gathered to inform environmental decisions, it is often not the right science. Among the consequences are heightened social conflict, delayed decisions, and mistrust.

Because of these pervasive problems at the junction of environmental analysis and decision making, several authoritative studies have recommended processes that integrate analysis with broadly based deliberative processes involving the range of parties interested in or affected by the decisions. The goal is to put analysis more directly into the service of those who may be affected by decisions. In these analytic-deliberative processes, participants with diverse perspectives and values contribute to decision making in many ways, including defining the environmental decisions that require analysis, framing the scientific analyses needed to gain insight into the decisions, and interpreting the results to illuminate the decisions at hand. Public agencies in the United States and elsewhere are increasingly committed to an analytic-deliberative approach to environmental understanding.

For example, EPA has made extensive efforts to implement and improve "science-based environmental stakeholder processes" in support of its decisions. The U.S. Climate Change Science Program, possibly the largest single environmental science program in the federal government and one involving 13 federal agencies, adopted "decision support" as one of four core approaches to meeting the program's goals in its current strategic plan. Among the implications of this emphasis are "early and continuing involvement of stakeholders ... in defining key science and observation questions" and "transparent public review of analysis questions, methods, and draft results".

Good environmental decision making requires both improved understanding of human-environment interactions and improved understanding and management of decision-making processes. The research we recommend will complement past efforts in the former area with expanded effort in the latter, using a decision science approach. Its central purpose is to identify and continually improve techniques for guiding and organizing practical environmental decision processes so that they achieve more of the ideal qualities of good decisions.

Approach of a Decision Science

A decision science approach analyzes decisions and the

processes for making them. In short, when science is gathered to inform environmental decisions, it is often not the right science. Among the consequences are heightened social conflict, delayed decisions, and mistrust. Because of these pervasive problems at the junction of environmental analysis and decision making, several authoritative studies have recommended processes that integrate analysis with broadly based deliberative processes involving the range of parties interested in or affected by the decisions. The goal is to put analysis more directly into the service of those who may be affected by decisions. In these analytic- deliberative processes, participants with diverse perspectives and values contribute to decision making in many ways, including defining the environmental decisions that require analysis, framing the scientific analyses needed to gain insight into the decisions, and interpreting the results to illuminate the decisions at hand.

Public agencies in the United States and elsewhere are increasingly committed to an analytic-deliberative approach to environmental understanding. For example, EPA has made extensive efforts to implement and improve "science- based environmental stakeholder processes" in support of its decisions. The U.S. Climate Change Science Program, possibly the largest single environmental science program in the federal government and one involving 13 federal agencies, adopted "decision support" as one of four core approaches to meeting the program's goals in its current strategic plan. Among the implications of this emphasis are "early and continuing involvement of stakeholders ... in defining key science and observation questions" and "transparent public review of analysis questions, methods, and draft results".

Good environmental decision making requires both improved understanding of human-environment interactions and improved understanding and management of decision-making processes. The research we recommend will complement past efforts in the former area with expanded effort in the latter, using a decision science approach. Its central purpose is to identify and continually improve techniques for guiding and organizing practical environmental decision processes so that they achieve more of the ideal qualities of good decisions.

A decision science approach analyzes decisions and the processes for making them. It considers the objectives of decision making and ways to evaluate decisions and decision processes against those objectives. It identifies the questions and kinds of information needed for good decision processes, and it develops knowledge about which decision processes are likely to produce desired outcomes. Basic research in decision sciences has focused primarily on unitary decision makers. Normative decision theory concerns hypothetical rational decision makers; behavioural decision theory concerns actual individuals. A smaller body of research has addressed the additional complications that arise when decisions are made in groups or when they must take into account the different and often conflicting perspectives and values of the people a decision will affect.

There is relevant work in the social psychology of small-group decisions and in studies of organizational decisions, mainly in business. There are also numerous case studies of actual environmental decision making, but few of these have systematically applied conceptual frameworks. This priority emphasizes research on what has been called prescriptive decision making, which we define as a science-based practice concerned with helping people to make good decisions. As already noted, our focus on the prescriptive presumes the continuation of basic research efforts on decision making that provide an essential foundation for prescriptive research. A decision science approach to practical decision making begins by identifying the elements of a responsible and competent decision-making process.

For example, an ideal decision process has been defined on normative grounds as one that includes the elements. These elements include some that are strongly dependent on participants' values (V) and some for which information from scientific and technical analysis (T) can provide participants with essential insight regardless of their values. Actual decisions vary widely in terms of how closely they approach these ideals. Many analysts argue that environmental decision processes should be iterative to accommodate changing human desires and the changing state of knowledge about the effects of environmental choices. This is the notion of learning over time embodied in concepts of adaptive management and governance.

From a decision science standpoint, good environ-mental decisions consider both physical and social phenomena — environmental processes, the available options, the effects of different options on environmental and social conditions, and so forth—and human values. Information about phenomena is often obtained from environmental scientists, health specialists, engineers, economists, and other experts on those phenomena. Information on values can legitimately come from a wide of array of interested parties. The need for both kinds of information is worth underlining because judgments about phenomena and about values are often intertwined, not least in the minds of analysts.

Good decisions require competent and socially acceptable ways to integrate information about phenomena with information about values. Decision science has developed some systematic techniques for doing this integration in ways that can be applied to environmental decision processes. As already noted, environmental policy additionally involves diverse, conflicting, and changing values; substantial scientific uncertainty and ignorance; and often mistrust among participants. Consequently, judgments about information can be hotly contested. There may be disagreement about which technical information is needed and what its practical significance is, how to interpret uncertain or disputed information, how to make tradeoffs between desired outcomes, whether seeking more information will be worth the cost, and even about the nature of the decision to be made.

Decision science can help improve decision processes by making these judgments more explicit and structuring the ways participants in decision processes make and consider their judgments. It can also help parse disagreements so that decision participants can distinguish those that might be resolved by more information and clear thinking from those that may also require bargaining, compromise, or other resolution strategies. Decision science approaches have long been applied to a variety of environmental decisions and used in training environmental policy analysts.

These aspects of decision process are considered important for several reasons: normative (they allow affected parties to exercise democratic rights), substantive (they generate better alternatives and choices), and instrumental (they increase the likelihood of timely implementation). A major challenge in applying a decision science approach to environmental decisions is the linked nature of these decisions. Prescriptive decision theory will need to be expanded from its past emphasis on one-time decisions with defined boundaries to decisions that require linkages among administrative or institutional levels that have implications at many physical scales, that have long time horizons, and that involve iteration. The application of decision science to problems of long-term adaptive management or governance is an important area for contributions. At the other extreme, applying decision science to time-pressured decisions, as during crisis, also presents an important challenge and opportunity.

Areas of Research

Developing Criteria of Decision Quality

The quality of an environmentally significant decision

cannot appropriately be defined by its outcomes because those outcomes may be highly dependent on factors that are unknown or uncontrollable when the decision is made. A decision may be well informed and well considered given what is known but may lead to unfortunate results because the system was not fully understood or because of the outcomes of key uncertainties. Thus, it is necessary to have internal criteria for judging the quality of decisions—criteria that are not dependent on ultimate outcomes. It is reasonable to expect that, on average, higher quality decisions (those based on the best available information, careful evaluation, adequate consideration of uncertainties and plausible worst cases, and so forth) are more likely than lower quality decisions to lead to desired outcomes in an uncertain world.

It also seems reasonable to expect that higher quality decisions will on average be more widely accepted. There is evidence, however, from energy decision making of a perverse and inverse relationship between the quality of decisions and their acceptance. The empirical relationships among different indicators of decision quality are a worthwhile research question. Researchers have proposed numerous internal criteria for decision quality. The problem of defining decision quality for practical environmental decisions, however, has not received the level of research attention it deserves. Both the normative and the behavioural traditions in decision science have difficulty with this problem.

The main difficulty in applying normative decision theory is that, in realistic situations, one cannot assess every consequence of every possible alternative and evaluate them all against the values of each decision participant. Decision makers seek the best practice not in the abstract, but under constraints of real people's cognitive capabilities, legislative mandates, limited time and resources, social conflict, and so forth: choices must be made and defended regarding what to include and what to exclude. Researchers in the behavioural tradition typically do not address issues of decision quality, in part because their approaches emphasize characterization rather than evaluation and improvement.

The recommended research would build on recent efforts to develop empirically supported knowledge about ways to organize high-quality decision-making processes under realistic constraints. It would inform the design of environmental decision processes by addressing questions such as these:

- What criteria do people use to evaluate decision quality? To what extent do these criteria differ for people from different cultural, socioeconomic, or educational backgrounds or for people representing different positions in environmental controversies? To what extent do they depend on past experience with related decisions?
- Which characteristics of decision processes are assciated with judgments of decision quality by the participants or outside observers? Which characteristics are associated with confidence in decisions? With acceptance of decisions?
- How do different ways of organizing decision processes fare in terms of the attention given to the elements of normatively good decision process (for example, do processes that involve more different stakeholders do a better job of identifying all relevant objectives, as is often claimed)?
- How do different levels of attention to particular elements of good decision process affect assessments of overall decision quality?
- How do different resolutions of trade-offs in the decision process (e.g., between getting more information and deciding quickly, or between broader representation and efficiency of decision) affect various indicators of decision quality?
- To what extent do interventions designed to ensure that decisions address certain elements of good

decision processes result in more positive assessments of decision quality? Which elements are most important to those judgments under which conditions?

- When decisions are highly constrained in terms of time, attention, or legal requirements, which elements of good public decision processes are most critical to the quality of the decisions?
- Are decisions of higher normative quality associated with preferred social and environmental outcomes?
- How can research results concerning good decision processes and ways to promote them best be disseminated to the users of these results (e.g., government agencies, stakeholder groups, corporations, partnership groups)?

This research might be conducted by various methods, including structured comparisons of naturally occurring cases, simulation, modeling, and quasi-experimental field research. Because environmental decisions present the full range of difficulties in decision making outlined above, they provide a good test bed for research on decision quality more generally.

Structuring Decision Processes

Behavioural decision research shows that individual decision makers typically omit key elements of good decision processes and that their decisions suffer as a result. People respond to complex tasks by using their judgmental instincts to simplify them in ways that seem adequate to the problem at hand. They respond to probabilistic infonnation or questions involving uncertainty with predictable biases that often ignore or distort important information. They have difficulty clarifying objectives, identifying all viable alternatives, and structuring decision tasks. When asked to consider value trade-offs or select among alternatives, they employ heuristic reasoning processes that are susceptible to a variety of contextual or task-related influences. Hence, there are many reasons to expect that, on their own, individuals (including experts) will often fall short of the normative ideal in making choices about complex issues involving uncertainties and value trade-offs.

Decision-making groups can, in principle, identify more elements of any decision than individuals and correct for individual members' errors, thus producing better decisions than individuals. Behavioural research on group decision processes indicates, however, that this potential is not necessarily realized in practice. Individuals who have relevant information that is not widely shared in the group must get others to take this information seriously. Whether this happens is highly contingent, depending for instance on the individual's social status, the group's norms (e.g., a value on originality opens the group to individuals' information, a value on agreement closes it), and the tactics the individual uses to propose the ideas. Moreover, social processes in groups sometimes lead to premature closure on a common perspective that ignores contrary information, resulting in tendencies toward "group think" or group polarization.

The decision sciences have developed a variety of tools to structure decisions and help decision makers and decision-making groups better approximate ideals of good decision processes. The recommended research will refine these tools and apply them more widely as a basis for improving environmental decisions. To illustrate the possibilities, we briefly describe progress on developing tools for three purposes: clarifying decision participants' values and preferences concerning alternatives, understanding and thinking through uncertainties and disagreements about the implications of choice options, and assisting in making collective choices when different individuals have conflicting understandings and competing preferences.

Clarifying Values and Preferences

The values and preferences people express regarding complex and unfamiliar environmental goods vary considerably according to how they are elicited. Hence, the task of clarifying preferences is one of helping people construct their preferences rather than simply revealing them. Tools concerned with preference construction and elicitation include formal methods based on precepts of measurement theory and decision theory and wisdom gleaned from applied experience. Perhaps the most well- known of these formal approaches is termed multi-attribute trade-off analysis, which involves an interview between an analyst and a decision participant. The result is a mathematical statement comprising a utility or value function that could be used to evaluate every possible alternative within the range of consequences used in the interview process.

The advantages of formal techniques of preference construction are that the judgments involved are made explicit, that the value information can be used in many ways to help clarify the decision process, and that decision makers in collective choice situations can learn a great deal through joint efforts to clarify preferences. The disadvantages are also substantial: the questions involved are difficult to answer and require decision makers to make their inchoate feelings explicit, the questioning process may be confusing, the process can be cognitively and analytically demanding and it may not be clear how the results will be used. This approach has other drawbacks, including the lack of trained people to implement such preference elicitation approaches, and the lack of a rigorous way to combine individuals' utility functions into guidance for collective decisions, such as the kind of social welfare function provided by welfare economics.

In part as a response to these drawbacks, several other approaches to preference elicitation have been developed and tested by researchers in order to make the task cognitively simpler, more transparent, or more closely matched to particular decisions. These include the analytic hierarchy process developed by Saaty (1980, 1991); strategies that focus on a choice among a set of possible policy alternatives to address a given environmental question; methods of clarifying preferences based on judgments of what would constitute "even swaps"; and techniques that emphasize key aspects of the decision problem, such as values, particular objectives, or finding an alternative that provides acceptable performance across all the objectives (satisfying).

Understanding Uncertainties and Disagreements

Decision scientists have been developing analytical tools and approaches for characterizing uncertainties. These include methods of eliciting and making use of probabilistic judgments or other sources of information about uncertainty, methods of combining probabilistic estimates through simulation, and methods of characterizing several different sources of uncertainty at once, all as a basis for estimating the effects of decision options. Decision researchers have also experimented with methods of conveying information from these methods to decision participants as a basis for better understanding, deliberation, and decision making. Morgan and Henrion (1990) provide a comprehensive review of such methods and how they are applied for complex problems.

Although probability estimation remains the major approach to characterizing uncertainties, other methods are being developed that involve less demanding judgments. Some are based on fuzzy set theory, on the presumption that highly precise probabilistic judgments are often unnecessary. Scenarios offer another widely applied approach to characterizing uncertainties for environmental decisions, although relatively little research has been conducted on their efficacy as a means to generate an appropriate comprehension of uncertainty.

Recent research using influence diagrams (a generic tool with wide application in model building, problem structuring, probability elicitation, knowledge mapping, and many other contexts) helps reveal the mental models of decision participants and the sources of some of their disagreements. Influence diagrams can reveal differences in the understandings of lay and expert participants or between participants with different stakes in the decision. They can help participants understand the bases of disagreements and perhaps see ways to resolve them.

Assisting in Collective Choice

One of the most difficult challenges in environmental decision making is how to arrive at a societal preference in a collective decision context. Since the writing of Arrow (1963), decision researchers have recognized that there is no unique rule for aggregating the ordinal preferences of individuals with different values across a range of alternatives. Research is warranted on a variety of techniques that may be useful for informing judgments about societal preference. Voting approaches could possibly provide a means of directly eliciting preferences and under specific rules provide affording a basis for aggregation, although such approaches are highly affected by how questions are framed, the set of alternatives, and the choice of aggregation rules.

New information technologies may also provide useful tools for expression of individual preference, even if a generalized rule for social choice on the basis of expressed ordinal preference may be impossible. Computer-based tools for knowledge and value elicitation may provide widely applicable approaches to obtaining high-quality judgments about subjective probabilities of consequences and the values people associate with different consequences. Problem-structuring tools such as influence diagrams may have enormous potential in conjunction with advanced information technologies. We are not recommending new research related to benefit-cost analysis, even though this approach is widely used to address the key issue of arriving at a social choice. We have two reasons for not doing so. One is that this line of research has its own momentum and seems less in need of increased research support than other, less developed areas. The current state of concepts and practice for benefit-cost analysis are discussed in several sources.

The other is that benefit-cost analysis is in some respects antithetical to the research program recommended here because it decides by assumption how to address at least two important issues that we think need to be decided empirically. It assumes that social value is nothing more or less than the sum of the values individuals express in markets or market-like contexts, and it assumes that the values of different kinds of consequences (for employment, endangered species, sacred spaces, etc.) can be compared by reducing them to a single monetary metric. There is growing literature documenting difficulties with these assumptions, particularly for large-scale problems involving long time horizons, non marginal changes, deeply held values, and equity issues. Moreover, because these assumptions are sometimes not shared by people affected by environmental decisions, attempts to employ them on actual environmental policy decisions have proved controversial and divisive.

A large literature on perceptions of justice and injustice, although not directly addiessed to environmental issues, makes it clear that for people in the United States and several other countries, concepts of just decisions do not reduce to the choice that is best for the individual making the judgment and that individuals' normative judgments about whether decisions are just can engender predictable emotional reactions (e g_, anger, resentment) that it may be risky for collective decision processes to ignore. The research recommended here would investigate ways to structure decision processes, develop empirical understanding of the effects of various decision rules and analytical assumptions, and identify ways to structure decisions that help actual decision processes more closely approach normative ideas of good decision making. Research on formal tools for structuring decision processes might address such questions as these:

- How can formal methods for improving decisions be made understandable and cognitively tractable for participants in complex environmental decisions? How can such methods be applied in real-world decision settings? How are the decisions affected?

- To what extent and under what conditions do the benefits of formal approaches to decision making outweigh their costs in time, money, and effort?
- How can judgments about the nature and likelihood of a range of outcomes be made more routine and workable through the use of information technologies? Do approaches such as influence diagrams and elicitation of subjective probability lead to clearer and more accurate understanding of uncertainty?
- How can learning be built into these formal tools through the potential for updating over time?
- How can methods for structuring decisions be applied effectively when decision processes overlap and involve multiple agencies, levels of organization, and sectors that jointly affect environmental outcomes?
- What systematic methods for aggregation of preferences can be developed and implemented in realistic environmental decision settings that do not require the strict assumptions of social benefit-cost analysis?
- How can risk communication methods be used to make the results of efforts to clarify preferences and uncertainty intelligible and useful to key decision makers and affected parties?
- Which values matter to individuals in important generic decision situations (e.g., purchase of energy services, housing, transportation, and consumer durables)? Can decision-aiding approaches help consumers by structuring the values and uncertainties in these choices as well as their links to other broader level decisions?

Creating Effective Analytic-Deliberative Processes

As already noted, several authoritative studies recommend that public policy decisions affecting environmental and associated public health risks be organized in ways that integrate analysis with broadly based deliberative processes involving the range of parties interested in or affected by the decisions. These studies conclude that better decisions can result when analysis is organized for decision relevance by giving decision participants a guiding role: "deliberation frames analysis, analysis informs deliberation, and the process benefits from feedback between the two". Many government agencies in the United States and elsewhere have made commitments to using broadly participatory processes involving analysis and deliberation to make or support environmental policy decisions and many have tried to implement those commitments.

Nevertheless, the quality of these decisions is only • beginning to be evaluated and the knowledge base for selecting the best process for a specific decision remains weak. By the late 1990s it was possible to demonstrate the potential of analytic deliberation, to identify some of the factors likely to affect its success, and to show that the best process depends on the situation. But because systematic analyses based on data from multiple cases are only beginning to appear and because most of these studies are restricted to specific decision contexts, understanding has not progressed to the point at which science-based input can be given to the design of processes affecting types of decision that have not yet been studied. As a result, organizations that convene such processes have been limited to improvising on the basis of the judgments of experienced practitioners and extrapolation from available case studies.

This situation is ripe for change. In recent years, researchers have begun to apply consistent methods to the study of multiple analytic-deliberative processes. Such studies have the potential to demonstrate generalities that apply across contexts and to specify ways in which outcomes are context-dependent. These studies, together with advances in theory and conceptualization, are making it possible to build much more nuanced understanding of desired outcomes, such as how decision quality and legitimacy are affected by the ways collective environmental decision-making processes are organized (e.g., whether and how the parties are represented, what resources they have available, how their input is structured, how decision makers are constrained in using external input). With this base of concepts and empirical knowledge, researchers are now poised to draw on preexisting bodies of basic social and behavioural science research that are clearly relevant to the design of environmental decision processes.

These include not only decision research, as already noted, but research on small-group processes, perceptions of justice and fairness, democratic deliberation and civic participation; organizational change, communications research, and conflict resolution. With clearer conceptual frameworks for examining environmental decisions, findings from these separate, older lines of research can be linked to the study of environmental decisions and can generate new and fruitful hypotheses to explore. An ongoing study on public participation in environmental assessment and decision making at the National Research Council is synthesizing knowledge in this rapidly moving field and the associated fields of basic social and behavioural science and developing recommendations for research and practice.

An organized research community is beginning to emerge that can generate the knowledge needed for a science-based practice of process design for environmental policy decisions. This research can improve the ability of decision-making organizations to deal in a competent and credible way with environmental complexity, incomplete and uncertain knowledge, diversity of human values and interests, and the other realities that make this field of decision making so difficult.

Research to build effective analytic-deliberative processes could address such questions as:

- What are good indicators for key attributes of success

for analytic-deliberative processes, such as decision quality, legitimacy, and improved decision capacity?

- How are these outcomes affected by the ways in which the processes are organized, the range and diversity of people involved, the rules used for deliberating and reaching conclusions, the ways technical information is organized and made available, and the environmental, social, organizational, and legal contexts of the decision at hand? What are effective ways to make technical analyses transparent to a wide range of decision participants, some of whom lack technical training?
- How can decision-analytic techniques for preference elicitation, characterizing uncertainty, and aggregating preferences be used to best advantage in broadly based analytic-deliberative processes?
- How can decision processes be organized to ensure that all sources of relevant information, including the local knowledge of nonscientists, are gathered and appropriately considered?
- How can analytic-deliberative decision processes be organized to reach closure effectively and with broad acceptance, especially when the processes involve a diversity of perspectives and interests? What tests could be applied to decisions and decision processes to support claims that they are ready for closure?

Rationale for the Science Priority

Likelihood of Scientific Advances

The recommended research can yield significant scientific advances by building on several recent developments in understanding. Recent efforts to identify and assess several elements of decision quality have established the groundwork for much improved understanding and measurement of this concept. Substantial recent work on decision-analytic tools for structuring decision processes, conducted mainly in laboratory and simulation settings, provides a basis for developing these tools further and testing and comparing their usefulness in realistic settings involving multiple and diverse participants. Recent theoretical, conceptual, and empirical work on analytic-deliberative processes and the increasing development of a self-identifying community of researchers and practitioners has set the stage for rapid progress through conceptually coherent empirical research on the design and study of processes for informing environmental decisions through analytic deliberation.

Continuing interest at the National Science Foundation in research on environment and decision making bodes well for scientific advances. Through its programs on decision, risk, and management science and human dimensions of global change and its initiatives on coupled human and natural systems and environmental research and education, the foundation is bringing together researchers from multiple disciplines with shared interests in environmental decision processes. These venues for communication are likely to provide good test beds for new research ideas.

Potential value

The long history of inadequately informed and incompletely deliberated environmental decisions, as well as the cost in delay, decisional gridlock, social conflict, and mistrust of government, make clear the importance and value of finding more competent and legitimate ways to organize the processes that lead to public policy decisions affecting environmental quality. Moreover, the increasingly widespread practice among federal agencies and other governmental and nongovernmental entities of opening environmental decision-making processes to a range of stakeholders and potentially affected parties has raised the stakes for managing decision-making processes well. A decision science approach can increase the likelihood of success with such processes.

Likelihood of use

The increasingly widespread use in government of

participatory processes requiring both analysis and broadly based deliberation indicates the potential demand for scientifically informed guidance on how to make decision processes work better. Despite the public commitments of various government agencies to openness, however, significant barriers remain to the use of results from the recommended scientific research on decision-making processes. These include commitment to standard procedures or past practices, perceptions of statutory constraints, and a shortage of organizational capability to conform to principles of sound process design. Key decision makers may not recognize that it is possible to put the design of decision processes on a scientific footing. Perhaps the most serious barrier to use of the results of the recommended research lies in the potential unwillingness of some decision makers to delegate responsibility for the design of decision processes or to involve a full range of affected parties in decision making in a serious way for fear that the ultimate decision might not fit their preconceived ideas or serve interests they wish to promote.

Despite such potential barriers, many environmental agencies clearly have backed their stated commitments to better and more open decision processes with significant investments of time, money, and institutional reputation, for example, in seeking out and responding to the input of a variety of stakeholders in these processes. Some have also shown serious interest in designing these processes with the help of sound knowledge. Such agencies are likely to take research results seriously if researchers are given incentives to disseminate their findings and if good lines of communication are established between researchers and practitioners. To make best use of research results, decisionmaking organizations should create internal incentives and assign responsibility within the organization for incorporating the best science into the deliberative part of decision making, and not only the analytical part. To the extent that these efforts are successful in some public-sector organizations, they are likely to diffuse to others over time.

Forested Landscapes in Perspective

Forest Values and Benefits

Nonfederal forests provide a wide variety of benefits that are important to the sustainability of the nation's economies, communities, and natural environments. For example, nonfederal owners of forests often benefit directly from the income they receive from forests and from the pleasure they experience when using and managing their forests. In a broader context, society may be the recipient of benefits provided by nonfederal forests, namely income and employment for its citizens and opportunities for them to exercise their interests in leisure and recreational activities. Obtaining these and many other benefits depends on the nation's willingness to invest in the sustainable management of nonfederal forests. A brief description of the many benefits provided by these forests is presented in this chapter.

Employment and Income

Forests are sources of employment and income for the nation's citizens. However, with the exception of data on Native American forests, there is little information that directly links these benefits to nonfederal forests on a national scale. For all forest ownerships in the United States, the U.S. Bureau of the Census estimates that nearly 1.3 million people were employed by U.S. wood-based industries in 1992 (GAO 1992). The total payroll received by these employees was $33.9 billion, while the value of shipments made by the industries was estimated to be $209 billion. The American Forest and Paper Association (1995b) also has estimated the economic importance of the nation's wood-based industries. In 1990, they employed more than 1.6 million people, of whom 59,100 worked in forestry, 701,800 in the paper industry, and 852,200 in the lumber industry.

Tribal forests are a source of considerable economic wealth for Native Americans. In 1991, these forests and associated programs provided more than 3,000 full-time and 28,000 part-time jobs for Native Americans. The Intertribal Timber Council (1993) estimated that economic benefits accruing from tribal forests were more than $284 million to Native Americans and an additional $180 million to non Native Americans. Most of these economic benefits result from the harvesting of timber—nearly 810 million board-feet of timber in 1990—on tribal lands. Fuel wood, pinion nuts, range forage, and other products also have provided a substantial portion ($38 million annually) of the economic benefits provided by tribal forests (Intertribal Timber Council 1993).

The public sector is also an important source of employment for citizens. For example, the U.S. Department of Agriculture (USDA) Forest Service had 31,135 permanent and excepted conditional employees on its payroll as of September 30, 1995. When seasonal and other types of employees are added, total USDA Forest Service employment in that year was the equivalent of full-time employment for 38,330 individuals. Information from the National Association of State Foresters indicates that in 1994 the state forestry agencies in the 50 states plus the District of Columbia and Guam employed 16,865 permanent employees. This total includes managerial, professional, technical, and clerical employees. Another 7,680 seasonal and temporary employees were employed by these state agencies in 1994. Other forest-related employment can be found within counties, municipalities, private consulting firms, colleges and universities, and nonprofit organizations.

Timber and Wood Products

Timber and wood products are major contributors to the high quality of life experienced by the nation's citizens. More often than not, these materials come from nonfederal forests. In 1991, the softwood and hardwood timber harvest in the United States exceeded 16.3 billion cubic feet. Of this total, 82 percent (13.4 million cubic feet) originated from industrial and non industrial private forestland. Timber harvested from city, state, or county land would increase this amount. [Estimates of timber harvest commonly are made available for four major ownership categories: national forest, other public forest, forest industry, and farm and other private forest. The "other public forest" category is a diverse group of federal (for example, Bureau of Land Management, and Department of Defense) and nonfederal public (for example, city, county, and state) land management agencies.

A breakdown of timber supply and demand information for the nonfederal public portion of this category is not readily available from existing sources.] If timber taken from this land is included, harvests from nonfederal forests would likely be in the range of 13.7 to 14.0 billion cubic feet. Since 1952, timber harvested from forest industry and farm and other privately owned forestland has decreased from 86 to 83 percent of the nation's total. More recently (1986-1991), the proportion has increased, primarily as a result of increased harvesting on industrial forestlands. Nationwide harvest of timber is expected to increase from slightly more than 16 billion cubic feet in 1991 to nearly 22 billion cubic feet in 2040.

Timber harvest from nonfederal forests is expected to rise through 2040 by 47 percent over 1991 levels, an additional 6.3 billion cubic feet of harvested wood. Expected declines in harvest from national forests and other public ownerships will temper the overall increase in harvest from all ownerships. More than 80 percent of the increase in harvest from nonfederal forests (5.0 billion cubic feet) will originate from non industrial private forests. Softwood timber harvest from industrial forests is expected to steadily increase as industrial softwood inventories increase through 2040. Regional shifts in harvested timber volumes are likely to occur during the next four decades.

By the year 2020, the Southern United States, a region

with a large proportion of the nation's nonfederal forests, will produce more than half of the nation's harvested timber volume. Southern timber harvest is expected to rise sharply in response to harvest reductions on Western public lands. Of special concern is the anticipated temporary reduction in harvestable acres on non industrial private forests between 2000 and 2010 —the result of sharply reduced planting and accelerated loss of non industrial forestland to non forest uses in the 1970s; this activity did not occur on Southern industrial forestlands. Because of the age structure of industrial forests in the South, these forests will not augment the expected reduced harvest on non industrial private forests. Timber management will become more intense on industrial forestlands, with the intent of reducing delays in stand regeneration and increasing tree growth once stands are established. This activity will accelerate site occupancy and hasten closure of stand canopies.

As a result of federal timber harvest cutbacks, harvests in the Pacific (Northwest and Southwest) region are projected to decline from 21 percent (1991) to 14 percent (2020) of the nation's total volume harvested. This regional shift is in large part caused by the substantial reductions in harvest that occurred on federal public forestland in the Pacific Northwest and Southwest. In 1991, growing stock inventories nationwide exceeded 785 billion cubic feet, of which 491 billion cubic feet (62 percent) was situated on nonfederal forest-ownerships. Of the latter, 316 billion cubic feet were held on non industrial private forestland. Nearly 70 percent of industrial growing stock is softwood, and more than 60 percent of non industrial growing stock is hardwood. Growing-stock inventories (hardwoods and softwoods) are projected to increase by 21 percent (165 billion cubic feet) nationwide between 1991 and 2040.

Forest-industry softwood inventories are expected to decline between 1991 and 2000 but increase by nearly 47 percent between 2000 and 2040. In contrast, softwood inventories on non industrial private lands will fluctuate minimally between 1991 and 2040 because of an approximate balance between timber removal and grow'th. The trend for private hardwood inventories is unclear; however, industrial and non industrial hardwood inventories are anticipated to be lower in 2040 than in 1991. On industrial and non industrial lands, inventories will be concentrated in timber ages near or below minimal merchantable limits. Although regional variations will occur, private forests will be younger and, on average, smaller in diameter than in the past. In addition,

Nonfederal forests accounted for more than 75 percent of the nation's net annual growth of growing stock in 1991. Of the nonfederal portion (16 billion cubic feet), one- quarter was held on industrial forestlands. In general, hardwood net annual growth is expected to decline and softwood growth to rise through 2040 on industrial and non industrial forestland. Growth and inventory trends on nonfederal forests are likely to have important impacts on water quality, wildlife populations, and recreation values. For example, on private lands, habitat will shift to favor species that can use early-and mid-successional stages of forest development; on public nonfederal forestlands, mid- to-late successional habitat will become more abundant.

Non-timber Forest Products

Nonfederal forests are also a source of non-timber products, such as pine cones, honey, mushrooms, and maple syrup. Currently, more than 450 special forest products in 18 categories are harvested from American forests. In the Northeast, for example, the gathering of pine cones for seed or decorative purposes is common on private forestland. From state-owned public forestland, Minnesota has sold between $8,000 and $10,000 worth of pine cones annually. Traditional food products (pine nuts, camas, and huckleberries) are gathered by tribal members, wild crafters, and recreational visitors on nonfederal forestlands.

In 1990, the value of honey production in Florida was

an estimated $10 million, most of which is attributable to an apiary in the Apalachicola National Forest near Tallahassee. Forest industry leases bee rights on substantial portions of the Atlantic Coastal Plain and Flatwoods, providing a significant base of honey production. In the Pacific Northwest, harvesting of mushrooms is an economically and socially important activity in many nonfederal forests. For example, the Washington Department of Natural Resources leases land to individuals to harvest mushrooms. Mushrooms are currently generating sales over $125 million in the Pacific Northwest, with a wTork force of over 10,000 people. Little is known about the conditions that produce these fungi, yet harvests continue to increase.

Much of the production of maple syrup, including the tapping of trees, is carried out on non industrial forestlands, especially those that are privately owned. Nationwide, the value of maple syrup production in 1991 was in excess of $39 million. Floral greenery is an established special forest product, and forestlands can be managed specifically to encourage favored species and environmental conditions. Basket weaving by Native peoples, such as the basket weavers of California, is another important example of the production of non-timber forest products. Non-timber forest products are easily identified with particular land parcels or regions of the United States.

These products present the landowners with comm-ercial opportunities or opportunities to use the activities of gatherers as management tools to manipulate vegetation by species or by product quality. Harvest of special forest products on federal and nonfederal lands is likely to increase. Annual income from visually non intrusive harvesting of such products is an incentive for nonfederal landowners to be involved.

Urban and Community Benefits

Although urban residents use wild lands beyond city limits, they spend comparatively more time in urban and community forests. This is especially true for the disabled, the elderly, young, or those who have low incomes. Urban and community forests provide a variety of important social and environmental benefits, the economic value of which has been estimated to be $3 billion per year nationwide. Urban and community forests moderate climate; protect air quality; control rain runoff; lower noise levels; provide wildlife habitat; improve the aesthetics of cities; and, in some instances, conserve energy, carbon dioxide, and water. They also provide social benefits, which include medical, psychological, social, and managerial benefits.

Medical benefits accrue from reduced stress and general improvement in public health. Psychological benefits result from the improved aesthetics of residential streets and community parks as well as from communities' enhanced sense of social identity and self-esteem, particularly in areas with active community involvement in tree-planting programs. Urban and community forests also provide benefits that are directly appropriable by landowners, such as the value of timber located near urban areas. For example, in Alabama, Florida, Georgia, South Carolina, North Carolina, and Virginia approximately 26 percent of the timberland is located in Metropolitan Statistical Areas. Landowners also benefit from increases in real estate value, increases that are directly attributable to trees. A conservative estimate is that the value of trees surrounding detached housing units in the United States is the source of an additional $1.5 billion per year in property tax revenue. Various studies also suggest that property owners benefit from energy conserved as a result of properly located and sized trees.

Recreational Opportunities

Nonfederal forests provide citizens with a wide variety of recreational benefits, particularly on public non federal forestland. In 1989, an estimated 52.6 million acres of state land was available for recreational use, nearly half of which was managed by state forestry agencies. State park and state fish and game agencies managed 19 percent and 31 percent of this area, respectively. Despite their relatively small land base, local governments managed the other half of outdoor recreational use. This is due to the close proximity of recreational public-land sites to people's homes. Recreational pursuits are also available on private forestland.

In the contiguous United States, for example, an estimated 23 percent of non industrial private forestland is available for recreational use by the general public. In addition to the 23 percent of non industrial private forestland that is accessible by the general public, another 45 percent is open to people personally acquainted with the landowner, and 26 percent is open only to landowners and their immediate families. The aesthetic values of non industrial forestland are also important to landowners and citizens alike. Along major travel corridors, private groups have coordinated efforts to manage forest landscapes in manners that will preserve important scenic amenities.

Fishing and hunting in forested environments provide substantial personal enjoyment to citizens and economic returns to rural communities. Fishing and hunting rights are sold on many nonfederal forestlands. Non-consumptive uses of forest wildlife are expected to grow twice as fast as the nation's population to 2000, with all forms of cold-water fishing activity to increase at about the same rate as the population. Citizens are also experiencing benefits from increases in wildlife species that thrive in forest-edge environments (e.g., deer, elk, turkey). Public lands, including nonfederal public forestlands, are expected to become relatively more important for big-game hunting and cold water fishing, assuming that access remains generally unrestricted and free. Hunting on private forestlands for a fee is also expected to increase.

Tribal forests are sanctuaries for worship and religious ceremonies and contain burial sites and other culturally significant areas for Native Americans. Forest wildlife contributes to the religious, cultural, and medicinal needs of many tribal members. Although not necessarily focused on securing recreational benefits, citizens frequently seek to preserve forests, including certain nonfederal forests, as a means of ensuring that future generations will be in a position to make choices about their use, management, and protection. Citizens' general interest in preserving forests that they will probably never lay claim to is an indication that they value these forests and the benefits provided by them.

Ecological Benefits

Nonfederal forests provide a wide variety of ecological services and benefits. For example, they are storehouses of large amounts of carbon. In the continental United States, nonfederal forests store an estimated 38.6 billion metric tons of carbon (90 percent of the national total), and Alaskan forests store an additional 16 billion metric tons. Approximately 90 percent of this continental storage capacity is provided by timberland —55 percent in non industrial private forests and 15 percent in industrial forests. Between 1987 and 2000, non industrial private timberland is projected to sequester an average of 61 million metric tons of carbon annually in living trees and under story vegetation. Carbon sequestration front removals (for example, wood products) is estimated to be 58 million metric tons annually during the same period-although the fate of carbon stored in these products is unclear.

Nonfederal forests provide habitat for important threatened and endangered species. Of 712 listed species, 609 (86 percent) have their habitat on private individual or corporate property, much of which is forested. Public non federal lands provide habitat to 516 species (72 percent), while nonprofit-owned land and tribal land provide habitat to 181 and 61 species (25 and 9 percent), respectively. Fifty-two species are found on other nonfederal lands (GAO 1994a). Considering all ownerships, forests provide approximately half the habitat for the nation's threatened and endangered species. More than 90 percent of these listed species have some or their entire habitat on nonfederal lands, although not necessarily on forested lands (GAO 1994a). Nearly three-quarters have at least 60 percent of their habitat on nonfederal lands; 37 percent are completely dependent on nonfederal lands.

Forests are also the source of approximately 60 percent of the nation's total stream flow, the primary means by which high-quality water is provided for industrial, municipal, and recreational uses. As the nation's major forest ownership category, nonfederal forests play an especially important role in this respect. Analyses suggest that precipitation on all types of land currently provides enough surface and ground water (1.4 trillion gallons per day) to meet not only present but also prospective withdrawals: 500 billion gallons —only 10 percent of precipitation—by 2040. However, these estimates mask important regional supply-demand imbalances, which are caused primarily by geographic, seasonal, and annual variations in supplies. These are areas of the nation where ground water development, in stream use (e.g., navigation, recreational activities, and hydropower generation) and surface water development (e.g., municipal and industrial uses) are expected to be especially demanding. In areas where these conditions occur, nonfederal forests will be called upon to play an especially important role in providing quality water in sufficient quantities.

The quality of water flowing from forested land has been of special concern since the early 1970s when federal laws began to emphasize activities to deal with non point sources of water pollutants. The quality of water flowing from forest and rangelands is good—-in large measure, this is because of federal programs that encourage states to initiate plans and programs for addressing water quality issues. In response to these federal programs, state governments, in cooperation with private concerns, have established a wide variety of water-quality best management practices that are being delivered to landowners and timber harvesters via educational, technical assistance, financial, and regulatory programs, hi general, landowner and timber harvester compliance with these best management practices is quite high, often exceeding 90 percent.

The positive condition of water quality flowing from forests should not imply a lack of opportunities for improvement. With regard to fish and wildlife generally, it is estimated that about 80 percent of the nation's flowing water from forest and non forest sources can be improved in terms of quantity and quality, fish habitat, or composition of the fish community. However, an estimated two-thirds of U.S. streams have habitat conditions that are adequate for sports fish. Considering only forests as a land cover type, there continues to be concern over the impact that forestry activities have on nitrate levels, water temperature, and suspended sediment. The latter is of special concern, especially following road construction and the application of some harvesting and grazing practices. Some practices in riparian areas also have raised concerns, especially removal of over story along stream-banks, which can raise water temperatures enough to adversely affect fish survival.

Nonfederal forests provide a wide variety of benefits to the nation's citizens. These include employment and income opportunities, timber and wood products, non-timber forest products, urban and community benefits, recreational opportunities, and ecological benefits. In many cases, information regarding these benefits is limited because information on the type, magnitude, and value of benefits is not often collected or made available.

6

The Fuel Wood Situation in the Developing Countries

Before describing specific regional situations, the aim of this chapter is to sketch an overall picture and call attention to the general characteristics of the importance of fuel wood and its derivative, charcoal, as a source of energy in the developing countries. Is there any need to point out that only during the last two centuries has wood gradually ceased to be the fuel most used throughout the world? The replacement of wood by fossil fuels with a high energy content and easier to manipulate played an important role in the industrial revolution. Wood, therefore, plays only a marginal role in the energy supplies of the industrial countries, except in certain rural areas. But this is not the case in developing countries, where the vast majority of the people continue to depend on the fuel to which they traditionally have access: fuel wood. Up to the middle of the seventies it was possible to believe that fuel wood, particularly if it became scarce, would be more or less automatically replaced by fossil fuels. Since then, however, owing to the increase in the price of the latter, the conditions for such a substitution have become much more difficult and the fuel wood shortages which are occurring in many parts of the Third World have thus become much more serious.

When wood becomes scarce, agricultural and animal

waste is used as a supplement or substitute. When all the immediately accessible traditional fuels become scarcer, minimum energy needs for such essential purposes as cooking food and heating the home can no longer be covered; and those who suffer most directly from such situations are the poorest, and the weakest of the poor: the children, the old and the women. This study is the first attempt to ascertain the seriousness and extent of this other energy crisis, that of fuel wood. Hie shortage of fuel wood is not linked to the growing scarcity of other sources of energy and its impact, as will be seen, goes far beyond the single problem of energy supplies. In order to put the fuel wood crisis in its real perspective, we shall analyse in this chapter the importance of fuel wood through official statistics for both forestry and energy, the place of fuel wood in rural energy systems, and finally the trends in situations in the developing world as they emerge from an analysis of the results of the work carried out in connection with this study.

Fuel Wood Production

According to the data available to FAO, which have recently been subjected to critical review, fuel wood production represented 5.4% of world energy consumption in 1978: 15 x 10- TJ as against a total energy consumption of 257 x 106 TJ. At world level, therefore, wood is by far the most used renewable source of energy, coming just after oil, coal and gas. As regards the volume extracted, fuel wood is the most important product of the world's forest resources, because in 1978 it represented almost 60 percent of the total volume extracted for the world as a whole. And this refers only to fuel wood properly so-called, i.e. excluding industrial residues recycled in the industry itself for the production of energy, such as recycling of the waste from the manufacture of paper pulp. In the developing countries the biomass in its traditional solid form (fuel wood and agricultural residues) represents a considerable and often insufficiently recognized proportion of the total energy supply.

In 1978 fuel wood alone accounted for more than a fifth of the total energy consumption of the developing countries, although consumption by country varied widely according to the extent of the forest resources available and existence or otherwise of fossil energy sources; and fuel wood production reached 1 421 million m^3, or 85 percent of the total amount of round wood used in the developing countries. Since international trade in fuel wood is negligible or circumscribed to geographically very limited transfers, national fuel wood consumption is held to be equivalent to production. Some countries, particularly in Africa, are almost entirely dependent on fuel wood as a source of energy: a total of 21 countries, of which 16 belong to the group of least developed countries, depend for more than three-quarters of their energy consumption on fuel wood.

For some ten years now, energy consumption in the developing countries has been increasing at an annual rate of about 7 percent, and fuel wood consumption at about 2 percent, according to estimates. Bat although total energy consumption has continued to increase at a rate slightly below 7 percent since 1974, there has been a considerable slowing down in several countries and regions: in Africa, for example, with the exception of Algeria, Egypt, Libya and Nigeria, the growth in energy consumption has been only 3.5 percent a year. In conclusion, it is probable that the relative dependence on fuel wood of the developing countries as a whole is decreasing owing to greater use of commercial fuels: but this dependence remains considerable, particularly, as will be seen, in the rural areas. The more rapid increase in world energy consumption is essentially linked, in fact, to the growth of the transport and industry sectors, while domestic energy consumption continues to depend mainly on traditional fuels.

In national statistics, the fuel wood and charcoal production is assessed on the basis of the forestry data available, supplemented if necessary by estimates. But considerable amounts of fuel wood are also collected outside the actual forest lands, on uncultivated land or in rural areas, and are not accurately assessed. In many countries the data available are at best estimates or extrapolations based on partial consumption studies. In few cases do systematic surveys make it possible to know the present consumption of fuel wood and its trends, the importance of the various sources of supply, the respective share of the various sectors in consumption, and the relationship between consumption and economic and social level. Fuel wood is essentially used locally, without being transported over long distances and without passing through the commercial channels which form the object of official statistical inquiries. Despite its obvious importance, fuel wood rarely appears in national energy statistics, which usually mention only the conventional commercial fuels.

Despite considerable recent progress, considerable gaps remain in information on fuel wood production. It is essential that systematic efforts be made to improve the quality and coverage of this information in a way that corresponds to the real importance of this source of energy and in order to incorporate this information in national energy balances. There is a particular shortage of information on supplies and consumption of agricultural residues, the other fuel widely used as an addition to or direct substitute for fuel wood, particularly in Asia. In most countries only estimates based on agricultural production data are possible. But in a few countries, such as India, detailed studies have made it possible to determine precisely the importance of agricultural residues and dung in energy consumption.

Fuel Wood in Rural Energy Systems

Fuel wood plays a major role in supplying energy to the rural masses and the poorest groups in the towns. Fuel wood occupies a special place in rural energy systems owing to the importance of the domestic consumption for which it is mainly used and the fact that it is produced within the system itself. This reflects the extent of the demand for warmth in the traditional rural energy system as compared with that for propulsive energy. Wood is the fuel customarily preferred by rural people both because its decentralized method of production is suited to the scattered nature of rural habitation and usually makes it possible to obtain the fuel without added cost, and because production can be maintained on the basis of sustained yield and in combination with other goods and services.

Fuel-wood is thus pre-eminently a renewable source of energy whose decentralized nature is particularly suited to the characteristics of rural energy systems. In a rural community, the energy system reflects an integrated structure of relationships between resources and activities, and the role of fuel wood must be seen, as a complex function with many connections with the land tenure and land use systems, agricultural practices, the machinery for allocating resources, social structures, etc. The main characteristics of fuel wood in rural energy systems are outlined below. Domestic requirements, essentially for cooking food and heating the homes, usually account for the biggest percentage of overall energy consumption in the developing countries. This is even more marked for rural populations and poor households.

Fuel wood is usually the fuel preferred by rural people, who have very little access to other forms of energy. Wood, therefore, plays an essential role in meeting elementary energy requirements connected with the very subsistence of these people. In addition to its renewable and decentralized nature, fuel wood can be gathered and used by simple techniques, without recourse to expensive equipment and is, therefore, particularly suited to the requirements and possibilities of its users. Minimum energy requirements for cooking and heating may be estimated at 6 -10 GJ, or 0.5 - 1 m^3 of fuel wood per person per year, under present conditions; considerable variations are possible according to cooking habits, climate, way of life and social structure, and also the efficiency of the cooking equipment. If account is taken of the amount of heating necessary in cold mountain climates, total energy requirements for domestic purposes may reach 25 to 30 GJ, the equivalent of about 3 m^3 of wood, per person per year. Seasonal climatic variations, the nature of the wood and its availability may considerably modify effective consumption levels.

In addition to its main role in satisfying domestic energy requirements, fuel wood is also an important fuel for many rural industries: drying tea and tobacco, smoking fish, brick - making, lime kilns, smithies, potteries and various village handicrafts. Consumption levels may vary greatly: in Tanzania, for example, it is estimated that 50 m^3 of fuel wood are necessary to dry the yield of one hectare of tobacco; elsewhere, it is estimated that 2 kg of wood are necessary to produce 1 kg of cane sugar. Industries may consume considerable amounts of fuel wood, thus adding to domestic demand in these same rural areas. Recent developments and the difficulty of obtaining commercial fuel supplies have prompted rural industries in some countries to turn to wood, or to retain it as their main, if not sole fuel, where encouraged by local supply possibilities or induced by government efforts to limit the effects of energy consumption on the trade balance.

The use of fuel wood in rural areas for domestic purposes or village industries often still forms part of traditional subsistence economy systems. Tlie wood is usually gathered by the women and children for the family's own needs in the immediate vicinity of the home, Gathering the family's energy supply is an essential chore which may occupy a considerable part of thc working day. In many cases, owing precisely to the presence of the rural population, there are no real forest resources in the immediate vicinity. Fuel wood is then collected from the woody vegetation scattered throughout the area: isolated trees, shrubs, the yield from pruning fruit trees, etc. When demand increases and resources become less accessible, a current of activity usually develops that generates employment and income: some of the country people devote themselves to collecting, transporting and distributing fuel wood to the villages and towns. This current of activity may reach considerable proportions.

It has been calculated that millions of work-days are invested in supplying towns and villages in the Sahel: for example, just to supply the town of Bamako in 1978 involved 500 000 work - days simply to cut the wood, and a cash movement of US$7 million. This shows both the importance that fuel wood provisioning may have for employment in rural areas and the conversion of fuel wood from a material available to everyone free of charges to a product with a cash value and price. This latter aspect is symptomatic of growing supply problems, but also of a change of attitude of which advantage could be taken in seeking solutions and in using fuel wood in a process of development. The contribution of fuel wood as a source of energy is not limited to rural energy systems or to subsistence sectors.

In many countries urban areas account for an increasing share of fuel wood consumption, owing both to the migration of country people who conserve a rural way of life, and to the dependence of the poorest families, who continue to rely on wood for their domestic needs. Fuel wood then often tends to be replaced by its derivative, charcoal, which is easy to transport, store and use, but the production of which entails considerable loss of the energy contained in the raw material. In the absence of control, urban demand signifies a concentration of consumption leading not only to localized over - cutting of resources around the town, but also to diversion to the town of supplies indispensable for the people living in rural areas; the effects are felt for more than 100 km around the towns, and the distance is constantly increasing. Urban demand for fuel wood, therefore, may also constitute an important factor in disrupting rural energy supplies.

Since rural energy systems form part of a complex whole, the growing difficulty of obtaining sufficient fuel wood has serious repercussions of all kinds. First, it results in people who do not have access to any other sources of energy having to devote an increasing proportion of their limited time and money to obtaining the supply they need. This results in accelerated over-cutting of the remaining woody vegetation, which may even lead to its complete disappearance, and adds to all the other factors contributing to its degradation: bush fires, grazing, clearing for the introduction of new crops, periods of adverse climatic conditions. In extreme cases the consequences for the environment may be irreparable and endanger people's very existence it is known what effect deforestation has on fragile ecological areas, such as arid zones and mountains, as a result of desertification or erosion.

Deforestation itself is often the result of clearing the land for new crops, even modern mono cultural systems. When trees disappear from the countryside, and with them the possibility of obtaining fuel wood, the people have recourse to agricultural residues and animal waste, the only fuel to which it still has access. In some cases it has been calculated that the amounts annually burnt instead of being dug into the soil are equivalent to considerable amounts of fertilizer needed to maintain soil fertility. If loss of agricultural productivity is to be avoided, recourse to mineral fertilizers is necessary, but this increases dependence on fossil fuels for energy. The alternative is to use oil or gas as a fuel; and this, assuming that the rural user is able to procure them, will add to national requirements for fossil fuels. Ultimately the shortage of fuel wood has two consequences throughout the rural energy system: dependence on substitute fuels imported from outside the system, and greater recourse to fertilizers to compensate for the fertilizing elements not returned to the soil.

Should the situation be left to deteriorate without intervention, it has a direct effect on nutrition, owing to the impossibility of cooking food properly, and an indirect effect on the food supply, owing to the decrease in agricultural productivity. The impact is all the more marked in the more fragile ecological areas and on the poorest sectors of the population. When the situation has not reached an irreversible state, it is technically and economically feasible at least to preserve or restore fuel wood's contribution to the basic energy supply necessary for the subsistence of the rural population. It may even be possible to increase this contribution and thus help to provide the extra'-energy needed for this population's development. The various possibilities are covered in the last chapter of this document.

In concluding this section on the importance of fuel wood in rural energy systems, attention must be drawn to the role played by this fuel in meeting such essential energy needs as cooking, heating and rural industries in the developing countries. Its growing scarcity is making it more difficult for a great many people to subsist and is breaking up their energy system; in extreme cases it is upsetting the balance of the environment as a result of deforestation and the cutting of all woody vegetation. The problem of fuel wood thus has three important dimensions: forestry, energy and environment. That is why its role in rural energy systems must be clearly perceived as a problem not only of subsistence but also of development.

Evolution of the Overall Fuel Wood Situation

The survey showed that in 1980 some 2 thousand million people, or three-quarters of the population of the developing countries, had a traditional-type energy consumption and hence depended on fuel wood and other solid components of the biomass to meet their daily domestic energy requirements. Bat of these people dependent on traditional fuels, 1 160 million, or more than half, were unable to meet their minimum energy requirements from available fuel wood resources without compromising future supplies: demand has grown faster than supply and in certain cases even over-cutting of the resources does not suffice to guarantee the minimum amounts needed.

Acute Scarcity Situations

It is estimated that in 1980 more than 96 million in the three continents were living in a situation of acute energy shortage: over-cutting of the woody vegetation, or what remains of it, and where possible the use of agricultural residues, did not suffice to meet minimum requirements and consumption was, therefore, inevitably below the minimum required. The most serious situations were identified in: the arid and semi-arid zones south of the Sahara, the eastern and south-eastern parts of the continent, the mountainous areas and the islands in Africa; the Himalaya region in Asia, and the Andean plateau, the arid zones along the Pacific coast and the densely populated areas of Central America and the Caribbean in Latin America, These situations are characterized either by high levels of demand owing to severe climatic conditions, or by relatively high population density in rural areas in difficult ecological zones where the productivity of the fuel wood resources is low.

The total annual deficit of fuel wood has been estimated at 95 million m^3, or 1 m^3 per inhabitant per year; only a small proportion of the minimum needs is covered. In all these situations the fuel wood crisis endangers the development potential; incidence on the nutrition and health of populations who are not able to cook their food and protect themselves from the cold; disproportionate amount of time and money devoted to procuring fuel; maximum use of residues for combustion and consequence of this, added to erosion caused by deforestation, on soil productivity resulting tendency to clear more land for cultivation in zones usually even more fragile. It may therefore be stated without exaggeration that the areas identified really are in an emergency situation, the acute scarcity of fuel wood generating an energy shortage whose extent and consequences necessitate immediate and massive interventions.

Forestry solutions are indispensable both to resolve the energy problem and to restore and protect a productive environment, but they will be insufficient, at least in the short term, to make up the deficits and restore energy supplies to the level of minimum needs. Any strategy for these acute scarcity situations must therefore necessarily include complementary emergency measures to ensure minimum energy supplies in the short term, including even the subsidized provision of additional fuel throughout the period required for the introduction of lasting solutions.

Analysis of the evolution of these situations produces an even more disturbing picture: it is estimated that by 2000 population growth will have brought the numbers dependent on fuel wood in these areas up to more than 150 million. On the basis of recent trends observed in deforestation and of plantation programmes foreseen for the coming years, extrapolated to the year 2000, it is to be feared that the annual fuel wood deficit will reach 160 million m^3, resulting in aggravation of the deficit per inhabitant. The actions planned at present are, therefore, insufficient even to avoid further deterioration of the situation identified in 1980.

Deficit Situations

The number of people in a deficit situation in 1980 is estimated at 1052 million. These populations are able to meet their minimum needs only by over-cutting and thus endangering their future supplies; renewal of the resource is not ensured. Such situations have been identified in North Africa and the Middle Bast, in the savanna areas in West, Central and Bast Africa, in the Ganges and Indus plains, in certain plains and islands of South-Bast Asia, and in the semi-arid populated areas and the Andean zones in Latin

America and in Asia alone more than 700 million people are involved.

These situations are characterized by great diversity, but usually concern relatively populated zones where the ecological conditions are fairly favourable to forest resources but where the relative density of the rural populations subjects these resources to pressures which considerably exceed the available supply, resulting in deficit situations. The overall deficit in 1980 is evaluated at about 350 million m^3, or 0.3 m^3 per inhabitant per year: almost two-thirds of this deficit is connected with situations identified in Asia. Owing to the big population growth in most of these zones, and to clearing of land for cultivation, the situation is deteriorating rapidly. But forestry solutions are possible in view of the relatively favourable ecological conditions.

These solutions should form an integral part of rural development and be based on active participation by the people in protecting and managing their fuel wood resources. They must give priority to mixed agricultural- forestry system, intercropping, rural woodlots, community forests, etc. Analysis of present trends, though, arouses fear that the deficit situations may worsen, and that some may end in acute scarcity before the year 2000. Taking into account the number of people dependent on fuel wood in 1980, the zones in a deficit situation might involve 1 782 million people in 2000, 1 149 million in Asia alone.

It is difficult to identify the specific situations which may develop into acute scarcity, but the overall deficit might rise from 350 million m^3 in 1980 to 710 million m^3, i.e. double in twenty years. The average deficit per inhabitant may grow by 0.4 m^3/year. This calculation is based on present trends in deforestation and probable rates of plantation. For this category of situations too, the action projected at the moment is insufficient even to prevent further deterioration and at least make up for the growth in population.

Prospective Deficit Situations

Among the zones which had an excess of supply over demand, in 1980, a category of situations has been identified which on The basis of present trends might have to face more or less marked deficits in the year 2000. This category of situations, defined as prospective deficit, concerns some 280 million people dependent on fuel w'ood in 1980, who might become 464 million by the year 2000 owing to high population growth. From a surplus of supplies over needs of 108 million m^3 in 1980, this category might drop to a deficit of about 100 million m^3 in the year 2000. This category covers both the appearance of a deficit instead of a surplus, and the rapid degradation of surplus situations; therefore, certain Latin American situations which by the year 2000 will be very close to deficit, without having actually reached it yet, have been grouped under this category.

A number of these prospective deficit situations w'ere marked in 1980 by still relatively abundant forest resources, but also by rapid growth of the rural populations linked particularly to large population movements and hence the clearing and cultivation of new land, leading to a rapid decrease in fuel wood supplies for which penetration and access to new forest resources does not compensate. Appropriate programmes for maintaining fuel wood supplies within the framework of the rural development programmes themselves should make it possible to control these situations; but the action must be undertaken sufficiently far in advance to prevent these situations degenerating to the point where more intensive solutions, more difficult to put into effect, are required.

Recapitulation

The dimensions of the problem and the prospects which emerge from an analysis of fuel wood supplies and requirements in the developing countries show that the concern expressed on this subject in recent years is fully justified. Out of an approximate total of 2 thousand million people dependent on fuel wood in the developing countries in 1980, 1 148 million, or 57.5 percent, do not have access to sufficient supplies and of these, 96 million cannot even cover their minimum needs and live in situations marked by acute energy scarcity, with serious social, economic and ecological consequences. For this set of situations, the deficit is estimated at 445 million m^3, more than half in Asia alone.

Ertrapolation of present trends in population, deforestation and plantation work produces a picture of a gigantic problem by the year 2000: of some 2.7 thousand million people dependent on traditional fuels for their energy supply, situations of acute scarcity or deficit would involve 2.4 thousand million, or 89%. The deficit might reach nearly one thousand million m^3 of fuel wood, equivalent to 9 million GJ per year. In a growing number of situations fuel wood will probably no longer play more than a marginal role unless actions are rapidly intensified on a scale consonant with the size of the problem. Governments might have to organize large-scale emergency programmes in order to helpmeet the minimum energy needs of the populations - needs as essential for their survival as are food and shelter. The cost of such programmes might well endanger the development potential of the countries concerned.

The only zones to escape such a process will be the sparsely inhabited areas which still have immense forest resources, such as the Amazon basin, the basin of the Zaire River, the major islands of South-East Asia, and a small number of zones located in the three continents. Supplies there will remain greatly in excess of local requirements, to the point where the feasibility might be considered of using this potential to supply the neighbouring deficit zones. The analysis and results presented here as regards the year 2000 are of a purely indicative nature, aimed at pr ompting reflection on what may happen if no major effort is undertaken.

It is probable that the extent and the seriousness of the

scarcity in developing Countries will force governments and populations to act and to adopt solutions whose impact will have to be monitored. What emerges particularly from this analysis is the magnitude of the task that has to be carried out in order to resolve the energy problem of the populations dependent on fuel wood, whose supplies will henceforth have to be ensured by deliberate action and no longer left to the people to gather as and where they can, thus making it possible for the problem to be ignored.

Special Regional Characteristics

It is necessary to complete this overall picture of the fuel wood situation in the developing countries by a few indications of the main characteristics of the regional situations. The survey showed in fact, that there are noticeable differences between the regions with regard to such things as the relative importance of fuel wood, ways of using resources, distribution of population in relation to resources, etc.

Africa- South of the Sahara is the region in which dependence on fuel wood is the most marked: between 90 and 98 percent of energy needs in the rural areas are met by fuel - wood, which may also account for more than 90 percent of national energy supplies.

Natural woody formations, which provide most of the supplies, seem to be used in a relatively inefficient way, perhaps because they have remained abundant until recent years. Populations are usually concentrated in savanna areas where the ecological conditions are not very favourable to forests. There is often a marked contrast between savanna zones with a big deficit and neighbouring forest zones with a surplus, clearly connected with accessibility and lack of infrastructure. Even in relatively populated zones, fuel wood sources other than the conventional forest ones play only an accessory role: trees seem, in general, to form a less integral part of the rural landscape and cultivation practices than in other regions; the type of farming or of plants grown seems, too, to make available smaller amounts of residue for energy.

All these characteristics lead to situations of considerable deficit, particularly in arid and semi-arid zones and mountainous areas, without the number of people involved being very high: big deficits often appear where there are more than 20 inhabitants per km. This reveals the severity of the ecological conditions, but also means that there is scope for forestry solutions by family groups and villagers, of which so far there have been very few. The importance of solutions which combine trees' role as a source of energy and their role as an important factor in rural economy and the stability of the environment must be emphasized.

North Africa and the Middle Hast present a great diversity of geographical, ecological and economic situations, and hence dependence on fuel wood reflects the existence or absence of a source of supply rather than whether or not the country has fossil fuels. In countries where the ecological conditions make possible a minimum of forest productivity, fuel wood consumption is growing at the same time as the consumption of other sources of energy. This is attributable to the continued dependence of the poorest sectors of the population on fuel wood, and also to a certain preference for this traditional fuel. Despite everything, fuel wood consumption is, with some exceptions, usually limited and wood is not the main fuel: the outstanding fact is the poverty of the groups using fuel wood, who do not have the possibility of acceding to other fuels.

Only a few countries with relatively big forest resources are characterized by a marked dependence on wood fuel, and here the deficit as compared with requirements is often considerable. Another characteristic peculiar to this region is the existence of marketing channels, in particular for charcoal, where financial possibilities permit importation of this traditional fuel preferred for certain domestic uses.

Asia is marked above all by two specific characteristics:

the size of the populations which are dependent on traditional fuels and the very complementary role usually played by fuel wood, agricultural residues and animal waste, to the extent that it is difficult to dissociate them.

Human settlements have existed here for so long that the people dependent on fuel wood arc often concentrated in densely-populated zones far from the forest resources. This makes it difficult to transfer supplies. In this region, therefore, fuel wood supplies from resources other than natural woody formations particularly farm woodlots, are particularly important: trees are often closely associated with cultivation systems and make appreciable contributions. The diversity of the fuel's used makes it difficult to evaluate the real minimum requirements for fuel wood. In some oases energy consumption is traditionally based on the use of agricultural and animal waste, which cannot, therefore, be considered as an indication of acute scarcity of fuel-wood.

The Indian sub-continent, together with certain areas in South-East Asia, is the main problem area as regards fuel wood; a population density of several hundred inhabitants per km^2, which continues to grow, gives rise to particularly complex rural energy supply problems, difficult to resolve owing to the possible repercussions on closely intertwined systems of energy and agricultural production and on the fragile equilibrium. It therefore in Asia that the deficit situations appear to be most serious, owes both to the size of the populations concerned and the extent of the deficits, and to the consequences of these deficits on the environment and on the natural resources both in the area concerned and even in the plains downstream.

In Latin America the situations seem more heterogeneous owing to the diversity of ways of life and customs and of physical and human conditions. A considerable proportion of the rural populations no longer uses wood fuel, but this is compensated for by a greater proportion of urban users. Dependence on fuel wood, therefore, remains high over extensive areas. The diversity of situations makes it difficult to estimate and apply parameters of fuel wood supplies and needs. Natural formations obviously play an important role in providing supplies, but the contribution of farm woodlots is more difficult to assess. The region is also marked by the fact that zones of acute scarcity generally coincide with difficult ecological conditions, and are so cut off that it is difficult to transfer supplies from surplus zones.

Mention must also be made of the extent of population movements towards newly settled areas and of deforestation in these zones. Finally, it must be added that in Latin America there are big industries using fuel wood and charcoal: it is in this region that the widest use is made of wood fuel for industrial purposes and this often has negative implications for the domestic fuel supply of the rural populations, particularly in Brasil. This overall picture of the fuel wood situation in the developing countries shows the full extent and seriousness of the problem. Fuel wood plays an essential role in the energy supplies of some 2 thousand million people, who use it mainly for cooking their food; of these some 100 million people cannot procure enough fuel for this elementary energy requirement and more than one thousand million are faced with increasingly acute scarcity.

Extrapolation of present trends shows that the populations dependent on fuel-wood who will be facing marked deficits in the year 2000 may double; at the same time the global deficit may reach one thousand million m^3„ The already serious fuel wood crisis is worsening and very few developing countries will be totally unaffected at the end of the century. In all regions the impact of the fuel wood problem is particularly severe on low-income groups and within these groups on the most vulnerable members: the children, the old and the women in general: it jeopardizes economic and social development prospects insofar as energy supplies are not covered and the ecological consequences of deforestation affect agricultural productivity. This study aims at arousing sufficient awareness of the problem to prompt the general mobilization of efforts called for by the scale of the problem.

Improving the Situations

The results of the analyses presented have demonstrated the seriousness and the size of the gap between accessible supplies compatible with sustained production and the present minimum levels of fuel wood needs. About 920 million rural people were affected by such situations in 1980 and this figure might be two and a half times greater by the year 2000 should present trends persist. In vast zones of western and eastern Africa and in the Indian subcontinent, fuel wood may well be playing no more than a marginal role by then. But all recent experience has shown that no substitute energy is able, under acceptable technical and socio-economic conditions, to replace fuel wood on a scale able to have a real impact on these gloomy prospects. This means that at least for the last two decades of this century the rural populations in the Third World, and probably the poorest urban sectors, will continue to depend to an over-whelming extent on the plant fuels immediately available in their environment.

This situation will continue until the conditions for a mass substitution of another energy source for fuel wood are met: and even then considerable time will have to elapse before a new technology can noticeably change a situation, so that it will take that much longer to have an impact. However, the fact that the real nature and extent of the problem is now being increasingly recognized already constitutes a first important step towards resolving it, or at least reversing the present trends. The problem is, then, of exceptional gravity, and it is essential to examine, however briefly, the possible solutions. Up to the energy crisis of the seventies, it was assumed that the transition from traditional fuel wood to commercial energies was automatic, and few deliberate efforts were made to control, far less improve, fuel wood supplies.

But now fuel wood, a renewable source of energy of local origin, has strategic as well as social importance. It is therefore essential that forestry's full potential to resolve the problem and maintain supplies be mobilized. This chapter will therefore analyse the feasibility of forestry solutions aimed at increasing fuel wood supplies. It will also show that no single or simple solution will suffice and that a number of actions will have to be combined in strategies adapted to the specific situation. It will also emphasize that in most cases there is a common denominator of similar constraints which hinder action. The removal of these constraints can set in motion a dynamic process of development.

The Feasibility of Forestry Solutions

Forestry solutions to the problem of increasing the amount of wood available for energy rely either on increased mobilization of the potential of existing natural formations or on the provision of new resources. These two types of solution must usually be applied simultaneously in view of the need to produce effective results as soon as possible in situations of fuel wood deficit. Ecological conditions constitute a serious limiting factor in many cases of aridity or difficult terrain; but even if the impact of forestry solutions on energy supplies remains limited, the role of trees in conserving the environment and in local agricultural and pastoral economies makes recourse to these solutions equally necessary, it is essential, in fact, that the fuel wood problem and its solutions be tackled in close coordination with integrated land management and cultivation systems, since for the populations concerned they constitute an indivisible whole.

In fact, any forestry solution to the problem of fuel wood supplies cannot and should not be considered in isolation from the overall problem of the complex role of forest resources in the rural economy and of their various contributions, productive and protective. Forestry solutions to the fuel wood crisis are inseparable from forest policy and management, to which they contribute fresh impulse and importance. The forestry solutions contemplated must therefore affect not only woody vegetation and stands of all sizes, but also the association of forest trees, even isolated ones, with agricultural or pastoral practices, in view of the role that all these elements may play in ensuring supplies.

The Productivity of the Natural Formations

The combined effects of logging, grazing and destruction by fire or other agents, particularly climatic ones, limit or reduce the potential yield of the natural formations, in particular open forest, savanna and steppe. The productivity of these formations can usually be increased considerably by more rational use of the available woody biomass and by applying relatively simple protection methods. Recent studies, particularly by FAO, have shown that 75 m^3 per hectare of fuel wood are available in the Terai region in Nepal, more than 80 m^3 per hectare in the Brazilian "cerrado" and 30 m^3 in the central southern part of Upper Volta.

A considerable percentage of these supplies is frequently wasted either during commercial felling or through burning by shifting cultivators or shepherds, or even during official deforestation and settlement programmes. The productivity of the natural formations can be improved by relatively simple means: tests with protection measures have resulted in a doubling of the yield from savanna formations; in other cases it is necessary only to include the production of energy as an additional objective in forest management. What makes these actions complex is the necessity of reconciling them with the local population's need for new arable land or pasture, and of obtaining the indispensable adherence of this population.

There are, however, very important obstacles:

- the difficulty of managing vast stretches of natural formations, of low to average productivity, for forestry services that are not very well established and have limited staff and means;

- possible lack of interest on the part of populations who have traditionally been excluded from management of the forest resources and who see these resources as a form of land use in competition with the uses that meet their immediate needs;
- the difficulty of controlling fires and preventing them spreading;
- the difficulty of organizing grazing and avoiding destruction of the woody vegetation by a livestock population that far exceeds the capacity of the grass cover;
- the lack of information both on existing resources and on the possibilities of improving their fuel wood yield by, among other things, associating it with other production and protection functions;
- the sometimes very advanced state of degradation of the woody vegetation, which despite the protection measures is no longer able to reconstitute itself, particularly if the ecological conditions are not favourable.

To ensure that forest land is managed effectively, forestry services must work in cooperation with the rural development and livestock services and with the direct participation by the people concerned. A positive attitude, indeed active participation by the people in the protection and management of the forest resources on which their supplies depend, is indispensable: they must therefore be made continuously aware of the role of the forest in their well-being and in the local economy. In many cases a particularly effective way of getting rural populations to adopt a responsible attitude towards their forest resources is to entrust them with the management of these resources, with the technical assistance of the forestrv service, and to allow them to reap the benefits.

The task of the forestry service is thus radically altered: direct action on forest stands is replaced by support for actions undertaken by the people themselves in accordance with what they themselves see as their needs - actions which require technical and logistical assistance in order to improve their chances of success. In the initial stage the forestry service must devote itself to showing the people what can and should be done and the benefits that would result. This new orientation of forestry action and the far- reaching changes it necessitates has been discussed in several FAO documents, and more particularly in "The role of forests in the development of local communities", FAO, Rome, 1978.

However, forest resources situated near big markets, such as large towns, will have to continue, in the main, to be directly managed by the forestry service in order to ensure regular supplies for consumers under satisfactory economic conditions. At the same time it is necessary to avoid fuel wood supplies being diverted to town dwellers to the detriment of the rural people, who are usually poorer. If a big effort is made to overcome the difficulties that have been enumerated, in many situations characterized by the existence of still relatively extensive natural formations improved management could result in a perceptible increase in the output of wood fuels within 10 to 15 years.

If this action is conducted in conjunction with actions to increase output of the other forest products, improve agricultural productivity and, where applicable, introduce a settled type of farming, the annual rate of deforestation could be markedly reduced and fuel wood supplies considerably increased. In many situations a relatively simple calculation is possible: an average increase of 20 percent in the yield of the accessible natural formations as a whole constitutes a realistic target that does not require large investments.

The increase in supplies can easily be compared with the total area of plantations that would have to be established to provide the same amount, assuming average yields, and the generally high cost of such an operation. This comparison often illustrates how advisable it would be to accord prior attention to improving the productivity of the natural formations - a solution difficult to implement successfully but which gives particularly rewarding results.

Creating New Resources

The creation of additional wood energy resources is frequently essential, all the more so because the populations which depend on this source of energy are usually concentrated in regions which by force of circumstances have been subjected to intensive deforestation: the remaining natural formations are not able to ensure sufficient supplies even if their productivity is improved. Forest plantations have often been preferred too, because they are relatively easy to establish and manage successfully. However, the feasibility and impact of these plantations are limited by major difficulties: ecological conditions, the lack of sufficiently favourable land, the attitude of the populations concerned, and the costs.

1. Ecological conditions in the deficit zones, in particular the climate and the soils, are often not very favourable to plantations, whose survival and yield is affected by unfavourable and unforeseeable variations. It is relatively easy to make a success of the first few years, but more difficult to maintain a satisfactory level of productivity up to the end. Information and basic research on exotic and indigenous species, planting and management techniques, tending, and the prevention of diseases and shortages are often inadequate and the distribution of such information often leaves something to be desired. These obstacles are often underestimated and many large-scale projects are drawn up on the basis of an extrapolation of the results obtained in research plots benefiting from special care under site and scale conditions that make them irrelevant. In addition, the real complexity of combining protection and tending with the achievement of maximum productivity is not always fully grasped.

All these technical aspects require priority attention:

forest plantations must be approached in the same way as other agricultural undertakings. The trees constitute a crop, requiring selection of species and provenances, choice of site and follow-up action that guarantees the best possible results, if the operation is to be profitable.

2. The lack of land where conditions are favourable to forest plantations is a widespread problem, because it is often the need for arable land that has led to the deforestation which makes it necessary to plant trees: farmers are rarely willing to release land for plantations unless their low fertility renders them marginal for agricultural purposes. Various solutions are possible:

    - Establish plantations in marginal zones where they will have the double purpose of restoring denuded or eroded land and producing: results from the point of view of production alone are rarely encouraging.
    - Replant forest areas previously cleared of their natural vegetation. This solution often proves expensive owing to the cost of clearing and can only be justified if it has been ascertained by careful study that the existing vegetation is too degraded or unproductive and that it is preferable to incur the costs and the risks inherent in a new plantation rather than attempt to increase the yield from a vegetation that has the merit of being adapted to the local ecological conditions. In all cases the site conditions must be such as to enable a reasonable yield to be expected. It is usually this solution that lends itself to large-scale plantations established by forestry administrations on State-owned lands.
    - Increase the number of trees grown outside forest lands. Widespread distribution of trees in every vacant spot throughout the countryside undoubtedly represents a particularly promising way of increasing the supply of fuel wood. The integration of trees and agriculture, in particular agro-forestry, constitutes

an extension of the management of forest resources and a remarkably flexible way of resolving the conflict between agriculture and forestry by fusing the populations' various interests and multiplying the benefits they can obtain directly from the same plot. In many cases the traditional land-use systems already provide for such integration.

Mention should also be made of the decisive effect that the improvement and intensification of agricultural productivity can have on land use, with the result that land may be made available for fuel wood plantations.

3. The attitude of the people is a determining factor. People do not feel concerned by or interested in plantations in the form of blocks of a certain size, immobilized for forestry use for a long period of time, about which they have not been consulted and the yield from which will not provide them with any direct, substantial and equitably divided benefits. At best the most that can be expected is a passive attitude: often there is more or less open hostility, resulting in illegal felling and degradation. In addition, it is relatively easy to plant a tree but notoriously more difficult to convince a peasant to assign part of his land to this purpose and to protect and tend the tree until it reaches maturity. There is only one, many-sided solution: active participation by the people from the earliest stage up to the time when the final benefits are reaped. A plantation must meet the people's needs as they themselves see them and constitute for them an interesting line of production whose protection and management will produce more direct benefits than would its destruction and replacement by some other way of using the same piece of land.

   Pull advantage must be taken of two determining aspects: the capacity of any forest plantation, through a judicious choice of species and techniques, to fulfil a number of objectives (provision of wood, fruit and fodder, protection, etc.); and the people's undoubted interest in plantations whose principal aim is to satisfy their domestic requirements for energy and other products. Beyond this, the major condition for the success of plantation programmes is that the people be aware of the importance of the fuel wood problem and of their role and interest in improving supplies. Before organizing and training the people, foresters have an essential role to play in stimulating such awareness by providing information and acting as animators.

4. The costs of implementation undoubtedly constitute an obstacle to increasing the areas planted in proportion to needs and probable deficits. Concordant observations made by FAO, the World Bank and other bodies indicate that in 1981 the costs of establishing and tending large-scale plantations in the Sahelian region, were well over US$1 000 per hectare, for an expected average yield of 4 to 7 m^3/ha/year. Two solutions are possible: recourse to external financing, or mobilization of local resources with the agreement of the populations concerned.

   In the first case the benefits to be expected from programmes financed by loans must be carefully evaluated, particularly as regards the solidity of the factors (yields, quality and value of products, time span, etc.) that condition financial profitability. The accompanying measures, human resources, infrastructure and institutions must also be considered with particular attention, owing to their decisive role in ensuring that the operation is conducted to a successful conclusion. Profitability can also be improved by modifying the traditional concept of forest production, adopting shorter rotations and producing more small w ood.

Active participation by the local people in operations of which they obtain the benefits makes it possible to cover a considerable part of the costs of installation from local resources, in particular labour. Not including the value of the land, the cost of the inputs at market price that the State has to provide for a community plantation programme usually represents between one- third and one-quarter per cubic metre produced of that for a standard large-scale programme . Here again it is necessary to motivate the population and to provide real support through appropriate incentive measures and technical assistance.

Coordination of Forestry solutions

In most cases improvements and increases in fuel wood supplies will depend on a complex programme ranging from actions to increase the yield of natural formations to the creation of new resources. The specific conditions of each situation will determine the result to be expected and the respective importance to be given to these forestry solutions. The effective importance of fuel wood in the rural economy and a detailed analysis of costs and benefits will provide valuable indications for improving the effectiveness of the actions. In cases where the ecological situation is particularly difficult or population density particularly high, these forestry solutions will probably be able to play only a limited role and require complementary action.

Bat it must be emphasized that in all cases the forestry solutions should be incorporated into a supply and distribution plan which guarantees access by the people to the fuel they need under economic and stable conditions. Given the weight and bulkiness of wood fuel, the spatial distribution of the resources as compared with the demand, the transport infrastructure and the organization of distribution are important aspects inseparable from the feasibility and impact of the forestry solutions.

It is necessary to ensure, in particular, that supplies for large towns or more heavily populated zones are not guaranteed at the expense of the people in the neighbouring rural areas. Because of their complexity and the importance of what is at stake, the forestry solutions to be implemented must constitute an important and integral part of a country's forest policy: this should simultaneously reveal effective acknowledgements of the extent of the energy contribution of forest resources and demonstrate the political authorities' commitment to voluntarist actions at all levels in this field.

Strategic action Guidelines

In most of the situations that have been identified, the deferred impact of the forestry solutions alone will not make it possible to resolve in the short term the tensions and problems resulting from insufficient fuel wood supplies. In practice it will always be necessary to resort to a combination of measures affecting the main parameters of supply and demand. What is needed is a real strategy for attacking the problem; the general outlines of this can be indicated, but the specific ingredients will have to be combined in accordance with the particular situations.

And it must be emphasized from the start that any strategy concerning fuel wood must be closely linked with the national energy situation and in particular with clear recognition of the importance of this source of energy as compared with the other forms of energy available and according to the various groups of users and requirements. The production of wood-energy must also be set within the wider context of the overall contribution of forest vegetation and trees to the rural and national economy and to the maintenance of productive environmental conditions. The production of energy is only one aspect, important but not unique, of the forestry sector's contribution to development.

As part of the preparations for the United Nations Conference on New and Renewable Sources of Energy, Nairobi 1981, a technical panel went very fully into the problem of fuel wood and charcoal. This panel's main contribution to the Conference consisted of the; formulation of a "Strategy for fuel wood as a source of energy for survival and development. The salient features and implications of this strategy are briefly reviewed in the following paragraphs in order to emphasize both the extent and the complexity of the tasks to be carried out.

A strategy for fuel wood has to recognize the absolute necessity of combining short-term actions with longer-term ones, those aimed at increasing supplies with those aimed at lowering demand, so as to tackle the problem from all sides at once and prevent it assuming unmanageable proportions before the more far-reaching solutions can produce their effect. Six main types of action were thus identified, affecting both supply and demand of fuel wood.

Short to medium-term actions

Substitution or supplement by other sources of energy, particularly commercial ones, may be indispensable in the worst situations in order to supplement fuel wood resources that are clearly insufficient to cover even minimum requirements. This may even be just a temporary measure to alleviate pressure on the remaining resources and gain time in which to establish new resources and await their entry into production. So far such actions have been limited to urban areas - e.g. the campaign to introduce butane in Senegal; and even here they have come up against the obstacles of the cost of the substitute fuel and the equipment for using it, and the difficulties of getting the people to accept a fuel with characteristics different to the traditional one. Substitution proves particularly difficult for domestic uses, and recent surveys have shown housewives attachment to the traditional fuels.

There is no doubt, however, that in situations of acute scarcity the use of substitute fuels will be more and more necessary in order to assure coverage of the minimum energy requirements. Efforts to encourage substitution should be aimed initially at uses for which such fuels are best adapted, such as rural industries, brick-making plants, pottery works, etc., which it is easier to influence owing to their concentration, provided a regular supply is guaranteed. In the longer term all possible uses of a renewable substitute fuel should be encouraged as the technology and equipment become available under technical, social and economic conditions appropriate to the specific uses. The distribution of wood fuels must be organized and controlled in order to ensure regular supplies and thus avoid both acute seasonal fluctuations and the appearance of localized shortages a short distance away from surplus areas, which often marks the situations observed, particularly in Africa.

In most cases this poses the problems of absence or inadequacy of a communication and transport infrastructure, change-over from a traditional, informal organization to a modern, structured organization for distribu tion, control of the machinery for fixing prices and the possible disturbing effect of big concentrations of demand, such as large towns, or situations of oligopoly. These aspects rarely form the object of voluntarist action, although they are fundamental if rational use is to be made of resources in the face of demand. The transformation of fuel-wood from a traditionally free product into an item with a monetary value should draw increasing attention to the importance of marketing and the need to encourage effective distribution under regular and equitable economic conditions.

The transformation of fuel-wood into a normal economic commodity cannot but encourage greater efficiency in production and use. The improvement of conversion techniques covers a number of operations, from harvesting to charcoal-making, including packaging for transport and processing for making available to the user a fuel with the highest possible energy yield. These techniques aim at better utilization of the existing resources and include drying of the fuel, the improvement of transport and storage conditions through densification or agglomeration, and the promotion of higher-yielding charcoal-making techniques. All these measures result in the provision of a better-quality fuel, extension of the range of the biomass utilizabie as fuel and improvement of the handling and transportation conditions, and the production of more charcoal of similar or higher quality from the same woody mass.

Improved processing techniques can make possible considerable savings by reducing the demand for wood for the same energy use. These measures should include a particular effort to disseminate knowledge and appropriate techniques, regroup procedures in order to improve their productivity and their investment capacity, and establish distribution circuits promoting effective economic organization while safeguarding employment. The improvement of wood-burning stoves is of particular importance because of the low thermic yield usually obtained from the fuel by traditional methods - seldom over 10 percent of wood's calorific value.

In view of the amount of wood used for domestic purposes, efforts should be concentrated mainly on domestic stoves, but without ignoring other uses such as tea and tobacco-drying equipment, ovens for smoking fish, bread-ovens, etc. It is technically possible, without major difficulties, to save one-third or more of fuel, and hence to lower fuel wood requirements by this amount, by using stoves that are better designed and better used. For this it is necessary to tackle all aspects, including the characteristics and preparation of the fuel, and cooking and heating methods and equipment. The use of locally available materials and technical skills makes it possible to produce improved stoves at very modest prices - less than US$10 per unit: an investment which, at the current price of wood, is usually amortized very quickly.

However, experience has demonstrated that social,

cultural and nutritional customs, and resistance to change in an important aspect of the household's life, constitute determining factors in the acceptability of an appropriate technical solution and may considerably slow down its dissemination and hence its impact. The short-term effect should not be overestimated, therefore: considerable results are possible, but they require close attention to local conditions, prior designing, jointly with the users, of appropriate and well-tried models, testing under real conditions of use, considerable technical assistance and the participation of local organizations and associations in the promotional campaign. However, in the most serious situations it is the solution with the greatest potential short-term impact; it therefore warrants full attention, but also serious preparation in order to ensure success.

Medium - to Long-term actions

Measures able to improve the fuel wood situation rapidly are an important way of reducing tensions so as to facilitate the introduction of measures whose effect will be longer-lasting and slower to appear. These consist essentially of actions to increase the amount of fuel wood available by improving the productivity of the existing resources or establishing new ones. The feasibility of these actions was discussed in the previous section, and they are now briefly taken up again here. Increasing the productivity of the existing natural formations_should receive an attention proportionate to the usually considerable contribution of these formations to supplies. The analysis of many situations shows that these natural formations constitute the bulk of the supplies and that a considerable proportion of them is still almost inaccessible.

In those which are accessible, productivity can often be increased by between 50 and 100 percent. Except in cases of severe degradation, natural formations (forests, tree and shrub formations) afford the possibility of increasing fuel-wood supplies through relatively simple protection methods and rational management. Three aspects are involved: fuller mobilization of the available biomass, avoiding the abandonment of waste and small, recuperable elements; increasing the actual productivity of the existing biomass by methods which stimulate its growth; improvement and simultaneous control of access to the resources.

Conditions for people's access to the fuel wood resources are of particular importance because they condition not only the effective mobilization of the resources but also the people's attitude towards them. Accessibility is determined by a complex set of physical, economic and juridical factors and is often inseparable from rational use of the resources. Improvement of the economic conditions for the production and marketing of fuel wood can undoubtedly increase access to resources that have been marginal to date under current conditions of collection on the basis of rights of usage.

If the local people are involved in harvesting the fuel wood and obtain direct employment and benefits under conditions of accessibility defined in a more positive, less rigid fashion, they will take an interest and eventually an active part in conserving and even managing the fuel - wood resources. This applies not only to actual forests, but also to the open or shrub formations which often constitute the only resource available locally. The production of wood - energy was a traditional aspect of forest management that has been overlooked in recent decades.

It needs to be rediscovered to benefit from technical advances and information. It is necessary above all to support it in national policies, allot it means proportional to the results expected, and rely on the people to gear down the effort needed. Innovatory solutions are undoubtedly necessary and human investment is probably at least as important as financial investment. The creation of new resources through plantations is, in the long run, an indispensable element in the strategy in many cases, as a complement to measures affecting the remaining resources.

In accordance with the specific nature of the situations and problems, there is a wide range of possible actions, which can be combined; large-scale plantations, costly but geared to a concentrated and usually monetized market, such as a town; community or village plantations able to meet the needs of a community; individual or family stands.

In the last two cases, part of the output is consumed locally and the surplus may be put on the market and provide cash incomes. A complex set of technical and socio-economic factors guide the decision regarding the relative weight to be given to each type of plantation. In all cases it is essential to integrate the plantation programme in land-use planning taking into account the other requirements and uses of the land. In most of the situations studied, and hence of the countries concerned, the analysis showed the inadequacy of the present plantation programmes. On the basis of this analysis, the Technical panel on Fuel wood and Charcoal recommended "a five-fold increase in current levels of tree - planting for fuel". This recommendation was endorsed by the Nairobi Conference and forms part of the Nairobi Programme of Action.

The effort required is considerable, and enormous financial resources would be needed should the traditional method of implementation by official bodies be used. Such an acceleration in the rate of planting is possible only if a mass appeal is made for active collaboration by the rural people; if the effort required is distributed among individuals and based on increasing the number of trees planted in any non-utilized space; and if the maximum amount of local resources, land and labour, is mobilized by individuals and local communities' for their own benefit and within the wider framework of the multiple contribution that forestry can make to meeting their requirements. Such programmes have recently been undertaken in China, India, Indonesia, and the Republic of. Korea and Tanzania, and show the path to be followed.

However, in order to be really large-scale and hence

lead to the results desired, such an effort must be based on a clearly expressed political commitment, supported by a set of technical, financial and institutional means. A solid technical basis is indispensable, and the approaches used must be those best adapted to the possibilities, means, requirements and structures of the people concerned. The rate at which such plantation activities are carried out should be stimulated and accelerated both by systems of loans and incentives and by emphasizing the other benefits and functions that the trees planted can provide within the context of the rural economy. It is also necessary to know how to take advantage of the opportunities offered by other aspects of rural development, such as the rationalization of land-use planning, greater integration among various forms of land use, the search for a more productive type of agriculture, social programmes for combating under-employment and rural poverty, etc.

In fact it is clear from all the analyses that a real strategy has to be defined case by case, in accordance with the specific conditions. But all strategies will have four basic characteristics in common:

1. they will lay down a set of actions affecting needs and consumption as well as supplies;
2. they will associate actions with immediate effects with longer-term ones, but will in all cases programme them on the basis of a critical assessment of the time factor;
3. they will be on a sufficiently large scale: there is little risk of over-estimating the scope of the action, because only massive programmes can have an appreciable impact;
4. they will mobilize the people en masse and induce them to play an active part in implementing actions for which they should be responsible and from which they should reap the benefits.

Implementation of the programmes required poses a real challenge, in view of their complexity and size: but there is no doubt that if the situations are allowed to worsen, an even greater and more expensive effort will be needed, not to mention the effect on the people's lives and on the natural resources.

Scope of the Strategies Concerning Fuel Wood

After having stressed the seriousness of the energy crisis situations caused by the scarcity of fuel wood, and the relative complexity of the solutions to be adopted, the last section of this chapter is intended to show both the magnitude of the existing constraints and the role that the fuel wood problem can play in stimulating development. It would be a serious mistake to regard the problem of fuel wood and its solutions as a mere subsistence problem affecting only the poorest, most isolated, least developed sections of Third World societies, a problem connected with that of the transition towards more advanced sources of energy and technologies.

Although it is true that the poorest are the ones most affected, the importance of fuel wood in national energy balances, and its intrinsic qualities as a renewable, decentralized and inexpensive system for storing solar energy, make it a real, strategic energy source whose potential should be fully mobilized in the service of development. In assessing the effort required it is important to stress how much the mobilization of efforts and of human and financial resources, always in demand for a multitude of tasks and priorities, goes beyond the mere provision of an energy supply, essential and difficult to replace though this is.

The scope of the strategies recommended should be seen as an ideal opportunity for removing certain constraints that are constraints on development, by, for example, adapting and strengthening institutional structures, mobilizing and training human resources, and strengthening applied research: it is not just a question of resolving a serious problem, but of taking the opportunity to stimulate a drive towards development among the people concerned through an active and responsible effort to achieve energy self-sufficiency, in conformity with the criteria of rural development.

Strengthening of Institutional Structures

The social dimension of forestry is now being increasingly recognized, and the essential contribution of fuel wood to the energy supply constitutes one of the most obvious examples of the importance of forestry for the development of rural people. But in many cases the major concern of forest policies remains conservation of the forest domain and industrial development; the forest is normally still considered State property, the people are excluded from this part of the land and know nothing about forestry; the benefits of the forestry actions which they can undertake or in which they car participate are marginal for them; and they are deprived, without compensation, of usage rights and other products in areas under forest management.

The drawbacks of the traditional structures in a changing world marked by population growth and the requirements of development are obvious in these instances and call for change; hence the new trends towards community forestry that are now spreading. Foresters were the first to become aware of the rural energy crisis caused by the growing shortage of fuel wood and saw in this one of the most important social dimensions of forestry. Fuel wood strategies call for modification and adaptation of the existing structures. The importance of fuel wood for energy supplies makes it necessary to revise the conditions for access to the resources: this must be controlled, but at the same time guarantee supplies.

The inflexibility of, or changes in, land tenure structures must not constitute a major growing obstacle to access to fuel wood supplies, far less discourage people from planting trees because they will not be the acknowledged owners or because this will tie to one use a plot which might be needed tomorrow for other purposes. The legislative and regulatory framework must evolve in the same direction, no longer closing the forest to the people dependent on it but making forestry an integral part of land-use planning in order to meet their needs and help in their development.

The role of the forestry services is of primary importance and constitutes a real departure from their traditional function as the direct executive of programmes drawn up within their own sector. Fuel wood strategies can only be successful if the people are the main protagonists and the forestry services provide active, comprehensive and constant technical support. This presupposes both changes in capacities, the aim now being to stimulate action by others as much as to take direct action, and greater technical efficiency, in order to multiply the examples of success which will provide the best tool for persuasion.

If the people are to feel really concerned in action to protect and increase the fuel wood resources, they must perceive these as responding to their needs and benefiting them directly. This is only possible if administrations decentralize the decision-making process and operational responsibilities to the field, where it is easier to perceive the people's needs and establish a dialogue with them, and where innovatory solutions can be implemented to solve specific local problems. For example, socio-cultural factors may result in collective forestry plantations being promoted on a large scale in one region, while in another the emphasis will be on individual tree-planting, using fruit-bearing as well as forestry species.

Actions concerned with fuel wood therefore constitute a particularly good opportunity for changing the traditional relations between forestry administrations and the people and developing direct approaches which uphold their interests and respond to their needs. In most cases the solution to fuel wood problems will have to be implemented within a wider framework embracing not only the other productive and protective contributions of the forest vegetation but also close association with other uses of the land and integration in rural development programmes.

This entails dialogue and coordination with the other agricultural technical services in the field, so that the integration of trees into the rural environment may be evidenced also by the coordinated approach adopted by the various disciplines and authorities concerned with this environment. The ultimate purpose must be to illustrate to the peasants the advantages of a system of land use that combines trees and crops. Adaptation of the institutional structures as briefly suggested here is not only indispensable for translating fuel wood strategies rapidly into actions and concrete results: it will also show the degree of commitment by governments to these strategies and the amount of political support, an essential factor in motivating the people.

Training

The institutional framework cannot undergo a significant and tangible change unless the staff who translate this change into reality are themselves prepared for the new tasks and evince new attitudes. But almost everywhere the large-scale actions required come up against the problem of lack of personnel and inadequate qualification of the staff that do exist. In many cases the inadequacy of the existing forestry staff constitutes the major constraint to any intensification of forestry activities and this deficiency is most marked among the technical field staff, which is the most indispensable. Implementation of a fuel wood strategy will therefore have to entail critical analysis of the capacities of the existing personnel and of the indispensable training measures required.

In order to increase the number of qualified personnel it will be necessary not only to increase the training capacities of the existing institutions, but also to make use of flexible, perhaps more economic, solutions which will enlarge the number of technicians without simultaneously enlarging the number of officials. Because of the decisive role of the technical field staff, their training must receive prior attention. The capacities for normal long training will generally have to be strengthened, and courses for accelerated, refresher and advanced training will have to be increased. Where the national institutions are not immediately able to meet training requirements, multinational actions can resolve the problem during the transitional period, either by recourse to institutions existing in neighbouring countries with similar conditions, or by the organization of special programmes to train instructors.

The novelty of the strategic guidelines for action as compared with the traditional forestry actions requires thorough revision of the contents of forestry training. This revision must cover the socio-economic as well as the technical contents, particular importance must be given to the insertion of wooded elements or trees into the landscape, to knowledge of local species and quick-growing, multiple-purpose species, to methods for regenerating and increasing the productivity of natural formations and for planting and managing artificial stands, and to the relationship between agriculture, grazing and forestry, to cite only a few outstanding aspects.

The staff are obviously even more important than the techniques for the success of programmes connected with wood energy, and it is essential that they receive preparation in sociological and economic aspects, oriented towards understanding of the specific social, cultural and economic background of the people on whose behalf the programmes are to be undertaken: the particular characteristics of the subsistence or transition economies, the function of the tree and its integration into the rural environment, the structures and processes of decision-making and allocation of resources and benefits are just a few of the aspects it is essential to know in order to understand the needs and motivation of the people and guide the technicians in their approach. An in-depth revision of forestry training is therefore essential for the successful implementation of actions concerned with fuel wood; and it is urgent that this revision be undertaken quickly, so that these actions can be implemented before irreversible degradation occurs in too many situations.

The People

The interest and active participation of the people are essential factors that have conditioned the success, or in their absence the failure, of all programmes undertaken to date: moreover, they alone are able to scale down the effort needed to obtain the large-scale impact desired. Interest and participation are encouraged by information and extension work; but also by internal factors such as social organization, equitable procedures for decision-making and distribution of costs and benefits, a real awareness of the consequences of a scarcity of fuel wood and of deforestation, the dynamic role that can be played by those particularly concerned, the women; and by inserting the effort regarding fuel wood within an overall development framework.

In many situations in which fuel wood is a problem, the rural people are concerned with many other acute survival problems and give immediate priority to the problems of water and food production: the supply of wood for energy and the negative consequences of deforestation are not seen as an important priority, at least not until degradation has become so serious as to be practically irreversible. It is therefore essential to inform these people about the process of degradation into which they may find themselves led, and on its dangers; at the same time they must be brought to realize, by demonstration and extension work, that they can play an active role and even assume responsibility for reversing these situations, and that such actions may also respond to their other requirements.

It is therefore essential that the species to be planted be carefully chosen so as to include species known locally, increase the amount of fodder or feed as well as of wood available, lead to the creation of jobs and income, produce the first products or services in as short a time as possible, etc. At the same time, the diffusion of simple appropriate techniques will increase awareness of the active role that each individual can play. Information and extension work should be aimed in the first place at those members of the population who are most directly concerned with the supply and use of wood fuel. In this connection the women can play a vital role both in increasing awareness and in promoting action, because it is they who are most directly affected by the fuel wood problem: not only are they usually responsible for collecting the fuel wood and using it in the home, they also play in some cases an essential role in marketing it.

Recent studies have also shown women's potential impact at the production level, in the form of individual stands associated with the gardens around their houses or in the fields. The women must be systematically considered as a dynamic element in decision-making and action at all stages, because of their energy needs and their normal active role in traditional societies. The people will become more quickly and keenly aware of the situation the more opinion - forming activities are backed up by incentive measures. These could consist of providing compensation for the immediate losses in land, available labour or agricultural production resulting from plantations, or encouraging the rural people to protect their sources of fuel wood, or complementing forestry measures with actions to meet needs more immediately felt (roads, schools, health centres).

These incentive measures can take many different forms, monetary and non-monetary, subsidies or loans, etc. They constitute a powerful means of motivation, to be framed according to the specific requirements and characteristics of each rural community. Finally, it is necessary to emphasize the impact that the process of mobilizing efforts around the problem of fuel wood can have on the dynamics of development in a rural community.-This is linked first of all with the multiple effects of forest vegetation, from supply of the wood indispensable for fire and construction to the maintenance of a viable and productive environment, including the supply of food for people and their livestock.

Bat examples such as that of the Republic of Korea or of Gujarat in India have shown that an organized effort, with the participation of the local inhabitants, to improve the fuel wood situation, can act as the catalyzer for a process of development, economic growth and social transformation. These programmes possess many of the conditions for success. But there are also other, more limited examples, in such difficult conditions as in the Sahel, which show that the task, though arduous, is possible. Owing to the complexity of the fuel wood problem and the need to combine actions over the entire chain from production to utilization, any programme of action on a certain scale touches in one way or another many aspects of the life and organization of a rural community: land-use planning, intensification of agriculture and integration of trees, silvo-pastoral organization, collection and marketing of wood fuel, organization of its domestic use, grouping or association of individuals to carry out the work and share the products, participation of women and children, etc.

Apart from supplying- energy, such a programme has an impact that coincides with the fundamental guidelines for development, such as improving conditions of life for the poorest sectors, helping to achieve self-sufficiency, strengthening the process of participation and decision - making at local level, diversifying activities and creating or increasing employment and income, stabilizing or improving environmental conditions suitable for life and economic activities, facilitating the transition towards a structured economic organization ensuring equitable distribution of efforts, production and benefits. Such programmes are therefore particularly suitable for encouraging initiative and the organization of individual and collective efforts in rural areas and for promoting a dynamic process of development.

The main solutions to the technical problems of fuel wood are more or less known. They are based on relatively simple technologies, which makes it easier to apply them and get them accepted in the developing countries than is the case for any other form of renewable energy. However, research has accorded too little importance to the production and use of wood energy in recent years: considerable research is needed if programmes of action are to be launched without delay on the scale necessary.

Research requirements have been reviewed in several recent studies, in particular a joint document by FAO and the World Bank published in 1981. These studies emphasize the absolute necessity of intensifying research on technical aspects in order to increase the productivity of woody formations in biomass and energy and promote more efficient use of the supplies available. At the same time the newer aspects of the integration of forestry into rural development, as regards both the protective and the productive functions of the forest, must be the subject of systematic attention.

In this connection the development of integrated agro-silvicultural systems based on the use of quick-growing, multipurpose species, possibly leguminous, is of top priority. The third essential aspect of this research effort concerns the human sciences; the social and economic features of local communities, their present organization and their potential engagement in activities concerned with producing and using wood fuel. Understanding of the needs and aptitudes of the local people conditions the success of any action, but the most elementary information is still too often lacking.

In addition to reorienting research efforts, it is indispensable to increase the research staff and equipment in the countries where the programmes are to be carried out. Only thus can particular local conditions really be taken into account and suitable solution devised. Systematic exchange and accelerated distribution of information on results, successes and failures, and new developments can stimulate and accelerate the impact of the programmes. But in most cases the training of research workers constitutes the necessary precondition to any strengthening of research.

Immediate solutions are possible to situations of obvious seriousness, provided these solutions are based on a stratification of specific local characteristics and use appropriate combinations of actions concerned not only with supplies but also with their distribution and use. Two key factors can accelerate implementation of the solutions: a) the advantages of the forest biomass as a local, renewable source of energy which at the same time provides other important goods and services, such as stabilizing the environment; b) the relative simplicity of the techniques to be employed, which do not require any basically new technology, but merely a special effort to spread information and knowledge and to motivate the executors.

There are many obstacles, but the actions required can and should be implemented using locally available resources and with the active participation of the people. Both because of the nature of the institutional, economic and social constraints to be overcome, and because of the manifold aspects of production, distribution and use of wood fuel, any fuel wood programme goes well beyond the sole dimension of supplying energy. It constitutes a special opportunity to mobilize efforts and help to stimulate development by improving the energy situation within the framework of a more solid economic basis and better conditions of life.

In conformity with its objectives, this study has made it possible to assess the situation regarding fuel wood supplies in the developing countries in 1980. This assessment is necessarily only a rough one, given the abundance of 'the information to be handled and its often heterogeneous nature, and also because of the specific character of the situations to be analysed, strongly influenced by local ecological and human conditions. However, in many cases the analysis made has not only been confirmed by those with experience and direct knowledge of the situations identified, but has proved sufficient to identify the main lines of action. The first important conclusion to be drawn, therefore, is that the information available on the parameters of fuel wood supply and demand is usually sufficient to enable difficult situations to be identified and actions launched: the fuller and more detailed information that is still necessary can be gathered when the programmes of action are being designed, and not prior to this. The implication of this is important, because the time factor is critical and any delay will result in a worsening of the situation and hence the need for more expensive ar d larger-scale action.

However, attention must be drawn to the limits and approximations of this study, to avoid there being any ambiguity regarding the possible uses of the figures provided in the tables. This is a global study intended to illustrate the average situations in each region (region = sub-continent) regarding the balance between fuel wood supplies and needs, In making these evaluations use has been made of the most commonly accepted average figures for the productivity of the various sources of fuel wood and the needs of the populations according to their habitat and way of life. In addition, in order to identify in each region geographically representable categories of situations, it has been necessary to limit the number of categories, smooth out the contours, and ignore certain particular local situations. It is therefore risky to use the figures supplied by this study on a particular region to assess a local situation within this region, even though concern for truth and accuracy has led the authors to base their methodological approach on the most precise and detailed local analysis possible by zoning within each country.

The study covers 95 developing countries in tropical and temperate zones, for which the uniform application of a methodology based on the same concepts and classification and the same reference years has made it possible to obtain relatively homogeneous results which then lend themselves to representation on an overall thematic map. In these 95 countries fuel wood played a very significant energy role in 1980, accounting in 12 of them for nine-tenths of total energy supplies. Of these 12 countries, 9 are in Africa. More than half the least developed countries are almost totally dependent on fuel wood: and in most of the others, it is usually because of inadequate local supplies of fuel wood that the people turn to other fuels, usually plant waste.

The total population involved in the study amounted in 1980 to 2.1 thousand million people. It is estimated that more than 80′ percent of these either live in rural areas or have conserved a rural type of energy consumption and depend to an overwhelming extent on plant fuels, mainly fuel wood, for such elementary needs as cooking food and heating the home. Domestic needs and requirements of small rural industries constitute the bulk of the energy needs indispensable for the survival of the rural populations and of urban dwellers with low to medium incomes.

In 1980 marked symptoms of fuel wood supply difficulties were detected in all or part of 39 African countries, 18 countries in the Middle East and Asia, and 14 Latin American countries.

A total of 1.15 thousand million people are affected by these situations, in which their energy needs can only be met by over-utilization of the woody vegetation, sometimes to the point of its complete destruction. In the worst situations, about 100 million people, half of them in Africa, are obviously unable to cover their minimum needs and are therefore faced with a really acute scarcity. In many cases the situations of acute scarcity correspond to difficult climatic and ecological zones, where the shortage of fuel wood leads to the destruction of all woody vegetation, resulting in destabilization of the environment and the risk of erosion, the consequences of which are felt beyond the zone directly concerned by the energy problem. Such situations have been identified mainly in the Himalayas, and in the mountainous areas of eastern and central Africa and of Latin America.

Elsewhere, in the arid and semi-arid areas of Africa and Asia, the deforestation resulting from, the search for fuel makes a dangerous contribution to desertification. Finally, in the most densely populated zones of Asia and Africa, the need for fuel leads to use being made of all possible plant elements, including crop residues indispensable for fertilization. The search for fuel-wood in these scarcity zones represents a threat to the natural resources indispensable for agricultural production, and therefore directly affects the objectives of food self-sufficiency fixed by the governments of the countries concerned.

The deficit situations detected affect more than a thousand million people, who are finding increasing difficulty in meeting their minimum energy needs as regards fuel wood. They manage to meet these needs only by over-cutting the woody vegetation, and this, combined with the effects of the population growth, presents an increasing danger to future supplies. Many deficit situations are evolving rapidly towards a situation of acute scarcity. The degeneration is perceptible, but it is difficult to measure its rate, and often there is no full awareness of the situation until it has reached an almost irreversible stage. It is in the Indian sub-continent that this process gives most cause for alarm, because of the size of the populations concerned,

The study of the effect of the prolongation of present trends up to the year 2000 dramatically illustrates what is happening. In what are now situations of acute scarcity, wood will be of no more than marginal use as fuel; while the deficit situations are evolving towards real scarcity. Under the pressure of the population growth and with forest resources decreasing, new deficit situations appear in Latin America and throughout most of Africa and Asia. Because of its very dimensions the problem must constitute a major concern which goes beyond the mere problem of fuel wood supplies. What other source of energy, and at what price, would be able to replace fuel wood on such a scale and within such a short lapse of time so as to guarantee coverage of the daily energy needs of the populations concerned?

The main results of the study can be summarized as follows:

1. In Asia, some 30 million people, mainly in the coldest zones of the Himalayas, were unable to ensure their energy supply in 1980, despite over-utilization of all the wood available. Approximately 710 million people were in a situation of decidedly inadequate fuel wood supplies, mainly in the highly populated zones of the Ganges and Indus plains and in the lowlands and islands of South-East Asia. It is estimated that by 2000, if present trends continue, 1.4 thousand million people in this region will be living in zones where fuel wood supplies are completely inadequate to cover their minimum energy needs. The deficit might reach 500 million m^3 of wood. A total of 11 heavily populated countries are mainly concerned.
2. In Africa south of the Sahara, 50 million people, mainly in the arid zones and the sparsely inhabited mountainous areas, were unable to cover their minimum energy needs in 1980, although the existing woody vegetation was over-utilized.. Approximately 130 million people, mainly in the relatively densely populated savanna zones, could cover their minimum energy needs only by over-cutting the existing

vegetation. It is estimated that in this region, as a whole about 500 million people will be faced with marked fuel wood supply difficulties in the year 2000 unless present trends are modified. The deficit might reach 300 million m^3 and concern 37 countries of the region.

3. In North Africa and the Middle East the situations of fuel wood deficit concern approximately 70 million people spread over all the countries in varying degrees. On the basis of present trends, by the year 2000 about 160 million people will be affected by a deficit of over 37 million m^3.

4. In Latin America, about 20 million people were unable to cover their minimum energy needs in 1980, even by over-cutting the vegetation to which they had access. The zones concerned are arid or at high altitudes in the Andean region, and particularly densely populated zones in Central America and the Caribbean. About 150 million people, mainly in the rest of the Andean region, were able to cover their minimum needs only by over - utilizing the existing resources. If present trends continue, by the year 2000 the fuel wood deficit might reach 135 million m^3 and affect about 340 million people in 17 countries of the region.

The study has demonstrated once again the specific nature of the situations, problems and solutions. It has resulted in a classification of the critical situations which provides a basis for reflection on the strategies and actions to be employed. This classification shows the relative importance of the various types of supplies in the various categories of situations. It therefore provides indications on the actions to be undertaken, while making it clear that a combination of actions affecting the various parameters of supply and demand will in practice always be necessary. This approach highlights three important points:

1. Even in the situations where forestry solutions seem both more difficult and less likely to have a major impact

on the energy situation, they are indispensable because of their other productive and protective functions where the environment is particularly fragile.

2. Although the natural forest vegetation in all its forms constitutes the most important part of the supplies on which a high proportion of the population depends, much of it is often not accessible to the people. Very serious attention should therefore be given to the accessibility and distribution of these supplies, in fact to including the energy aspect in the management of these resources.

3. The rate at which plantations for the production of fuel wood are being established at present is clearly insufficient to have a real impact by the end of the century. Considerable acceleration is necessary in all types of tree-planting, but above all in spreading trees throughout agricultural areas. This is the most, promising measure and the one most likely to receive the support of the populations, thus decreasing the amount of effort needed.

The study has also demonstrated the extent of certain gaps in information which show how inadequate has been the attention given to the energy role of the forest resource in recent years. These gaps relate in particular to:

1. The productivity of natural formations other than closed forests producing mainly for industry: specific data on tree and shrub formations - an important source of fuel - are often lacking, and this limits assessment of the real possibilities for action and hence a serious management effort;
2. The actual area covered by non-industrial plantations and their real state and productivity;
3. The actual amounts of agricultural and industrial residues available and used for energy purposes as substitutes for or additions to wood fuels;
4. The legal, physical and economic conditions for access to the fuel wood resources, which condition the real

availability of wood fuels for the population; essentially linked to specific local conditions, they seem to have attracted little attention on the whole.

It would be particularly useful to go further into these aspects, because they would provide better knowledge of fuel wood supplies and understanding of the solutions to be adopted. But they are closely linked with specific local conditions and cannot be satisfactorily grasped from a global study like this one. It is here that this study must play its full role and draw the attention of all those concerned by the problem to the need to devote prior attention to the zones where situations of acute scarcity have been identified. In these zones the various supply parameters should be investigated more thoroughly so as to understand the problem better and analyse the feasibility of appropriate solutions.

At the same time it is essential to understand the underlying causes of the degradation of supplies: urban growth, the impact of certain trends in modern agriculture, the transformation of wood fuel from a free good available to all into an important commercial commodity, the effect of the energy supply of the over-utilization of the woody resources for other agricultural or grazing purposes, the spread of uncontrolled production of charcoal, etc. The study has therefore brought out a major point: the situation regarding fuel wood supplies is deteriorating ever more rapidly in many regions owing to the growth in population and the dependence of the people on this fuel. The actions undertaken so far are, without exception, completely inadequate.

But the implications of the scarcity and the actions aimed at restoring supplies go well beyond the energy question alone, important though this is: they concern the other effects of forestry actions, whether maintenance of the conditions for productivity of the natural resources or of the conditions for life, or survival, of the populations concerned. Owing to the many aspects involved, actions to improve fuel wood supplies can stimulate and induce a dynamic development movement based essentially on active participation and assumption of responsibility by the people concerned in efforts to meet their own needs. Awareness of the seriousness and extent of the fuel wood crisis constitutes a first step towards ensuring the commitment of all - the populations concerned, governments, the international community - to immediate, large- scale action. The fuel wood crisis is not the energy crisis of the poor; it is a particularly serious element in the energy crisis of the rural areas in the developing countries.

Efforts must be made in many different fields: management of the remaining resources, even the degraded ones; planting and multiplication of trees in agricultural areas; stabilization of supplies; improvement of conversion techniques, etc. If the actions undertaken are to be successful and sufficiently massive to attain the impact required, it is indispensable to train personnel, strengthen structures, intensify applied research, instil new capacities for development and new enthusiasm in the populations concerned, and combine the efforts of various disciplines in an approach that is typically that of rural development. This is the challenge that is posed. Its scope goes beyond the energy situation and concerns the potential for expanding food production. In many cases it is already an emergency problem, calling for immediate action before the situation deteriorates so far as to become irreversible.

7

The Effects of Global Trends on the Environment

The Information Revolution

The end of the 20th century is characterized by a profound technological revolution that has profound effects on the environment and the socioeconomic state of the world. It has been referred to as the "information age," the "third wave", and the "post-industrial society". I believe the term "information revolution" is more appropriate. The two major phenomena promoting this revolution are the development and increasing use of computers, which make possible the storage and processing of large volumes of information, and new telecommunications technologies, which permit the transmission of this information over long distances almost instantaneously. This technology is being integrated to produce powerful tools and systems, increasing by several orders of magnitude humankind's capacity for collective memory and providing a worldwide arena for social interaction.

In addition, these systems have become inexpensive, require a small amount of energy and human effort to use, and are becoming more accessible to more and more people all over the world. The information -telecommunications revolution is generating a "global intelligence" — a computerized neural network with increasing numbers of information producers and users. The producers are not only the public and private institutionalized information packaging and delivery systems, but also scores of smaller groups and individuals with computer terminals and the will to be connected to networks.

Consequently, billions of bytes of information are being exchanged every minute among information producers, relay stations, and users and receivers of various kinds. Along with these advances, and in large measure as a result of them, accessory facilities for production and reproduction of information and ideas, such as photocopiers, home printers, and faxes, have become widely available. Using these resources, many more social groups are now able, even at the local level, to express themselves in new and complex ways — electronic bulletin boards, community newspapers, and local cable television channels. At the national level, too, media are developing locally customized views.

General Effects of the Information Revolution

The global networks provide wider public access to more sources of information than ever before, not only from central information streams, but also from myriad local sources. The possibilities for interaction are multiplying accordingly. Many social contacts are becoming independent of distance, giving rise to a new spectrum of relations that were not previously possible. Internet, the worldwide computer network, currently links more than 20 million users and is growing at a rate of 20% per month! It was built in an extremely democratic fashion, following the basic principles of decentralization, unlimited and total access, and freedom of information. Although it is not yet clear if the Internet will remain a central element of the information age over the long term, it definitely appears that it will continue to play a key role in the development of new social tools of communication for some time to come..

One overall effect of the information revolution appears

to be a general democratization of information flow, both at the producer and at the receiver ends, with loss of power by the monopolistic information holders. The increasing availability of knowledge, technical and non technical, about how to get things done is particularly important. We assume (and hope) that information networks will remain free of control or censorship by any existing or newly created "information power" as has often been the case in the past.[1] Keeping them open is going to be a ongoing global challenge.

Control of information for political purposes was common during the Cold War and, in large measure, still is today. Major world powers have strongly influenced the flow of news through press agencies that, often subtly, censor "inconvenient" information. Information is also controlled by the use of "authorized" television networks, which are regularly used as political tools both by governments and by wealthy elites. The information revolution will probably also result in increasing di versification of expressed points of view and approaches. This diversification effect is critical. In fact, it may be the most effective antidote to the forces of uniformity that are coming into play in the globalized world.

The complex processes of globalization have promoted the development of a mainstream standardized culture that includes not only widespread homogenization of production and consumption systems and patterns, but also greater cultural uniformity, including expression codes, attitudes, and beliefs. The new trend toward diversification and differentiation is building on the flow of information that allows freer expression of alternative perspectives, including those of social minorities and disadvantaged groups who are finding relevant and accessible channels for expressing their opinions and disseminating information.

The creation of new methods for public participation is producing an immense potential for the generation and use of knowledge and innovation at the grass-roots level. Many traditions that had been eliminated, forgotten, or discredited by mainstream culture may now be revived. Traditional knowledge can be rescued, revived, adapted, and sustained.

The more marginalized aspects of complex cultures, often intentionally or by omission wiped out by the forces of standardization, may also stand a chance of survival if enough of their representatives are determined to use these newly developing mechanisms. In all likelihood, meso and micro cultures (as well as subcultures) will survive at a different level than the mainstream culture. The future coexistence of several cultures, on different planes or levels, will likely become more common and important. Smaller, usually weaker cultures should be able to transcend their limited spheres, however, to claim more extended "virtual" territories. People will be able to belong to a specific culture without abandoning their rights as part of the wider standard culture.

The potential of this development is enormous. People will be able to become more homogeneous on one level, but increasingly heterogeneous on another. Meso and micro cultures and nations will no longer disappear under the shadow of a mainstream culture. The industrial nation-state that has arisen through the smothering of less powerful national or local groups will lose its main source of power. Unavoidably, this will lead to fragmentation of power and perhaps instability; but it will surely lead to more and different forms of democratization as well.

Effects on Environmental Management

Processes that degrade the environment have often developed as a result of central decisions based on the views of powerful groups about how to control or use natural (and human) resources and territory. Typically, in the centralized industrial states of the world, local groups are among the least powerful; their environments and cultures are often undermined or destroyed without their being able to do anything about it. The reigning ideology tends to equate almost any transformation of nature with progress and progress with modernization, and assumes that both are desirable. In consequence, local communities must often choose between their immediate convenience, on the one hand, and their long-term welfare, on the other. To make matters worse, they have little accurate information about the potential long-term effects of proposed natural and socio- cultural transformations.

Even where communities do not agree with proposed measures, they often have few effective channels through which to communicate their views. The right of communities to define their own destinies has not been properly acknowledged in practice, even when present in policy. In most cases, national decision-makers do not wish to change this situation. Circumstances may now be changing, however, and, in some cases, radically. Development paradigms are being re-examined, probably because of negative experiences throughout the world and changes in mainstream culture as a result of the early effects of the information revolution. New and alternative approaches are now being considered, typically under the rubric of "sustainable development."

The information revolution is opening many new channels of communication to local groups in, among other things, the field of environmental management. People are becoming more involved in their communities, better informed about options, and more determined to have a say in their future — be it in devising new development models at the local level, formulating policies on local issues, or advocating decisions at the central level about issues affecting them. Because of the wide proliferation of more, and more diverse, information, environmental management can no longer be considered the reserve of a few.

Now, if authorities want to engage in environmentally unfriendly actions in communities, they must often first convince ombudsmen, local groups, senior citizens, schoolchildren, and women and men of all professions of the positive impact of their projects. In addition, more people are acquiring the means to propose their own solutions, based on both their own traditional and empirical knowledge, which is gradually becoming properly validated, and the scientific and technological knowledge that is becoming increasingly available to all.

Development of Global Financial Markets

Times have changed since wealth was measured in terms of salt, corn, or gold coins. Even paper money is losing value as the nearly 200 million Visa credit cards accepted in 6.5 million stores throughout the world are used to transact about $650 million[2] in business every day. Including other credit cards, the figure is five times this amount. In addition, a huge number of transactions are carried out using cheques, shares, money orders, and so on. As a result of the information revolution, a growing volume of financial operations is carried out with "electronic money." The trend is clearly toward more widespread substitution of paper-based transactions with electronic operations.

The development of this "virtual" framework has made international monetary systems more volatile; financial and commercial transactions can be carried out at a speed that is changing the rhythm of political and economic events. Financial decisions are made at a moment's notice, at any hour of the day or night. Global markets never close. Effects are almost instantaneous. When a major financial operation takes place or an economic policy announced, repercussions can be felt throughout the world in a matter of minutes. A further consequence of the information-based management of money has been the internationalization of money markets and a subsequent blurring of financial borders. There are increasing ties between currencies and national governments are experiencing greater difficulty in defining autonomous policies.

Somewhat paradoxically, however, financial trends are developing "on their own." It is becoming increasingly difficult to control markets, as many more people, acting on their own, are making many more decisions over short periods of time. Central banks are having problems ensuring the stability of national currencies or the behaviour of other financial parameters. This situation is exacerbated by the similarly widespread automation of markets and the development of new, early forecasting programs. There are "a dozen firms managing more than 100 million dollars [US] each on the basis of advice generated by computers".

Growing numbers of mathematicians and computer experts are dedicated to predicting market trends by computerized nonlinear forecasting and other tools that increase the speed and accuracy of financial decisions. The effects of this practice are not yet wholly understood, but they are already playing a role in the globalization trend and in liberating at least some aspects of the financial market from monopolistic control. All dollar values in this book are expressed in US currency.

More Effective Transportation Networks

Although to a much lesser degree than the flow of information, the transportation of merchandise has been deeply affected by post-industrial changes. The internationalization of air traffic allows for the rapid transportation of a wide range of lightweight, high-value, perishable, or time-sensitive merchandise, such as electronic equipment and parts, food, flowers, and newsprint. The movement of freight by sea has also become more efficient with the development of computerized shipping and the associated improvement of commercial systems, faster ships, and modular packaging. The effectiveness and safety of shipping has been improved considerably by the worldwide adoption of container systems, which reduce the risk of theft and spoilage and significantly accelerate the loading and unloading of goods.

These improvements have promoted the growth of trade worldwide by reducing shipping costs and facilitating redistribution of production. Production occurs more and more often at the most "convenient" place, that is, the most economic, simplest, and safest site available. This is making it more difficult for governments and lobby groups to retain industries or other economic activities artificially in non economic situations. The "lubrication" of merchandise transport systems is also playing a role in the uniformity-diversity dichotomy. On the one hand, there is movement toward uniformity, through stricter and more widespread application of standards, specifications, and quality control. On the other hand, container systems permit the movement of diverse products within a highly standardized system. As with information, the final result will likely display both characteristics.

Movement of People

Another element in this changing world is the increased speed, volume, and accessibility of transportation for people, mainly by air travel. At any moment, throughout the world, several thousand planes are in the air, transporting tens if not hundreds of thousands of people over hundreds or thousands of kilometres. In addition, ground transportation (by automobile, bus, or train) has also become much more flexible, accessible, and rapid, increasing several fold the number of kilometres that people travel during their lives. The effects of this increase in travel are felt in many ways. First, there has been phenomenal growth in the tourist industry. Many countries receive over 10 million visitors annually (mainly tourists); in some popular tourist destinations, such as Spain, Italy, the United States, and Mexico, the number of visitors can sur pass 30 or 40 million per year. Second, business travel has similarly increased.

Business dealings are carried out more frequently and effectively by complementing telecommunications with face-to-face contact. Third, previously difficult international and national social contacts are now becoming commonplace. Thousands of international or interstate sports competitions, conferences, and other events are becoming the rule rather than the exception. Last, but not least, the ease of international travel has increased the flow of international migrants. The main emigration routes, over which people are driven by social, economic, and political situations and events, have been made more accessible by better transportation.

This increase in the transnational flow of people is a major factor in globalization. Visitors interact in many ways with their host countries, exchanging money, purchasing products, influencing (and being influenced by) culture. Migrants interact still more. They affect local job markets, they experience and produce cultural changes, and they mix socially and genetically. The result is an unprecedented mixture of cultures and groups, with the subsequent acquisition or loss of knowledge, changes in outlook, more rapid evolution of processes, behaviour, and attitudes. Like other global trends, increased travel has produced uniformity, while also fostering diversity. The two processes are taking place simultaneously, although probably at different levels of social systems and consciousness.

The unequal Distribution of Wealth

As described above, globalization is resulting in less differentiation among many aspects of society and life. At the same time, a rebirth of diversification is being promoted by the democratization of information through the expansion of electronic networks and the increasing number of channels of communication. Some important elements in both national and international spheres, however, do not seem to be profiting from either trend. Instead, these processes lead to the unequal distribution of resources, products, and access to money among much of the world's population. International economic disparities do not appear to be decreasing as a result of recent developments; on the contrary, they seem to be growing. The difference between the real incomes of the poorest and richest people in the world is huge. Annual per-capita income in the 16 richest countries varies from $10 420 to $21 250, averaging about $15 000.

At the other extreme, the annual per-capita income in the 25 poorest countries ranges from $80 (Mozambique) to $350 (India), with an average of about $220. Five days' accumulation of per-capita income in the 16 richest countries (total population, 725 million) is equal to 1 year of per-capita income in the 25 poorest (total population, 1 575 million). These figures are averages, however. The income of the poorest people in the poorest countries is considerably lower than the national average. It is estimated to be less than $60 or $80 a year and, in the poorest tenth of the population, probably does not exceed $40. The hourly wage of a well-paid professional in a developed country is often over $100; this can represent 2 or even 3 years' earnings for someone in the poorest sectors of the poorest countries.

Differences in Quality of Life

Do such quantitative comparisons reflect differences of the same order of magnitude in the quality of life of populations? The answ'er to this question is as varied as the criteria for evaluating such an elusive concept as quality of life. From one point of view, the quality of life of an itinerant farmer in the highlands of New Guinea may be higher than that of a neurotic Wall Street executive, despite the astronomical difference in income. The United Nations Development Programme (UNDP) has defined a "human development index" (HDI), which gives a rough idea of the differences in quality of life in the richest and poorest countries of the world (UNDP 1994).

The HDI is based on life expectancy, adult literacy, schooling, and income. The maximum value of the HDI is 1.0. UNDP results show 19 countries with an HDI exceeding 0.9; 25 have an HDI below 0.3. Although this measure provides only a general idea of quality of life and cannot be assumed to be a mathematical expression, the great variance in HDIs further demonstrates the abysmal gap that exists between the richest and poorest countries in terms of quality of life. People in developed countries are better fed and live in a healthier, less contaminated environment, with fewer infectious diseases. Therefore, they are sick much less frequently; in addition, these relatively healthy people have easier access to a much more efficient health-care system containing the best human resources, expensive medicine, and sophisticated equipment for diagnosis and treatment of illnesses.

This is not always true, however. Some forms of contamination that are not easily detectable are found more frequently in the developed world than in Third World countries, although these examples are becoming less common because of globalization. The average person in a poor country often works long hours in an unhealthy environment, in a confined space, and in an uncomfortable position; breathes toxic substances; is faced with long trips on crowded buses or trains; and must support a large family on an insufficient salary. In addition, he or she frequently lives in a degraded environment, where there is a high risk of natural catastrophes, such as landslides or floods.

The average person in a rich country has more free time and more options for using it. He or she can take up a sport or other exercise and has access to a range of health products that allow him or her to maintain a healthy lifestyle. A person in a poor country has little free time; he or she has an unbalanced diet and less resistance to disease. Often, living in high-density areas where appropriate hygiene may be difficult or impossible, the poor are faced with a much higher prevalence of infectious diseases. To be objective, we must recognize that these situations and evaluations do not apply to all social sectors in rich and poor countries. There are poor sectors in rich countries and very rich sectors in poor countries. The standard of living of the upper classes in some poor countries may seem sumptuous, even compared with that of the average person in developed countries. However, a huge gap exists between the two worlds that appear to be increasing daily.

There are several reasons for the increase. First, the populations of poor countries are growing much faster than those in rich countries, making it increasingly more difficult to provide employment and services for all. Second, the environment of poor countries is being degraded faster and, as a result, their production base is shrinking. Third, poor countries are losing their best human resources to the North. Finally, goods and wealth produced in poor countries are being systematically transferred to the rich through export of capital; payment of royalties, profits, loans, and interest; deterioration of the terms of exchange; and processes of cultural alienation that are promoting unnecessary and frivolous types of consumption, again favouring the transfer of money and resources from the poor to the rich.

Effects of International Disparities on the Environment

The huge differences separating the rich and poor populations of the world are having an unmistakable effect on the environment at all levels. Poverty is a prime cause of many of the world's serious environmental problems. In most countries, the urban poor must survive in crowded conditions, without appropriate sanitation and waste-disposal services. As a result, poor neighbourhoods are becoming a major cause of water and soil degradation, both in their immediate areas and "down slope" or downstream. In some countries, landless rural poor are forced to move into inappropriate locations, cutting and burning trees to clear land for subsistence farming or raising cattle, or excavating the soil and sediments to extract the minerals that allow them to survive.

A large part of environmental degradation, including desertification, erosion, and contamination processes, is the direct result of the efforts of poor people to make a living — often, simply to survive. The issue, however, is not why these people are harming the environment and how they can change their behaviour; the real issue is why they are in a situation where this is their only recourse. Not all environmental problems are the result of poverty. Many (perhaps the most acute and wide-ranging problems) result from economic affluence and indiscriminate consumption. Wealthy countries are responsible for burning most of the world's non renewable fuel.

They produce the largest volumes of solid and liquid wastes, produce enormous volumes of unnatural gaseous emissions, possess the largest depredatory fishing fleets, and consume most of the goods produced in environmentally unfriendly ways in the poorer countries. Finally, through the promotion of export-driven economics in developing countries, the wealthy nations force these countries into positions in which environmental degradation becomes unavoidable. There is a strong relation between the inequitable social structure of the world and the main processes of environmental degradation that are taking place across the planet. A sustainable approach to environmental management must address the paramount need to restructure the distribution of wealth among countries and among people. Harmonization of production-consumption and the more equitable distribution of wealth are preconditions for sustainable environmental management.

International Migration

Differences in quality of life are increasing in an epoch of intense globalization of communications and transport. As a result, for the first time in history, most inhabitants of poorer countries have become aware that people in other places live not only differently, but much better. Third World people, representing 80% of the world's population, increasingly want to immigrate to the developed world. Salvadoreans, Nicaraguans, Peruvians, and many other Latin

American people dream of emigrating to the United States and Canada. Thousands of North Africans would like to move to France, Belgium, and Switzerland. Many Indians and Pakistanis would like to emigrate to Britain or Saudi Arabia. Each year, several million people attempt to fulfill this wish, and a considerable number succeed.

They use the most varied and imaginative methods. Some cross a desert or river; others cross larger bodies of water in small boats. Still others try their luck by legal means, hoping to be included in the quotas of Canada or the United States, or through agreements between governments. Professional people and entrepreneurs have an advantage. Those who possess special expertise or belong to the qualified professions are accepted with relative ease. One result of these migratory fluxes is the development of stricter policies and strategies by the rich countries to prevent uncontrolled arrivals. Careful controls, visa requirements, and financial guarantees are all geared toward closing borders.

Despite these measures, however, migratory pressure is so great that large numbers manage to squeeze through or around the various "filters," and settle in the targeted countries where their situation is often secured after several years through one of the periodic amnesties, which, in a way, are a recognition of the impotence of the police and immigration systems in preventing people from escaping living conditions in the South. Currently, the main recipient countries for immigrants are the largest and least densely populated: the United States, Canada, and Australia. These three countries absorb about 1.5 million immigrants every year, that is, approximately half of the total migration to developed countries.

Immigration to the United States

The United States alone receives more than 1 million immigrants a year. California, the richest and most populated state in the country, increased its population from less than

26 million in 1980 to the current 31.5 million. Foreign immigration accounted for about 40% of the increase. In the area of San Diego alone, legal immigrants constitute more than half the population, and it is estimated that there are 200 thousand illegal immigrants in the population of 2 million. Similar situations are found in other southern US cities, such as Houston, Los Angeles, and San Antonio. A significant segment of the immigrant population ends up in the sector of American society living in poverty.

The shantytowns of San Diego are typical poor neighbourhoods, composed of recent, mainly illegal immigrants. The Los Diablos slum in San Diego County is "a wasteland of rusting cars and makeshift housing, acreage owned by the city and squatted on for many years". These squatters work at small construction projects or pick tomatoes and cucumbers for below-minimum wages; they earn about $3 per hour, compared with the minimum wage of $4.50 per hour (in Mexico, however, the same work pays one-tenth that amount). Squatter camps like Los Diablos can be found throughout southern California, Arizona, New Mexico, Texas, and Florida in the inner cities or suburbs of many large metropolitan areas. In some ways, they represent the Third World inside the developed world.

In 1992, over 1 million people immigrated to the United States, of which 841 thousand were classified as "legal". Almost half were from Latin America, with 23% coming from Mexico, the country "sending" the most migrants to its northern neighbours. Of the remainder, 13.1% came from the Caribbean and 11.1% came from Central and South America. More than a third (35.2%) of the remaining legal immigrants came from Asia. During recent years there has been an increase in immigration from eastern Europe, which previously had not exceeded 8%, and a relatively small amount of immigration from Africa (about 2%).

These legal immigrants include a considerable number of people with high levels of education: 26.6% have university degrees, although in their own countries people with degrees make up only a small percentage of the population. This phenomenon has been referred to as the brain drain." It tends to accentuate North-South disparities, strengthening human resources m countries with well-developed capacities and reducing the already weak professional base of poorer countries. The countries of origin of migrants with the highest education are India (average schooling, 15 years), Philippines (14 years), and Korea (13 years). The lowest level of education is found in Mexican immigrants (7 years).

Most of the poor in the country are born in the United States, usually as members of ethnic minorities (Afro-Americans, Hispanic-Americans, and American Indians). Not only do these immigrants possess relatively high levels of education, they are also often trained and experienced in highly specialized occupations. For example 40 h of AT&T's researchers were bom outside the United States. A similar proportion of the professionals in the Silicon Valley are also immigrants. According to *Business Week,* the next generation of engineers in highly sophisticated US companies will be dominated by immigrants.

While these immigration trends continue, there is evidence of a change in the types of jobs available in the United States As the country moves toward a post-industrial, third- wave society and redistribution of its global productive roles, a large number of labour-intensive production activities are being transferred to less-developed countries like Mexico. Many jobs that were once performed by immigrants or unspecialized American workers have disappeared, a situation that is affecting the segment of the American work force that depends on these jobs for its survival.

One frequently hears that it is the continuous influx of immigrants that is creating job scarcity. Although research has shown that immigrants create more jobs than they take, their presence can contribute to the level of frustration in society. There is widespread feeling among American citizens that, to solve the unemployment problem, immigration must be stopped or drastically reduced. In some areas, however, the lack of inexpensive immigrant labour may promote the transfer of many jobs to sites in Brazil, Guatemala, Mexico, or other countries, including some jobs now performed by American workers.

Immigration to Other Developed Countries

The population density in Canada and Australia is less than 3 people per square kilometre. Immigration to Canada has ranged from 100 to 200 thousand people a year over the last few years. Australia has accepted slightly fewer people than Canada. Lately, a large proportion of Canadian immigrants have come from Asia (especially those in Vancouver, Toronto, and other large cities), Eastern Europe, and, to a lesser degree, the Middle East and Latin America. As a result of the recent war in Somalia, many citizens from this country have also come to Canada, many of them as refugees.

In Australia, the immigrant population includes a considerable number of people from neighbouring Far Eastern countries (China, India, Indonesia, Melanesia, Pakistan, the Philippines, Polynesia, and Vietnam), as well as Eastern Europe. In Europe, immigration patterns are closely related to the affiliations of former Third World colonies. France and Belgium have received many immigrants from the Francophone countries of Africa (Algeria, Morocco, and Tunisia); the United Kingdom is the destination of Indians and Pakistanis; Holland of Indonesians; Portugal of people from Angola, Cape Verde Islands, Guinea, and Mozambique; and Spain of Spanish-Americans, Moroccans, and other Africans.

The southern coast of Spain, in Andalucia near Tarifa, is the destination of tens of thousands of illegal immigrants who cross the Strait of Gibraltar in *pateras*. Moroccans, Mauritanians, Senegalese, and other Africans from south of the Sahara cross the strait with the help of *pasadores* or *lobos*. Once they reach Spain, some manage to move into other countries, such as France and Germany, but many remain on the Iberian Peninsula. In Europe, African and Asian workers are a source of inexpensive labour for jobs not attractive to nationals. As a result, it has become increasingly difficult for some of the richer European countries to do without their work. In addition to the large number of immigrants with low professional qualifications, Europe receives a significant number of immigrants with higher qualifications (generally through legal or semi-legal channels), arriving as students, invited professors, professionals, and qualified technicians.

A portion of the earnings of immigrants is transferred to their countries of origin. For example, it is estimated that Morocco receives over $1 billion as a result of these remittances. Similar figures have been reported for Algeria, Tunisia, and, to a lesser degree, sub-Saharan countries. As in North America, a significant sector of the immigrant population has a high level of education, strengthening the knowledge base of European countries, while reducing such resources in the countries of origin. Third World countries spend their limited financial resources training their professionals, only to have the few well-trained people who complete their studies quickly absorbed by the much richer North.

The Development of Free Markets

Immediately after the Second World War, the main political powers began negotiations to reduce tariffs and duties worldwide, giving birth to GATT (the General Agreement on Tariffs and Trade). With the participation of 23 countries, this agreement was concluded in Geneva, Switzerland, in 1947, and took effect in 1948. At that time, the objective was to approve an interim agreement until an international agency could assume responsibility for coordination and management of international trade relations. However, such an agency was never formed and GATT remains the principal tool for liberalizing world trade. Since its inception, GATT has expanded to include more than 100 countries by the early 1990s.

An attempt to liberalize regional trade took place in Western Europe after 1958 when the European Common Market was formed by Belgium, France, Germany, Italy, Luxembourg, and the Netherlands. This trading bloc, now know as the European Community (EC), grew further to include Denmark, Ireland, and the United Kingdom (1973), Greece (1981), and Spain and Portugal (1986). By 1993, other European countries were negotiating entry and, before the end of the century, it is likely that the remaining Scandinavian countries and Austria will join. The Czech Republic, Estonia, Hungary, Latvia, Lithuania, Malta, Poland, and Slovenia are also interested, although their incorporation will probably not occur before the year 2000.

The EC countries trade mainly with their economic partners (78% of the Netherlands' exports remain in the EC; Belgium and Luxembourg, 75%; Ireland, 75%; Portugal, 74%; Spain, 71%; France, 62%; Italy, 59%; United Kingdom, 55%; Germany, 53%). Most of the remaining commerce is directed to North America and the Far East. The role of Third World countries in European commerce is less important. Starting in 1988, a second major commercial bloc was formed in North America when the United States and Canada negotiated a free trade agreement. In 1993, an agreement was reached between these two countries and Mexico to ensure its integration into the process through the North American Free Trade Agreement (NAFTA).

The formalization of this treaty has generated strong opposition from some sectors of both the Canadian and the American public who believe that opening the borders will release a flood of companies moving south to Mexico in search of a less-expensive environment, while posing the risk of increased immigration to the United States and Canada. A recent article (*Economist* 1993b) expressed the view of many who think that there may be exactly the opposite effect. It cites the case of a General Motors plant planning to move a large portion of the production of Cavalier vehicles from Ramos Arizpe, Mexico, to Lansing, Michigan. According to the article, Mexican labour costs are only 35% lower than those in the United States and 40% lower than Canada's, when average wages are adjusted for benefits and lower productivity.

The effect of NAFTA may thus be less pronounced than feared by those who oppose it. Following a proposal of then President of the United States, George Bush (the 1990 "Initiative for the Americas"), and other Latin American countries are also making progress toward similar agreements. The most important regional block is the MERCOSUR, comprising Argentina, Brazil, Paraguay, and Uruguay, complemented by the Central American Free Market (Costa Rica, Guatemala, Honduras, Nicaragua, and El Salvador) and the Andean Group (Bolivia, Colombia, Ecuador, and Venezuela). Chile and Peru have not joined any of these liberalization initiatives.

Since the 1960s, attempts have been made to create a Latin American free market — after the formation of the Asociacion Latino-Americana de Libre Comercio, which became Asociacion Latino-Americana de Integration (ALADI) after the treaty of Montevideo. ALADI's role has been mainly to provide an institutional framework for regional agreements dealing with integration processes, including trade liberalization. Recent GATT negotiations took place in this environment of globalization.

Many difficulties were encountered during the "Uruguay round," particularly because of the insistence of some EC countries on maintaining certain farming subsidies. The document resulting from the Uruguay round of GATT was approved and signed by the 117 member countries on 15

December 1993 in Geneva, Switzerland. Although the final agreement was not as wide ranging as expected, tariffs will decrease by an average 40%. The relatively successful conclusion of this agreement shows that the world continues to move toward globalization and that, although international commerce is complex, the barriers that used to prevent the development of open trade relations are gradually being dismantled.

International Commerce and their Effects on Globalization

Evidence from recent history shows that globalization processes are unstoppable because they tend to feed on each other. Current globalization trends are based on a framework of unidirectional openings (liberal approaches in developing countries, continued protectionism in developed economies). It is an internationalization controlled from the financial decision-making centres in the North. Farming systems in the United States and the EC remain supported by direct and indirect subsidies. In Europe, this is viewed by some as overt protectionism; in the United States, the subsidies are more indirect — for example, subsidized water for irrigated agriculture in California and other western states.

Third World countries, on the other hand, pressured by the need to service large debts and conditioned by liberalizing programs imposed by the International Monetary Fund (IMF) and other lending agencies, have been drawn into export-promotion campaigns. These have forced them to accept unfavourable terms of exchange because of import quotas, used as instruments of political pressure, or in relation to refinancing their foreign debt. The desperate need to export, coupled with the necessity of creating new sources of employment, has compelled many developing countries to be less selective in their acceptance of new industries transferred from developed countries, including the rapidly spreading *mcicjuiladoras,* which generally use production systems that are not only highly exploitive of the work force, detrimental to health, and environmentally unfriendly, but also teach workers almost nothing that can be applied elsewhere.

Economic Globalization and Environmental Degradation

Economic globalization and liberalization of trade are having a strong impact on the environment at local, regional, and global levels. Whenever trade barriers are lowered or eliminated, many economic activities that had previously been carried out under their protection also tend to disappear, often to relocate in other areas where economic survival is easier. Generally, the dominant factor in competitive production is cost. Developed countries must compensate for their high labour, tax, and environmental costs through more productive technologies, higher production levels, and more efficient management strategies. Despite the high costs, there are clear advantages to producing certain goods in developed countries: well-organized and efficient infrastructures, high capacity of existing human resources, better quality control, and proximity to markets.

However, a number of productive activities in developed countries would not be able to survive for long without the shields of protectionist trade barriers and subsidies. Because globalization processes tend to remove these barriers, many productive activities traditionally associated with developed economies are gradually being transferred to developing countries. In some cases, this happens through partial transfer of some operations in the productive chain, such as assembly or production of parts for industrial use. Such transferred operations can be carried out at a lower cost at the receiving site because of lower labour and environmental costs.

Normally, this transfer involves agreements between the countries to allow productive complementarities. In most cases, the transferring country charges duty only on the value added in the host country, and the host country opens "free zones" to allow entry and exit of raw materials and merchandise with minimal or no import-export duty. These industries are called *maquiladoras* and are common in Costa Rica, the Dominican Republic, Guatemala, Mexico, and, with slight modifications, in some countries of East Asia and North Africa.

Often, when the whole economic activity becomes uneconomical in the developed country, the entire productive process can be transferred to the partner country. Many metallurgical, textile, and electronics industries, among others, has been transferred in this way. Similar arrangements are being made in relation to agricultural activities (some Californian crops have been transferred to Brazil, Chile, and Mexico), forestry (the Canadian forest industry is having trouble competing with counterparts in Brazil and Chile), and aquaculture (shrimp farms have been established in Ecuador and the Philippines).

This global restructuring of production is having a profound effect on the environment. Most of the industries or activities moving to developing countries have some potential for environmental degradation. A considerable number of them produce toxic wastes or emissions that can introduce negative elements into water, air, or soils. When these industries or activities are located in developed countries, a long social learning process has contributed to the development of a set of environmental laws to address, more or less efficiently, their potentially hazardous effects. Developed countries have preventive and reactive systems, including technical solutions to environmental degradation, policies and rules for that purpose, definitions of responsibility and accountability, and appropriate institutions, to deal with environmental problems.

Many developing countries lack these systems. Some laws may exist, but they are poorly applied (if at all).

Recently, progress has been made in several countries, butit is insufficient to prevent serious environmental degradation. Thus, the restructuring of production appears to be threatening the environment at local, national, regional, and global levels. For example, acid rain, which was once common only in north-eastern North America and Western Europe, has become a serious issue in several Third World countries, including Brazil, China, and India. Industrial procedures to check environmental degradation are often bypassed as industries relocate to Third World countries where such requirements do not apply or can be circumvented.

New irrigated-farming projects in developing countries are using water at a rate well above the renewability potential of aquifers or surface water bodies. Farming and neo- forestry activities are being carried out on land from which rich and diverse native forests have been eliminated. The balance is systematically negative: less care is exercised or responsibility taken; fewer resources are applied to environmental protection; soil is eroded; aquifers, streams, lakes, and coastal waters are contaminated; forests are disappearing; exotic species are introduced without consideration of their ecological effects; and the atmosphere is polluted. Any long-term approach to environmentally sustainable development must consider these effects of globalization. The problems must be addressed before they become impossible or too expensive to reverse.

8

Managing the Environment

The Environmental Challenge Facing Asia

Asia's rich environmental management traditions sustained its people for centuries. Practical examples include the rice terraces of Indonesia and the Philippines, and common property management of Japanese inland fisheries. Some of the greatest Asian thinkers - the Buddha, Confucius and Gandhi - had a profound appreciation of the dependence of people on the natural world. Perhaps such traditions, in part, explain why the Asian public is more concerned about current environmental impacts on health and well-being than people in any other region. In the early stages of Asia's drive for economic development, Asian environmental traditions were challenged by economic development models which promoted the exploitation of natural resources for export. Forests were cleared, first for high-value hardwoods and then for tea, coffee and rubber. Mines were developed ir previously remote areas. Environmental change accelerated with rapid agricultural and industrial growth in the twentieth century, becoming more extreme in recent years. Asian agricultural production rose 62 per cent from 1990 to 2002..

Forests were cleared rapidly, in part to make way for food production - Indonesia alone lost *1.7* M ha a year of forests during the 1990s. Large areas were irrigated for food production, with high amounts of water and agrochemicals being applied. Asian industrial production rose 40 per cent from 1995 to 2002, compared with 23 per cent globally. As in other regions that experienced industrial revolutions, early industrial developments have involved highly polluting industries. Further developments constantly generate new types of environmental burden - e.g. the heavy metal hazards from 'e-waste' (computers, phones, televisions, etc.), one of the fastest growing sources of waste (UNEP 2004; World Bank 2005a). Asian urbanization, the fastest in the world, is posing massive environmental challenges.

Today, most of the world's mega-cities are in Asia, and so also are the world's biggest slums. By 2020, Asia's urban population is projected to double to 2.2 billion from a little over 1 billion in 1990, and nearly half of Asia's population will live in cities. Water supply, housing, wastewater treatment, solid waste management and transport infrastructure already cannot keep pace. For example, municipalities will face a more than ten-fold increase in solid waste burdens by 2025 (with China, Indonesia and Philippines facing the largest increases). Pollution may reach intolerable levels: already, eight of the world's ten most polluted cities are in China, where 3- 6 million life-years are lost each year from pollution.

Despite having the fourth largest fresh water reserves in the world, the Ministry of Water Resources states that more than 400 Chinese cities, including the capital, face severe water shortages - and people are being forced to migrate because of lack of water. Such dynamics have brought about enormous benefits through fuelling the Asian economies and supporting Asian livelihoods. Many development indicators have directly improved as a result - notably GDP, exports, food security, nutritional status, employment, and levels of poverty. However, these changes are reaching unprecedented levels, increasing the severity of four major environmental problems, which may themselves undermine growth and poverty reduction:

- Decline in quantity or quality of natural resources - such as fisheries or soils - which threatens many livelihoods and economic activities, and thus growth
- Degradation of fundamental ecosystem processes, e.g. natural cycling of water and nutrients, and biological dynamics such as pollination - which threatens all livelihoods and most economic activity
- Increased climate-related environmental hazards such as floods and droughts - which imposes major costs to life and property
- Water and air pollution - which damages both health and infrastructure. Environmental problems are increasingly felt at the regional level.

Trans-boundary resources are often managed unsustainably, e.g. the diminishing fish stocks of the South Pacific or Bay of Bengal; risks to clean air from Indonesian forest fires or East Asian sand and dust storms; and pollution in shared rivers (e.g. the Indus, Mekong and recently, the Songha river where a toxic benzene spill threatens Russia). Cross-border trade may cause over-exploitation of timber or wildlife (e.g. in South-east Asia and East Asia). Growing demands by the region's growth centers for resources such as timber, metals and oil are putting other regions under increasing environmental pressure. Regional hazards are also-emerging, such as floods and droughts, and zoonotic diseases such as Avian bird 'flu and SARS. Asia has also progressed in some areas of environmental management.

Exposure to water pollution and indoor air pollution has, in general, fallen across the region as investment in clean water and electricity has improved. Safe drinking water now reaches a majority of the population in South Asia - increasing more rapidly over the last decade than in any other region. Many Asian countries have phased out or banned the most dangerous pesticides. Energy efficiency has improved rapidly, particularly in China. Reuse of waste products is increasingly handled at the regional level, with waste reprocessing a rapidly growing industry in China. The increase in Asian land area officially protected for biodiversity (up to 7.6 per cent by 2003) is an overlooked environmental success story - even if there is often much to be done to ensure local poor people benefit. Yet most environmental trends remain negative, and more poor people are suffering from them. There are many promising political, social and economic processes in Asia that are driving pro-poor environmental outcomes:

- Poor people themselves have organized to demand better access to natural resources and improved environmental services - and subsequently to manage resources sustainably and establish improved relations with the authorities. Sometimes this has been done in collaboration with government - as with the 89,000 forest protection committees in India, and 13,000 forest user groups in Nepal. Neighbourhood groups in the slums of South Asia have organized their own sanitation schemes on massive scales, at costs far lower than those provided inefficiently by municipalities.
- Asia's private sector, as the engine of growth, can play a vital role in responding to environmental challenges, and is already responding with real leadership and innovation. Japan's auto industry has sought to lead the world in low emission vehicles. Asian companies are rapidly adopting environmental management systems, aiming to meet international standards; 40 per cent of companies with the global environmental standard ISO- 14001 are from over 100 countries in Asia.
- Asia's vibrant civil society has mobilised to press government to manage natural resources wisely, with especially significant impacts in India and the Philippines. In many countries, faith groups are increasingly involved in environmental debate. The media in manv countries are increasing their coverage of environmental issues. And judicial activism, notably in India, has been driving better

implementation of government environmental policies through increasing both supply and demand for environmental justice.

- Asian governments are increasingly promoting better care of the environment: decentralising control over natural resources; entering management agreements with resource users; and promoting clean technologies through fiscal instruments. The resource intensity of consumption patterns is being addressed, e.g. Japan's 'Basic Law for a Recycling-Based Society' and its 'Reduce, Reuse and Recycle (3Rs) Initiative' began the trend, and today the Chinese Government is exploring ways to develop a 'Circular Economy' - recently committing to generate 15 per cent of China's power from renewable sources by 2020 (up from 7 per cent now). The 5th Asian Ministerial Conference on Environment and Development has concluded that 'long-term, effective poverty reduction requires that the natural environment be protected'. Held in Seoul in 2005, it called for pro-poor 'Green Growth' requiring significant governance, policy and system changes, supported by international partnerships.

The current discussion addresses three questions that are central to achieving this bold vision:

- How can environmental assets continue to contribute to pro-poor growth, especially in low- income countries in Asia?
- How might environmental degradation undermine Asia's growth, and particularly affect poor people?
- How can pro-poor environmental improvements be made, and how can Asia's development partners assist?
- How Can Environmental Assets Continue to Support Pro-Poor Growth, Especially in Low-Income Countries in Asia?

Water is for us what oil is to the Arabs' Natural assets, :h as fertile soils, rivers, forests, fisheries and mineral deposits, account for a very significant proportion of national wealth in Asia. Together, they are worth almost as much as the value of manmade assets such as infrastructure. The figure is typically higher for lower income countries, i.e. 25 per cent in South Asia, compared with 21 per cent in East Asia. Indeed, natural capital is the main asset of many of Asia's poorer countries (e.g. 64 per cent in Bhutan). The historical trend of using natural resources for growth is continuing. Lao PDR, Bhutan and Nepal are developing their water resources to generate hydropower exports to their neighbours.

While it remains controversial, the Nam Theun 2 hydropower project in Lao PDR may generate $2 billion in export revenue to Thailand over 25 years. Indonesia has used its oil and mineral wealth to diversify its economy, while Timor Leste sees its rich oil and gas resources as its main driver of growth. Nature tourism is a growing sector in Sri Lanka, Nepal, Kyrgyzstan and Thailand. For example, tourism provides 37 per cent of income in Chiang Mai, Thailand where forest trekking is popular (Thailand Environment Monitor 2004). The challenge is to use this natural wealth carefully, to (1) generate growth, and (2) enable the poor to benefit from this growth, while (3) sustaining the resource base and its continued capacity for pro-poor growth. There are two main ways in which natural resources can contribute to pro-poor growth:

- National economic growth, which creates jobs and adds to total income and government revenues - which can be used for pro-poor purposes
- Development of small and medium scale enterprises, through use of forests, fisheries, and other natural resources owned and managed by primary producers and processors of natural resources.

For natural resources to sustain pro-poor growth, their extraction should not be subsidised, processing should add real value, the poor must not be harmed by the extraction, and profits must be taxed and used for pro- poor spending. These objectives are not always mutually compatible and there are some difficult choices: Avoid subsidising large-scale resource extraction. Many countries lose money from subsidised exploitation, e.g. by loss-making state firms (e.g. Sri Lanka's state timber corporation), subsidies to government joint ventures (e.g. the Facific tuna processing industry), large tax write-offs (e.g. Indonesia's timber industry), permitting excessive logging (e.g. Cambodia) or land conversion (shrimp farming - Bangladesh, Vietnam). This leads to 'boom and bust': natural capital is asset- stripped and low resource prices encourage excessive, inefficient processing, which eventually destroys the viability of the industry. Key is to reduce incentives for overexploitation, notably by dismantling subsidies that harm the poor and the en vironment. Increase the value added by a competitive resource industry. With declining terms of trade for primary commodities, successful businesses have invested in technologies that enable increasingly sophisticated processing. Asian timber producers, for instance, once exported sawn-or round-wood, but now export furniture and mouldings. There is broad consensus that the aggregate worth to the economy of further processing is maximized by promoting competitive industry, i.e. without perverse subsidies such as artificially low log prices and log/rattan export bans. Access to technologies and markets is key, as are capacities to help set and meet appropriate international standards. Ensure that natural resource extraction does not harm neighbouring people but, preferably, supports their development. Many large-scale commercial mining, timber and hydropower investments can come to dominate remote areas with often poor and/or minority populations. They may compete with subsistence harvesters, for whom there is usually little legal recognition. Harm can be avoided

- and preferably opportunities realized - by careful zoning, local hiring and procurement policies, management agreements, and earmarking some of the profits for local level investments. Several corporate-community forestry partnerships in India and Indonesia offer good examples.

- Allocate natural resource revenue towards pro-poor growth. While some governments have failed to invest their natural resource wealth in pro-poor growth - and thus fall under the 'resource curse' - others have allocated natural resource revenues to poverty-reducing investments. Some have earmarked specific natural resource revenues (notably mineral and forest revenues) to the local administration or local people, as in some mining concessions in the Philippines.

Job creation is one of Asia's biggest challenges, and many new jobs will continue to be in the SME sector. To lift themselves out of poverty, poor people will wish to use their major assets - usually natural resources - and aim to add as much value as possible. They may need to group into associations, to help them negotiate better terms and improve the efficiency of environmental asset management. Past attempts at forming producer cooperatives around subsidised inputs, such as in fisheries, have often failed due to political interference and elite capture with the inputs not reaching the poor. A more successful approach is to provide an enabling business environment through secure resource rights, support for common property management, improved access to markets and transport, streamlined regulations and technical support. This is an area for further development: since they tend to be dispersed, natural resource-based SMEs are challenging to support, and difficult to regulate for their environmental impact.

How Can Natural Resource Conservation Benefit Poor People? Loss of natural resources can impose high economic and social costs. Thus some Asian countries have limited the extraction of key land and sea resources, as well as introducing completely protected areas where extraction is forbidden (such as national parks). These often represent significant conservation developments. But in some cases these have been introduced at high social costs for poor people, who may suffer from blanket harvesting restrictions, as in most national parks. Protected areas can be managed in ways which ensure that neighbouring poor people still receive substantial benefits, and are compensated for any loss of existing natural resource use rights. Nature tourism is a fast-growing industry with potential to provide revenues and employment for poor residents, as well as to preserve ecosystem services.

Rapid economic growth has exerted considerable pressure on the environmental sustainability of the region and ... could have an adverse effect on achieving sustainable development[7] Asia's rapid growth is, in some cases, being directly undermined by environmental degradation. In Pakistan, 16 per cent of the land is subject to salinisation resulting from excessive water application, with similar scales of this problem occurring in the Central Asian countries. The irrigation mismanagement in Pakistan costs over US$200 million per year in reduced food yields. In western India, groundwater pumping has enabled agricultural intensification, but water tables quickly dropped from 10-15 m below ground in the 1970s to 400-450 m by the 1990s. In many areas, wells have been abandoned and entire villages have become deserted.

Shrimp farming has declined in some countries, due primarily to pollution and weak environmental controls; resulting disease caused Asia's shrimp industry losses of over US$1 billion in the 1990s. Marine over fishing has also undermined economic returns. In the Gulf of Thailand, average hourly catch has fallen almost 10 times from 250 kg/h in 1961 to 18 kg/h in 1999. Such environmental damage can foment social and political unrest. South Korea saw over 70 anti-pollution protests in the 1990s. China has faced rural unrest because of increasing pollution. Investing Asia's drawdown of natural capital in other sectors of the economy can avoid 'boom and bust'.

This is particularly the case of minerals and other non-renewable resources which, by definition, are declining with extraction. It is clear that, if natural capital is simply liquidated as consumption, then it will not lead to sustained improvements to the economy. If, however, profits from natural capital extraction are invested in physical capital (e.g. infrastructure) and human capital (e.g. education) to drive further growth, they might make a sustained contribution to improved welfare. Where there is a windfall natural resource gain, such as a rapid oil price rise, this can be set aside in a special saving account. This in itself can be beneficial environmentally if future investments in physical and human capital lead to more efficient resource utilization, thus reducing further pressure on the resource base. Timing is crucial in shifting from pure resource extraction to resource management and diversified income sources, before it is too late and the resource collapses.

In many cases, the switch has not been made in time - such as gold mining in Kyrgyzstan, oil and gas in Indonesia, and some Asian timber enterprises and fishing fleets. But there are limits to how much drawdown of natural capital is economically desirable. Natural capital in Asia is already declining dramatically in both quality and quantity, while manmade and human capital continues to grow. Fisheries are depleted, soils eroded and made saline, aquifers dry up, and forests are denuded. These impacts are significant enough to reduce Gross National Savings by almost a third in China, Philippines and Cambodia, by almost a half in Mongolia and Malaysia, and by nearly 90 per cent in Indonesia. In addition, there are certain ecosystem processes which are critical for their life-supporting services, notably nutrient recycling, air and water purification, pollination and other biological mechanisms. Loss of this 'critical natural capital' is irreversible and represents a significant threat to the long term welfare of the human race. Yet, globally, the Millennium Ecosystem Assessment has identified that 60 per cent of environmental services (particularly freshwater, air and water purification, climate regulation, and pest regulation) have been degraded.

Most poor people in Asia, particularly women, are dependent on natural resources for their livelihoods, but suffer from inadequate access and declining resource quality. Most of Asia's rural poor depend on agriculture, for which access to fertile soil and predictable water supplies is essential. Yet 28 per cent of Asia's land is already degraded and water tables are declining (FAO 2004). World Bank studies in China, Cambodia, Lao PDR and Vietnam suggest that there is a strong overlap between highly degradable land and where the poor live. People without access to secure land are, perhaps paradoxically, even more dependent on a wide range of natural resources, as they cannot raise financial capital - and women are disproportionately dependent. In West Bengal, three times as many women as men are involved in gathering non-timber forest products, processing is done entirely by women, and twice as many women as men are involved in their marketing.

Fisheries are the key resource for more poor people in Asia than in any other region, notably in Bangladesh, India, and Indonesia and along the great Mekong River, and many farm households augment their food supplies and incomes by fishing. Many poor people in Asia are exposed to environmental health risks and hazards - both the traditional risks of dirty air and water, but also new risks from animal-transmitted (zoonotic) diseases such as bird 'flu. There have been major environmental health improvements over the last decades, with 80 per cent of people in low-income Asian countries now having access to improved water sources. However, access to sanitation remains much lower at 44 per cent - partly explaining why water pollution remains a significant problem: faecal coliforms in Asian rivers are 50 times the WHO safe maximum. In South Asia, the environmentally caused disease burden is now greater than that from malnutrition (20 per cent, compared to 15 per cent).

Many women and children suffer particularly from indoor air pollution (from dirty cooking fuels used in confined spaces), causing up to a million premature deaths each year across Asia. Young children and poorly educated women in poor households in Bangladesh suffer four times as much from indoor air pollution as men in higher income households. Animal health and human health are becoming increasingly linked in Asia, as people and livestock come into closer contact with wildlife when they move into new areas and intensify agricultural production. Wildlife acts as a 'pool' from which pathogens can emerge, as with avian bird flu and possibly SARS and HIV AIDS. Environmental changes have exacerbated Asia's high vulnerability to disasters - and this will increase with climate change.

Asia has always experienced wide climatic variation. Buildings, livelihoods and social networks have adapted to cope with natural events. Management of normal floods has been integral to the fishing and farming livelihoods of poor people in Bangladesh and Cambodia. However, these natural events are now becoming more frequent and extreme, leading to more lives lost, more property destroyed, and more conflict. In China, natural disasters are now the main direct cause of people falling back into poverty. The poor tend to suffer most, as they live in the most vulnerable areas, e.g. many slum dwellers live on land which is highly vulnerable to environmental hazards such as landslides, pollution and floods. Such vulnerabilities are exacerbated by damage to protective environmental assets, such as coral reefs, coastal mangrove forests and riverine wetlands, which increase exposure to floods - as illustrated in some areas by the devastating tsunami.

Asia includes several larger countries like China and India that are increasingly significant emitters of greenhouse gases. It is also the continent that will experience some of the greatest adverse impacts of climate change, which will affect millions of people in almost all countries. Asia already faces 90 per cent of all climate related disasters in the world, at a cost of half a million lives each year. Many development assistance investments have recently been shown to be vulnerable to climate change (OECD 2004). A further 2 rise in temperature is expected to cut farmers' incomes by 25 per cent (DFID 2004). There is an urgent need to balance energy provision with less pollution, and with investment in adapting land use, infrastructure and other systems to climate change (especially in the vulnerable agricultural dry lands of India and China, and the fragile coastal zones in Bangladesh and the South Pacific).

As Asian countries grow and trade increases, the world economy's environmental impact ('footprint') becomes heavier, with impacts felt well beyond the main centres of growth. For example, China is now responsible for half of global cement consumption, a third of coal and steel use, and is the biggest importer of timber. This boosts the revenues of resource producing countries in the region and beyond, but also increases the rate of resource depletion and carries significant environmental risk such as increased pollution, land degradation and climate change. A similar picture can be painted for large urban centres which obtain many of their supplies from far away, at significant environmental costs on the remote ecosystems on which their continued growth depends.

The next 10 years are likely to witness significant increases in consumer demand in Asia - in China alone it is expected to rise to the equivalent of four more 'USAs'. Added to the already high, and increasing consumer demand in the West, pressures on the world's natural resource base are also set to increase exponentially, unless rising commodity prices, increasing consumer awareness of 'footprints', and improved policies and market instruments start to dismantle predominant high-input/low- efficiency/high-waste production processes.

The global market for environmental goods and services is over $600 billion in 2005. Asia Pacific accounted for $37 billion of this total, but its growth is the fastest in the world, with the market expected to triple by 2015'. There is growing agreement that pro-poor environmental change is urgently needed - and moreover, emerging consensus about how to achieve it. The analysis above points to three key areas for improvement:

- Institutions and governance
- Investment
- International partnerships.

Institutional and governance changes are key to addressing natural resource management and pollution. Pollution is, in part, a governance issue, when there are few private incentives to protect public assets. While simple point-source pollution problems can be tackled by technological solutions, not all environmental problems can be dismissed by assuming that technical fixes will become available. On the one hand, investments are needed in Asian science, technology and innovation systems to generate effective technology. On the other hand, the underlying causes of many broader-scale environmental problems arise primarily from the political, economic and social systems that drive existing production and consumption patterns. For example, many natural assets - fisheries, minerals, forests, and aquifers - are both finite and of key importance, but they are effectively 'unowned', unvalued, and/or unmarketed.

Valuable natural resources are too easily seized by elites and contribute little to the national economy. Institutional change is thus at least as important as technological change (WRI 2005). Institutional change, to enable environmental management for pro-poor growth, has begun but may need scaling up. Progress has often been the result of changes in who controls the allocation and use of environmental assets, as well as better incorporation of environmental norms and incentives in mainstream institutions. It is remarkable how many institutional innovations have begun in Asia.

But there is scope for further governance and institutional changes to:

- improve poor people's access and rights to natural resources
- develop information, analysis and political capabilities to challenge those sectors that affect the environment most, including watchdogs
- empower poor people and local organisations to lead action on the ground
- form institutions and partnerships that link development and environment more closely - in debate, in planning, in accounting, and in investment.

Investment in environmental management is good for economic growth, good for quality of life, and good for the quality of the global commons. 'Investments into renewables and energy efficiency technologies are the best hedge against the economic risks of rising oil prices and declining reserves', says the Chief Executive of the Chinese investment banking specialists, London Asia Capital. As well as reducing risk, environmental investments can produce high rates of return. An extensive global review has revealed some very persuasive figures. In Thailand, more than 600 firms participating in an eco-efficiency investment programme achieved an aggregate 47 per cent rate of return.

In China, one of the world's largest land management investments, in the Loess Plateau, has improved the livelihoods of over 1.2 million farmers: combined with other initiatives, numbers living under the poverty line have halved from 59 per cent in 1993 to 27 per cent in 2001. There is scope for increased public investment on environmental management. The Chinese Government's environmental investment is set to increase from 1.3 per cent during 2001-2005 (based on China's Tenth Five-Year Plan: 2001-2005), to 1.5 per cent (based on China's Eleventh Five-Year Plan: 2006-2010). In most other countries, though, public investment in the environment remains low, at 0.3 per cent of GDP in Indonesia, Malaysia, Philippines, Thailand, Malaysia and Vietnam.

The private sector wills under-supply environmental services unless market and regulatory incentives are compelling. Investment by the public sector is often important for leveraging much larger private investment. For example China's State Environmental Protection Agency has only 300 full time staff members, but without their effective strengthening and enforcement - including means to value environmental assets and allocate appropriate funds - the private sector will be slow to invest in clean technology. Private sector environment investment requires an enabling context. There is a growing body of experience on introducing environmental fiscal reform (to reduce overuse of scarce, inefficiently priced resources, such as water) and payments for environmental services (to reward those who protect, e.g. biodiversity and watersheds). In essence, environmental 'bads' can be taxed and environmental 'goods' supported, especially where they are pro-poor. Transaction costs can be reduced to help small and medium enterprises are to benefit from environmental markets.

Micro-credit can help, enabling poor households to bear the risks of investing in environmental assets. International partnerships can provide important support to Asian countries' management of the environment for pro- poor growth. Many Asian countries are taking a lead in improving management of environmental assets, as we have described above. Their development partners can also play a key role. Development assistance to Asia could help 'mainstream' environment within partner governments' poverty reduction strategies or equivalent national and local planning processes, budget support, sector-wide programmes and projects.

Specific initiatives could be supported that help improve the capacity of Asian authorities to manage the environment. Together, Asian countries and development partners can share technology and knowledge, catalyse environmental investment, and forge institutional change in a number of priority areas. There are knowledge challenges in all the following suggested partnerships. Asian scientists and their colleagues from other regions need to play a key role in them, particularly to invigorate regional and national innovation systems.

There are also institutional and investment challenges - and it is important for them to build on existing Asian-led processes:

- Healthy Asia, healthy environment: Environmental health improvements in air and water pollution can lead to major reductions in mortality. Improvements in water quality and quantity also lead to significant health benefits. There is a number of promising public- private partnerships across the region to increase access to clean water and air.
- Transition to sustainable energy, and tackling climate change: A meaningful post-Kyoto regime is now within reach to limit the causes and effects of climate change. Global carbon trade needs to develop in ways that support investment in clean energy (through, e.g. the Clean Development Mechanism as well as bilateral arrangements). There are good potentials for partnerships within the region on clean energy, e.g. hydropower from Nepal and Bhutan, which could also form the hub of regional energy strategies - but these would have to be planned to minimize environmental risks. There is a strong need for partnerships to improve learning, innovation and investment in adapting to climate change. The G8

Gleneagles Plan of Action highlighted many such areas for partnership, and energy will be the theme of the next G8 assembly.

- Sustainable forestry and eradicating illegal logging: illegal logging costs countries billions of dollars in lost revenue, and harms poor people. The Asian Forest Law Enforcement and Governance initiative (AFLEG) addresses supply- and demand-side incentives for illegal logging, and assures wood is traded from legal sources alone. This process serves as a high-profile means to encourage radical institutional change. It may be usefully supplemented with efforts to encourage Asian consumers to discriminate in favour of good environmental practice, and fair trade, through certification.
- Sustainable fishing: Given the importance of both fish production and fish consumption in Asia, improved management is vital. One innovative approach is fisheries certification which is now beginning - but only covers 4 per cent of the world's catch. Without such approaches, the long-term future of Asia's fish producers is threatened.
- Asian rivers management: Trans-boundary rivers pose a major challenge: they are critical assets for growth in the countries that share them, but without effective cooperation, the environmental services they offer will be undermined. Where means for cooperation are secured such as in the Indus River Treaty and Mekong River Commission, they provide a powerful vehicle for larger regional cooperation. There is scope to strengthen work in these established forums, and to extend such approaches to other basins in the region.
- Greening Asia's financial markets and private sector: Asia's private sector is booming and interest in environmental management is growing. This can be stimulated through the commercial and investment banking sectors, export markets and private sector accreditation. OECD markets are vital for Asian

exports and can provide important incentives for environmental improvements.

- Disaster preparedness and risk reduction: The deaths of over 70,000 in the South Asian earthquake and of over 280,000 in the tsunami have brought home once again the vulnerability of Asia to disasters. Two things stand out: typically, it is the poor who suffer most and, with climate change, the risk of extreme weather events is increasing. Disaster preparedness requires strengthening the existing coping strategies of the poor combined with good information systems and appro-priate technical, financial and physical support. The response to the 2004 Asian Tsunami and 2005 South Asia Earthquake illustrated the strengths of (as well as the challenges of managing) multiple national-international partnerships, including with the UN and the military.
- Pro-poor conservation: Since Asia has already invested over 7 per cent of its land in protected areas, there is an urgent need to both demonstrate and secure their potential contributions to pro-poor growth. One approach is for development partners to capitalize local environmental conservation and nature tourism funds that can trigger larger environmental investments.

Forests under Attack

Management of forest ecosystems has always been one of the most difficult challenges presented to humans. During the agricultural revolution, societies inhabiting forest areas in Europe, the Middle East, and other parts of the world started clearing trees to prepare land for crop production. In Roman times, hundreds of thousands of square kilometres of Mediterranean forests with their deep and fertile soils were eliminated to make way for cereal crops, such as wheat and barley. In Sudanese Africa, during the first centuries of the Christian era, a considerable portion of forest gave way to locally domesticated sorghum and millet crops and itinerant cattle-raising. In America, many of the forests surrounding the valley of Mexico were gradually removed to make room for corn and bean farms. In Asia, rice paddies replaced the extensive forests of China, Indochina, and some of the largest Indonesian islands.

Despite this worldwide reduction in area, at the time of the industrial revolution forests still occupied nearly 30% of the continental landmass, typically concentrated in humid and sub humid areas. In the 1600s, more than half of Europe and more than 90% of the humid regions of North and South America were covered by trees. In Africa, although long-term human habitation had significantly reduced forest areas (mainly through burning), resulting in "savannization," large tracts of land in humid and sub humid regions remained covered by forests. In Europe, the industrial revolution brought about systematic and intense degradation of the forests.

The main causes were the increase in population and the burning of firewood by industries and individuals. During the 18th and 19th centuries, new villages were established in less productive environments, such as steep and stony slopes in the cooler mountain highlands of the Alps, the Massif Central of France, and the Apennines in Italy; these areas were slowly converted to agricultural production, significantly reducing the forest cover. In many areas of Europe, population growth outpaced the opening of new farmland. Often, this was simply because land was not available. In many cases, however, it was due to a concentration of land ownership in the hands of a few people. At the beginning of the industrial revolution, most of the surplus rural population had moved to cities to work in the new industries. Howlver, European industries soon proved insufficient to absorb all the migrants. This prompted the migration to America, which by the end of the 19th century and the first half of the 20th century became intensive.

In North America, the arrival of millions of Europeans meant the opening of new forestlands for farming. New

England was completely covered by forests in 1620 and largely deforested 150 years later. In the 18th century, more than 4 million hectares of Arkansas marsh and swamp forests were converted to farmland. Between 1848 and 1858, Minnesota's population, next to the Canadian border, increased from 10 to 150 thousand (it was promoted from a territory to a state at this time). A similar situation occurred in the 1870s in the territory of Dakota (*National Geographic* 1986). By the late 1870s, more than half the temperate forests of North America had been eliminated, and the process continued for many decades. Because land had become scarce in the east, most new arrivals and many older settlers or their descendants moved west, clearing new land for agriculture.

In South America, most forested areas were in the tropics, particularly in the Amazon basin and the upper basins of the Parana and Orinoco rivers. Early deforestation of tropical ecosystems occurred during the colonization period along the north-eastern coast of Brazil to make way for sugarcane plantations and, later, by the end of the 19th century, around Sao Paulo for coffee production. The deforestation of mountain areas, which had begun in pre- colonial times, continued after European colonization, reducing forested areas to only the steeper or cooler slopes by the end of the 19th century.

Well into the 20th century, however, a considerable portion of the continent's extensive tropical forests remained virtually untouched. This delay in deforestation was probably due to the abundance of grasslands in the more productive temperate areas (the pampas). The only forested areas in temperate climates were on the slopes and narrow plains along the Pacific coast in central and southern Chile and in the highlands of the Plana 1 to of southern Brazil.

Deforestation in the 20th Century

In this century, deforestation processes in Latin America have proceeded at a much faster rate. By the 1970s, most of the *Araucaria* forests of the Planalto in Brazil and the forests of the western foothills of the Amazon basin from Colombia to Bolivia had been partially or totally eliminated. More recently, new forest areas have been logged or burned in eastern Paraguay, Mato Grosso in Brazil, and Santa Cruz in Bolivia to make room for cattle and soybean and rice plantations. For the last decade, deforestation in the Brazilian Amazon region has been occurring at the rate of about 21 thousand square kilometres every year, bringing the total area cleared to more than half a million square kilometres in the last two centuries.

In Africa, deforestation activity was widespread, particularly along the Guinean coast, to make way for peanut, cocoa, coconut, and banana plantations. Other areas affected included the central highlands (from Rwanda and Burundi to Uganda) and the tropical forests of south-central Africa from Angola to southern Tanzania. Today, African rain forests are greatly reduced to less than 1 million square kilometres, barely 4% of the total area of the continent and less than 20% of their original area.

In Mali, the use of wood for firewood, charcoal, and construction has resulted in deforestation. Annual wood use in this region is estimated at about 300 kilograms per person (360 kilograms in urban areas and 270 kilograms in rural areas) for a total of 1.7 million tonnes per year. Of this amount, more than 200 thousand tonnes per year are used in the Bamako metropolitan area, which has resulted in the forest retreating toward the southern part of the country. In the Mopti region, the burning of wood to smoke fish is also contributing to rapid deforestation and environmental degradation. Although some reforestation projects have been carried out (often giving priority to exotic instead of more appropriate indigenous trees), the general trend has clearly been toward deforestation. In Sudan, more than 48 million cubic metres of wood is cut every year for charcoal production or for use as fuel.

Deforestation has also been intense in southern and

Southeast Asia. The trend has accelerated during the last few decades, particularly in Indonesia and Malaysia, where large, previously untouched areas of Sumatra, Borneo, New Guinea, and the Malaccan Peninsula have suffered extensive forest degradation. The increasing demand for timber during the first half of the 20th century was met by a resource base mainly composed of natural or semi-natural forests. During this period, the value of a forest was related to its logging potential. Over the last few decades, however, new potential values of forests have been emphasized: as eco-tourist resources, as sources of biodiversity, etc. This change in attitude has promoted a different approach to forest management and exploitation.

Native people in Canada and the United States, who are reluctant to allow logging on their traditional lands, have found important allies in many environmental groups. Pro-logging lobbies are losing their influence, and exploitation of temperate forests in North America and Scandinavia is becoming more difficult. Besides being "politically incorrect," logging in the North is also becoming uneconomic. In temperate climates, trees grow very slowly. In many areas downwind of industrial centres, wood stands are being affected by acid rain, further complicating things for forestry companies in the northern countries. Profitability among Canadian lumber companies decreased substantially from 1990 to 1993.

The growth of a strong paper-recycling industry is also affecting the forest business, accelerating this trend. These tendencies have resulted in a decrease in the production of timber and paper pulp from northern forests and a substitution of material from more competitive artificial plantations in warmer latitudes, such as the southern United States, Brazil, Chile, and Argentina.

In many Third World countries, natural forests have also been beset by continuous logging, without allowing Time for regeneration. As a result, the amount of material coming from natural tropical forests in these areas has also decreased. In some cases, new artificial forests were planted in place of the natural forests (southern Chile and Misiones in Argentina). In most cases, the newly planted areas are mono specific plantations of exotic trees. In some areas, cleared land has been converted to agriculture or animal production.

Globalization processes are promoting the gradual substitution of natural forests by artificial systems. The redistribution of economic roles is having an effect on the forestry industry at all levels. Some countries that were traditional producers are withdrawing from the international scene, while others that have not been producers are increasing their exports. These trends are taking place at a time when the demand for timber and paper pulp is increasing worldwide. In spite of this, increased production — from 2.7 billion cubic metres in 1977 to 3.4 billion in 1988 — has been sufficient to meet the demand. Particularly important was the increase in paper pulp production (about 30% for the same period), which appears to be related to the increasing worldwide consumption of paper promoted by the information revolution. Wood and charcoal production increased 33% between 1977 and 1988.

Rain-forest Environments

Tropical rain forests are located in areas where steady high temperatures and an abundance of water allow continuous growth of vegetation. Tropical rain forests grow year-round. Average daily temperatures remain between 20° and about 30°C and water shortages are infrequent. In addition, solar radiation is high, further favouring photosynthesis and associated biological processes. These environments are characterized by multilayered vegetation reaching maximum heights of 40 to 60 metres. Nutrients are mainly stored in living biomass, rather than in the soil. Because of this, when vegetation is removed, the chances of the system recovering to its former state are limited.

In addition, microclimatic changes — such as decreasing humidity, increasing temperature, and wind variations —

can produce dramatic effects and make germination or regeneration of most native plant species difficult or impossible. Soil erosion which is negligible under forest cover, increases radically when vegetation is removed. This further reduces the potential of the ecosystem to recover. In brief, these modifications — loss of nutrients, deterioration of air and soil microclimates, and soil erosion — bring about a complete change of the whole ecosystem. When such a change occurs in a 1- or 2-hectare plot, the system may recover. However, when the deforested area measures tens or hundreds of square kilometres, the process may be irreversible.

African Forests

In Africa, forests are mainly removed for two reasons: they are cleared for new farmlands and they are cut for lumber and firewood. When old-growth forests are eliminated, productivity of the soil decreases because of nutrient losses. In most cases, the decrease in fertility is so great that even applying fertilizers does not result in competitive agricultural activity. For poor farmers, fertilizers are unaffordable, except in rare cases where natural fertilizers or phosphate rock are available locally. Often, the only practical way to increase production is to clear more forest area for cultivation.

In earlier times, shifting cultivation from one small plot to another allowed the ecosystem to recuperate. With increasing population density and encroachment of commercial plantations, however, recuperation has become impossible, and the forest ecosystem disappears completely, with the consequent loss of bio- and cultural diversity and water resources. Such pressures are causing African forests to retreat at a sustained rate. In the 20th century, the main culprits have been commercial crops, such as bananas, oil palms, rubber, and cocoa.

In Nigeria, oil palm plantations have replaced forests over large areas, particularly in the eastern regions of the country. Coupled with the rapid growth and concentration of the population, this has left little forest remaining. In Cote d'lvoire, about half a million hectares of forest are cleared annually to make room for cocoa, coffee, and other food products. From an area of 14 million hectares in 1956, the forest had been reduced to less than 5 million hectares 30 years later. The export of commercial crops and lumber explains the relative success of the country's economy in the short term; however, its unsustainability is evident.

Southeast Asian Rain Forests

In Southeast Asia, the originally extensive rain forests have been greatly reduced. In Burma, Indochina, and Thailand, forests have been replaced by farms and plantations. The forests of the more densely populated Indonesian islands (Java, Madura, Lombok, and Bali) have been logged or burned to the point where there are few remaining relics. As a result of deforestation on fragile soils, erosion has become a serious and widespread problem. In Java, annual erosion rates ranging from 10 to 40 tonnes per hectare have been reported. Recently, the drive toward deforestation has affected some areas that had remained untouched in Peninsular Malaysia, Sumatra, Mindanao (Philippines), and other less-populated islands of the region.

Large tracts of forest can still be found in Borneo (Kalimantan), New Guinea, and Celebes (Sulawesi). The Indonesian government attempted to promote settlement on these islands to alleviate the problems associated with the extremely high population density in Java (nearly 900 people per square kilometre). The initiative produced mixed results. To some degree, it relieved the population pressure in Java (although only temporarily). At the local level, however, the effect was disastrous. Large areas of rain forest were destroyed and the native people on the islands were displaced from their land. Javanese are alien to New Guinea and Borneo; the traditional cultures of these two large islands have been profoundly affected, and the process still continues.

The situation on Borneo is particularly complex. It belongs to three countries: unevenly populated Indonesia, a large multi-island country; oil-producing Brunei, which is small, rich, and densely populated; and the Malaysian states of Sarawak and Sabah. Deforestation and the annihilation of wildlife are still going on at a fast rate in the Indonesian part of Borneo, where settlement strategies have compiled a very poor record. In Malaysia, until recently, authorities were not concerned with the preservation of the natural rain forests. In 1991, a Malaysian minister was quoted as saying: "It is not our business to supply the West with oxygen" (*Economist* 1993c).

This attitude has changed somewhat. In October 1993, however, a major business deal was announced by a large company (owned by the Minister for Environment and Tourism) that involved a logging concession on 200 thousand hectares of rain forest, along with a coal mine and other components. Sarawak forests produce 80% of Malaysia's timber-related products, and Malaysian environmentalists predict that Borneo's rain forests will disappear in 20 years. In other areas — for example, the Philippines, Thailand, and Sabah (on Borneo) — some tracts of rain forest are being conserved and the export of timber has been halted. Deforestation continues, but at a slower rate, mainly as a result of agricultural encroachment.

Until recently, the effects of deforestation were less pronounced in the eastern half of New Guinea (part of the republic of Papua New Guinea) and nearby islands (the Solomon Islands). In the last few years, however, the tropical hardwood timbers of these areas have been stripped beyond the level of sustainability. Francis Tilly, Prime Minister of the Solomon Islands, foresees the disappearance of all commercial timber from the islands in 15 years if this rate of deforestation continues. According to the *Economist* (1994a), landowners can get as little as $2.70 per cubic metre for their timber. The foreign buyer, however, can then sell this timber for as much as $350 per cubic metre! In the

Solomon Islands and Papua New Guinea, most foreign logging companies are of Malaysian origin, escaping the increasingly tight controls on logging in their own country.

The Amazon Rain Forest

The quest for rubber, mainly after 1840, was one of the main factors in the settlement of the Amazon. In 1844, only 367 tonnes of rubber was exported from the region; in 1851, exports had increased to 1 391 tonnes and by 1910 to 42 000 tonnes. During this period, 600 to 700 thousand new settlers immigrated to the Amazon region as a direct or indirect result of the establishment of the plantations. The total population of the area, which was about 137 thousand in 1820, increased to 323 thousand in 1870 and to more than 1.2 million by 1910. During this century, settlement of the Amazon has accelerated, mainly as a result of government policies promoting agriculture, cattle- raising, and logging in the region and bolstering a legal system that clearly favoured forest-clearing.

A key element in this system was land allocation based on the concept of "squatter's rights"; title was awarded to whoever could demonstrate occupation of the land for a given period. Because occupation could be demonstrated by partial or total deforestation of the land to be claimed, systematic and widespread clearing of land for cultivation or speculation ensued. Later, particularly after the discovery of the Serra Pelada gold deposits, mining activities developed, resulting in widespread degradation of the natural landscape and water resources. Gold was mined in open quarries, in mines, and in alluvial placers throughout the region, such as Mato Grosso and the Madeira River. Simultaneously, a number of other large-scale mining concerns, such as the iron and tin mines of Carajas, gradually spread throughout the region.

Another factor in the loss of forest habitat relates to the construction of large hydroelectric complexes, such as the Tucurui dam on the Tocantins River (with a flooded area of about 2 thousand square kilometres), the Samuel dam in Rondonia, and others. Satellite images show that 410 thousand square kilometres of forest was cleared between 1978 and 1988. This amounts to almost 10% of the whole area, reducing total forest cover to slightly more than 4.5 million square kilometres. Of the approximately 425 thousand square kilometres of the Amazon that was cleared by the early 1990s, about three-quarters was eliminated in the last two decades. At the same time, the Colombian Amazon forest (with a total area of about 280 thousand square kilometres) had been reduced by 7% to 260 thousand square kilometres, and the forests of the Peruvian Amazon had shrunk by about 60 thousand square kilometres.

Recent news from the Amazon region reveals a slowing of the deforestation process. In 1990, "only" 14 thousand square kilometres was cleared, compared with almost 20 thousand in 1989 and about 27 thousand square kilometres in 1988. In Ecuador, the main problems resulted from petroleum exploitation. Frequent spills in the Ecuadorean oil fields have had a critical effect on the environment. One of the largest spills took place in the region of La Joya de los Sachas, affecting the Napo River basin. Similar spills are frequent in Colombia, where the main oil pipelines are frequently attacked by guerrilla forces.

Significant effects of deforestation have been described by Salati and Nobre (1991) based on an empirical model developed by Shuttleworth (1988). From September 1983 to September 1985, about 10% of the rainfall in the study area of Salati and Nobre was intercepted by the forest canopy, accounting for 20 to 25% of the evaporation. The remainder of the water being returned to the air moved through the trees by transpiration. Over the same period, about half of the incoming precipitation returned to the atmosphere as evaporation, a process requiring 90% of the energy input. Of net radiation, 75% went into evaporating water and the remaining 25% was used to heat the air.

It is estimated that 50 to 60% of the rainfall in. the

region originates from the recirculated water vapour that arises through evapotranspiration. Thus, a reduction in the forest cover will decrease precipitation, perhaps up to one-half or more throughout the Amazon and in downwind regions, such as the Bolivian altiplano and the eastern slopes of the Andes. Palaeogeographic studies show that less-humid periods were relatively common during the Quaternary period in the Amazon region. Colinvaux (1989) thinks that these changes were one of the causes of the high level of biodiversity in the area and that they coincided approximately with the glacial period:

The contemporary reality is that much of the Amazon basin will be turned into pasture as people clear the land for cattle grazing. . . . History does suggest that parts of the Amazon can be exploited productively without causing mass extinction, but wise use must be the overriding theme.

Despite the modifications that the area suffered in previous eras, for the last few thousand years the core of the great forest has remained largely unchanged despite demonstrated human occupation. The production systems developed during that time did not bring about the general degradation that is occurring now in newly settled areas. It is generally accepted that indigenous production systems are sustainable over the long term. Although we are not certain what the forest was like before human occupation, we do know that the current forest ecosystem is the result of indigenous management for several millennia.

That management system was based on a careful slash-and-burn technique, where small patches of forest was cleared for planting, used for 3 or 4 years, and then abandoned, allowing the selective growth of new plants. Other areas were preserved as sources of medicinal plants, for example, or simply left alone. Under these management strategies, some areas of the forest were used without affecting their potential, and the rest of the ecosystem was protected, resulting in long-term conservation of local environments. In that way, people took advantage of the enormous diversity of the jungle; rather than attempting to obtain maximum immediate return, they ensured the optimum long-term benefits.

Temperate Forests

Despite a long history of deforestation, temperate forests still occupy a vast area: 1 933 million hectares, compared with the 1 700 million hectares of tropical forests that remains today. More than 80% of the world's remaining temperate forest is found in North America and Eurasia. Most temperate forests are managed using interventionist strategies. Some are managed reasonably well, maintaining many components of the original ecosystems. In others, the indigenous ecosystem has been completely replaced with "artificial" (often exotic) plantations. Exploitation of temperate forests for lumber and other resources has led not only to a decrease in forested areas but also to a loss of biodiversity.

In many cases, inappropriate management has produced negative effects on the living systems and on the supporting environment, such as substantial changes in the structure of the forest, a decrease in the number of species, and damage to wild fauna. In tree plantations, the negative effects are even greater because these "artificial ecosystems" are normally mono-specific. In southern Chile, for example, the indigenous temperate forests were rich and diverse. Traditionally, they were used by the Mapuche and other local populations.

Today, however, they are being supplanted by exotic mono-specific plantations of trees grown for export (such as *Pinus insigne).* The negative environmental effects and the loss of diversity (both biological and cultural) that this practice is producing are becoming widely recognized. Although temperate forests still cover large areas, their actual value has been reduced because of diminished diversity and other ecological changes. The continued use of forests in cool climates has recently become less economic because of their slow growth and increasing opposition from environmentalist groups (particularly in North America).

Soybeans and Deforestation

Health-conscious people of the developed countries have discovered a food staple that is the "remedy to all ills" — soybeans. Rich in protein and low in cholesterol, they have become the diet supplement of the 1990s for those who want to decrease their risk of cancer and heart disease. The soybean plant is native to East Asia. It was domesticated by the Chinese about 4 thousand years ago and has become a component of the diet of people in most East Asian countries. Per-capita consumption has traditionally been high in China, Indonesia, Japan, Korea, Myanmar, and Thailand, probably one of the reasons for the low rates of heart disease and cancer in this region.

Western countries have known about and consumed soybeans since the time of Marco Polo, but only recently has this staple become important in the diet of their populations. In the 1980s, the increase in soybean use was particularly dramatic as a result of its growing popularity as an animal feed. In the United States, soybean use doubled, and similar trends were observed in Canada and several countries of the European Community (in the Netherlands, for example, soybeans are widely used as pig feed).

World production has followed the trend, growing substantially in the last few years. In the United States, production of soybeans increased from 1.1 to 1.9 million bushels between 1970 and 1987. Some increase in production also occurred in Europe and Asia; however, most of the increased demand has been met by clearing forestland for soybean production in South America. Argentina and Brazil are the largest producers of soybeans on the continent; Bolivia and Paraguay have also substantially increased production recently. Other South American countries are important suppliers, but produce smaller volumes.

The crop — For higher productivity, soybeans require

well-drained, highly fertile soils; high temperatures; and abundant rainfall. The most appropriate soils for soybean production are sandy and salty tropical soils in humid areas that are not subject to regular flooding. The best results are obtained if soybeans are planted immediately after deforestation. For this reason, soybean producers have identified the large forest regions of South America as the best places for their farms. Normally, trees are cut and sold and the stumps removed using heavy machinery. After other vegetation is cleared away, plots are prepared for soybean cultivation. Often, soybeans are planted in combination with other crops on a semi-annual rotation.

Tine crop normally associated with soybeans is wheat. The additional demand on the soil resulting from multi cropping increases the rate at which some key nutrients (potassium and phosphorus) are depleted, although because soybean is a leguminous vegetable which replenishes nitrogen in the soil. Tropical soils can sustain soybeans and associated crops for 3 or 4 years before their fertility is affected. Once the level of key nutrients decreases, productivity and yields also decrease and fertilizers must be applied. Because using fertilizer increases costs and reduces competitiveness and earnings, soybean farming companies and entrepreneurs often prefers to clear new, inexpensive forestland.

This practice has resulted in systematic clearing of the tropical rain forest throughout the Ma to Grosso-Santa Cruz-Paraguay region. Tropical soybean production areas extend throughout central and south-eastern Brazil, eastern Bolivia, and Paraguay, in addition to temperate regions in Argentina, Uruguay, and the Brazilian state of Rio Grande do Sul. As of the mid-1990s, soybeans are the most important item in the commercial agricultural economy of South America.

Effects on Forest Soils

Soybean farming in tropical soils causes much damage.

Forest cover is eliminated, the soil remains bare or poorly protected for most of the year, erosion becomes widespread, rills and gullies develop, and gradually soil fertility is lost along with much of the soil itself. For this reason, the continued use of tropical soils requires heavy applications of fertilizer; when this is not possible, the land is used to raise cattle or is abandoned. Soybean crops are affected by a large number of plagues. Among the insects that attack the plant are *Auticassia gemmatalis, Rachiplusia mu, Pseudoplisin includens, N czar a viridida, Peizodums guildinii, Euschistus hews,* and others at a more local level. In addition, soybeans are attacked by numerous nematodes, fungi, bacteria, and viruses. The crops are also frequently invaded by several local and exotic weeds, reducing productivity levels.

To keep the crops healthy, farmers apply large volumes of agrochemicals to combat weeds, insects, and other pests.

Some of these chemicals find their wav into natural water systems, causing serious contamination not only in local streams but in swamplands as well. As a result, soybean cultivation is degrading local ecosystems, and its expansion can only be explained by a lack of concern at political and local levels about the long-term integrity of these systems. The e;rowth of soybean cultivation in South America has continued unabated for some time. Since the late 1970s, it has been the main crop in the upper Paraguay basin. In 1985, total production in Mato Grosso was 1.7 million tonnes and in Mato Grosso do Sul, 2.6 million tonnes. This represented over 20% of total Brazilian production or almost 5% of world production. If Bolivian and Paraguayan production are included, the total volume for the basin was about 6 million tonnes in 1985 (7% of world production).

During the last decade, expansion continued. In 1993-1994, annual production was 4.8 million tonnes for Mato Grosso (almost three times what it was 9 years earlier) and 2.3 million tonnes in Mato Grosso do Sul. Almost 10% of the current world supply of soybeans comes from the upper Paraguay basin, where the total area planted is about 3.5 million hectares and crop yields are about 2 tonnes per hectare.

Effects on Rivers

The radical change in vegetation cover over such a vast region is influencing the hydrologic regime in rivers downstream. The principal rivers affected are the upper tributaries of the Paraguay (the Taquari and Cuaiaba rivers) and Parana (the Iguazu, Grande, Paranapanema, and Tiete rivers) and, to a lesser extent, some Amazon tributaries flowing from the south (such as the Xingu and Tapajoz rivers). The main effects of deforestation have been increased runoff, higher flood peaks, soil erosion, larger amounts of suspended sediments in the water, rapid silting of dams, longer droughts, and generally more irregular flows in rivers throughout the year. However, a hydrologic feature of the region tends to even out these irregular flows — the Gran Pantanal wetland.

Gran Pantanal

Gran Pantanal is a large region of swamps and marshland in south-western Mato Grosso, Brazil. Extending for about 160 kilometres along the east bank of the upper Paraguay River, it resembles an interior delta formed as a result of Quaternary and pre-Quaternary sedimentation in a slowly sinking basin located to the west of the Gondwanic basalts and sandstones of Mesozoic and Cenozoic age (such as the Botucatu sandstones) and the Brazilian Shield.

Rivers descending from the north and east arrive at the plain and produce enormous alluvial fans that obstruct the development of river valleys. This causes the formation of a characteristic meandering pattern as the riverbeds frequently change direction, leaving abandoned crescent-shaped lakes. The landscape is dotted with hundreds of lakes where aquatic organisms, waterfowl, and many other species flourish. Several well-defined rivers can also be identified, such as the Paraguay (the main river) and the Cuiaba, Taquari, Miranda, and Aquidabuana.

Before occupation by Europeans and criollos, the region mainly consisted of humid forest in the lowlands and *cerrado* in the neighbouring highlands. The ecosystems are intermediate between the Atlantic forest and the Amazon rain forest. -*Cerrado* (the Spanish word for closed) is also a type of forest with a lower canopy and a bushier, grassier undergrowth. There is no sharp boundary between the *cerrado* and the humid forest; a gradual transition can be observed almost everywhere. The level of biodiversity in the region was (and to a large extent still is) high; it includes tens of thousands of plant species, hundreds of thousands of invertebrates, and many fish, birds, and mammals.

As a result of this natural richness, the area was densely populated during pre-colonial times. Conservative estimates put the population of the Gran Pantanal basin at no fewer than 1 million. The arrival of the Europeans was traumatic. Spaniards came from the west (upper areas of Peru) and the south (Asuncion) and established religious missions in the Guaira region about 500 kilometres southeast of the Pantanal. Paulist slave traders (the *Bandeirantes)* reached the Guaira region by the end of the 17th century. They captured tens of thousands of indigenous people in the missions and villages and sold them to the owners of the sugarcane plantations of Pernambuco.

Despite the conquest and colonization efforts, however, both the regional ecosystem and portions of the local populations managed to survive until well into the 20th century. Most of the Pantanal remained in the Empire and later Republic of Brazil, some lies in Bolivia, and Paraguay retained only the small area of wetlands in the Gran Chaco and Neembucu. During the first half of the 20th century, activity centred around the Paraguay River, as *quebracho* wood was harvested for tannin and *yerba mate* plantations were established. In the 1960s and 1970s, criollo occupation increased following new Brazilian "development" policies that made new highways and roads a priority and encouraged uncontrolled colonization.

Tens of thousands of migrants (from Rio Grande do Sul and other areas of Brazil) moved to Mato Grosso, establishing ranches throughout the region. One common "style" of occupation was to clear the *cerrado* and forest, plant grasses, and introduce cattle. Deforestation was also carried out to prepare land for planting grains, mainly soybeans, rice, and com. Rice plantations were established every w'here, mainly to obtain funding from the government. According to local agronomists, the rice plantations were a means to obtain easy credits. The forest was logged and removed or burned to make room for dry rice farming. After 3 or 4 years, grass seeds were included in the rice and, after 4 to 6 years, a new artificial grassy ecosystem was established.

On more fertile soils, the forest was cleared for soybean farming. In the early 1990s, soybean agriculture occupied 5 to 10% of the land in the Pantanal basin, and soybeans are the main agricultural export of the Brazilian states of Mato Grosso and Mato Grosso do Sul. Soybean production is also important in Santa Cruz (Bolivia) and eastern Paraguay.

Deforestation took place quickly; by the early 1990s, extensive areas had been cleared. In Mato Grosso do Sul, for example, 80% of the forest is gone. In the Gran Pantanal, deforestation was delayed somewhat because of the swampy conditions. Gradually, however, local ranchers have encroached on the natural ecosystem by burning trees or using "agrotoxic" substances. Many thousands of hectares of forest and swamp have been destroyed to make room for raising cattle.

The effects of this environmental degradation are being felt throughout the Pantanal region. The ancient, clear rivers have become brownish, muddy streams. Channels are being filled by sand, fishing is uncontrolled, and poaching of local animals is widespread (often organized by the ranchers themselves). The few remaining indigenous people have been dispossessed of their land and reduced to a situation of misery and desperation.

Impact of Changes in the Gran Pantanal

The Pantanal is a huge natural-flow regulator. The plain covers 90 thousand square kilometres and receives water from rivers on the west, north, and east during the rainy season. Some of the water is lost to evaporation; the rest moves toward the southern outlet to form a free-flowing river (the Paraguay) several hundred kilometres to the south. The summer rainy season occurs in January and February, but the surplus flow of water in the Paraguay River is spread over the next 6 months because of the presence of the Pantanal.

Because of the Gran Pantanal, the peak flow period for the Alto Parana and the Paraguay rivers occurs at different times of the year: the Alto Parana reaches its maximum level in March and the Paraguay a few months later between June and August. Without the dampening effect of the Pantanal, flooding would occur at the same time in these rivers, causing disastrous flooding downstream of their confluence. During the rest of the year, river levels would be much lower, affecting navigation and the movement of merchandise to and from Rosario, Santa Fe, Parana, and all of Paraguay.

The sediment-loaded waters of the Bermejo and Pilcomayo rivers also affect the level of the Paraguay. These rivers arise in the highlands of Salta, Jujuy, and the Bolivian altiplano. Their peak flow period occurs in late summer or early fall. Without the Pantanal, this peak would coincide with a period of heavy flow in the Paraguay, with potentially catastrophic consequences up- and downstream from their confluence. In brief, widespread deforestation in the Paraguay River basin combined with drainage of the Pantanal wetlands would significantly increase the flow in this river in summer and early fall. It would result in a much larger sediment load throughout the basin, and flood peaks in the river and its tributaries would be simultaneous. The volume that could be expected has not been calculated, but it would probably be at least twice the current highest flow in the Paraguay River and slightly less than twice the highest flow in the middle Parana.

The Hidrovia Project

In the midst of ever-increasing damage to local ecosystems, a new regional integration project — Hidrovia — has been proposed. The aim of the project is to ensure that soybeans and beef, among other products, can be transported from the river ports of Mato Grosso and Bolivia (in Gran Pantanal and upstream) down to Buenos Aires in Argentina and Nueva Palmira in Uruguay for export. Today, the Pantanal can be navigated only by small boats and barges. Its river channels are already shallow and are filling with silt and sand. In fact, this situation created the swamp in the first place.

For commercial navigation to be feasible, deeper canals and complementary hydro works may have to be built. Digging canals in the swamp, however, will have an impact on both the geo- and ecosystem. An immediate effect will be an increase in water velocity in the channels and erosion of the banks and riverbed. This process will occur first downstream, moving gradually upstream and resulting in widespread drainage of the swamp. The drier soils will then be available for use as rangeland. The aquatic ecosystem will be disturbed by noise, turbulence, and contamination from the expected heavy barge traffic.

The project may require the movement of millions of tonnes of earth and sediment and the use of heavy equipment and numerous labourers. One can only guess at the destructive effects of this work on wildlife and the ecological equilibrium. However, an independent investigation must be carried out to ensure that all factors are taken into account before a decision about the project can be made. This need is widely recognized by university researchers, local nongovernmental organizations (NGOs), and some political groups and authorities.

Winter and spring flows, on the other hand, would be greatly reduced (probably several times lower throughout the basin), affecting navigation and the water supply of certain cities — this is already occurring in Cuiaba, Mato Grosso. Several waterworks have been built in the Parana basin. The most important was the Itaipu dam, downstream of the largest falls (in terms of flow volume) in the world — Sete Quedas Falls. This dam, which cost over $10 billion, was completed around 1982, forming a 2 thousand square kilometre lake and producing a significant quantity of hydroelectric power. Although the energy produced is to be shared equally by

Brazil and Paraguay, Paraguay uses only 5% of its share. The remaining 95% is sometimes purchased by Brazil or, lately, not used at all. Selling this energy to other countries is not permitted under the binational treaty. Despite the huge amount of unused energy generated by the Itaipu dam, the governments of Argentina and Paraguay decided to construct a new mega-dam at Yacyreta Island (about 300 kilometres downstream of Itaipu). The cost of this dam may be over $5 billion and it will contribute a significant amount of energy to the already enormous surpluses existing in the region.

More recently, plans are under way to create a "hidrovia" or "hydro-way" to ensure river navigability through a complex array of dams, drainage and navigation canals, docks, piers, and other harbour structures. The cost of the project might reach several billion dollars, adding to the considerable foreign debt of the countries along the Paraguay and Parana rivers. There is concern that these works may result in the virtual elimination of the Pantanal and that they will be useless, as canals remain dry for most of the year and flood catastrophically during peak flow periods.

The final result of these mega-plans may not be "development" or even "modernization," but the complete annihilation of some of the world's largest ecosystems, together with their associated traditional cultures. Some foresee a significant loss of opportunities, natural and human resources, and future financing possibilities for the countries and cities of the basin.

Indigenous People of the Upper Paraguay Basin

Despite aggressive occupation of their lands, attempts to eliminate or enslave them, migration, and acculturation, about 60 thousand indigenous people belonging to 15 nations have managed to survive in the Pantanal-upper Paraguay region. These people were evicted from their land in most of the *cerrado* regions of Ma to Grosso, remaining only in isolated areas with less-fertile, stony soils or on steep hillsides and in the swamplands of Gran Pantanal. Several groups are in danger of extinction.

The Guarani were Right

Before "science," humans knew many things. Traditional knowledge was not supported by a theoretical framework, but it was rich and diverse. Tribes understood their environment: vegetation, insects, mammals, birds. They knew which plants could be used as medicines and which were poisonous. Knowledge was site-specific. In most cases, it was difficult to apply elsewhere; but locally, it allowed many groups to sustain a quality of life that should not be undervalued.

Scientific knowledge accumulated slowly. In many ways, it was nourished by the traditional or "empirical" knowledge of local groups. After many generations, scientists are still looking to traditional societies for elements of knowledge. Some scientists, however, possessing the knowledge accumulated over generations, prefer to ignore the fact that traditional knowledge, in one way or another, provides the basic insights that allow continuing enrichment of the paths of science and technology. In the meantime, a huge body of knowledge about nature and its ways is being lost with the death of each shaman, wise man, and medicine woman.

Agronomists have failed in their attempt to increase production indefinitely with their "green revolution." Twenty years later, whole ecosystems have disappeared, taking with them species that were not even recorded. Hundreds of crop varieties have been wiped from the face of the Earth and erosion has become widespread. Although more food was produced for a period of time, our children and our children's children will not be able to grow crops in eroded soils. Monospecific, artificial ecosystems are vulnerable to plagues and require large quantities of pesticides that are contaminating water resources.

Dead fish, eroded soils, unique animals and plants eliminated — the technologists have failed. The Guarani knew how to clear a parcel of land; what, when, where, and how to plant; how to leave large areas untouched to conserve the medicines and to keep the spirits happy. The Guarani called them "spirits"; scientists call it "genetic biodiversity." Basically, it is the same thing. The Guarani were right. The Guarani people of Mato Grosso do Sul number about 30 thousand; they live on about 20 reserves, but the population is concentrated in small areas. During colonization, their religious leaders were ignored by the government and *capitaos* were appointed to govern them. The Cjuaranis resisted this move by continuing their rituals in secret and, later, by reviving some of their traditional systems of self-government (like communal assembly).

The difficult situation in Guarani communities is reflected in the rate of suicides among the young people (31 cases in 1990, 21 in 1991, and 21 in 1992), which is among the highest in the world. The Guato people build canoes. They live by fishing and farming the islands of the Paraguay River. Only a few hundred Guatos still exist and only a few of these remember their own language. The Guaycuru-

Kadiweu belong to an ancient, large, seminomadic nation that became horseback riders in the 17th century. They lost some of their land in Mato Grosso in the 1950s and were left with a reserve of just over 500 thousand hectares. There are currently fewer than 1 500 Kadiweus living on their ancestral lands and a few hundred living elsewhere.

The Terena, who are descendants of the Arawak, are among the largest groups of indigenous people, numbering about 20 thousand. They farm (rice, beans, manioc, and corn) and display a high level of acculturation. Like other indigenous groups, they have had difficulty retaining enough land for survival. Today, they are virtually landless and depend largely on low-paying jobs on local ranches. As in many other areas of the continent the situation of the indigenous people of Mato Grosso is critical and, in many cases, desperate.

A wealth of traditional knowledge is being lost every day, human rights are violated, and many indigenous people who are unable to visualize a future for themselves take their own lives. Along with nature's riches, Mato Grosso is losing its rich ethnic and cultural diversity and the knowledge necessary to ensure a more sustainable and just future.

Civilized Man and its Evolution

A legitimate conclusion to draw from all this is that as civilization and brain development have gone on hand in hand, the lower races which have not taken part in it are forever unfitted for it, though specialized enough to take up some few special employments as an intruder in civilization, they cannot carry on the advance by themselves. They are also barred out more effectually the sooner they escaped from the factory of brain. The Negro is a survival of men who migrated too soon and whenever he is left alone he invariably reverts to ancestral life as in Haiti. His colour and physique bar him from the best parts of this country where he quickly perishes, and the struggle in a civilized environment is causing such degeneration that he is producing a tremendous crop of degenerates in the south from bad food, bad habits and exposure. Crime, consumption and insanity increase and hasten the inevitable extinction. He is sure to become extinct and is not an exception to the rules of acclimatization as Shaler states.

The domestic animals are also mentioned as exceptions to the law of acclimatization by change of type, yet almost every one is wholly unadjusted to the climate where man takes it, and would promptly perish were it not protected from the climate. Others, such as dogs, surviving in every climate without protection, have actually changed in type like the bears. Eskimo dogs and polar bears are both killed by the heat, and tropical bears, as well as Mexican dogs, will die in the Arctic unless housed. Human parasites follow the same law and would die unless kept alive in an artificial environment independent of climate. No living thing will stand marked change of climate without change of type through destruction of unfit.

When Morel wrote his great epoch-making work on human degeneration prior to the publication of Darwin's and Wallace's theories, he undoubtedly opened a mine of enormous value, but, he w^Tas woefully wrong in considering the lower races as degenerate forms of the higher—a mis:ake following from the general conception of a primitive high type of man. This mistake still tinctures scientific as well as popular literature. The low'er races are smaller brained though absolutely normal, and perfectly adjusted to an environment deadly to a Frenchman. I can add my own slight experience to the effect that among the lower races I have found as little or less evidence of degeneration as among the higher. This condition of nervous instability is merely one of the natural methods of cleaning any race of its most unfit. The Chinese seem to lead with the greatest per cent of degenerates and the races on the north shores of the Mediterranean are a close second.

Does it not seem also that evolution of brain stopped

in Asia long ages before it did in Europe and that all Asiatics are jetsam of evolution? The only ones who went ahead were the restless ones who were forced into Europe from the teeming areas of the north of Asia —and who became the ancestors of the Celto-Slavic or Alpine stock who certainly have helped civilization as much as any other race, and who are part of the newest and most vigorous of moderns—Russia. Our New[r] York Indians are doing very well, as they had evolved a large brain and were really the prehistoric Aryans of the new world, yet they are not able to do anything towards the advance of civilization, though far in advance of the Peruvians and Aztecs. Some of them are living about as the lower Italians, both survivors of lower races in a civilization built up around them by brainier intruders.

Comparative theology has long shown the strict relation between the kind of religion and the kind of civilization, and it really should not be necessary to call attention to the fact that they both depend upon brain development nor to deny that religion causes civilization as Dr. Reid states ("The Present Evolution of Man"), and as the clergy have been in the habit of preaching for generations. If there is any relation it is the other way, for in mediaeval times theology has done the most to retard civilization. The further natural selection increases the brain the higher are the religious concepts. Mohammedanism is always found no higher than barbarism because that is the limit of the religious conception of people who have not brain enough to go beyond barbarism after their migration south, and it is absurd to say that it is a cause of their civilization. These people refuse to accept Christianity because they are incapable of understanding it, and if they could accept it, then, if that religion is the cause of civilization, they should at once become highly civilized, which we know the Christian Abyssinians have not done.

When Christianity arose it was too abstract and advanced for the mass of Jews and it had to travel north in search of brain. The Romans too could not understand it and they only accepted it as a political measure from outside influence from the north. Indeed races accepting Christianity invariably change it to accord with their own mental state, our own Negroes even mixing it with voodooism. Taylor has shown that in Europe ("Orig. of the Aryans") there is a close relation between race and religions, that Italy cannot become Protestant nor Scandinavia accept the southern form, and that religious wars have always been race wars and we know that the latter are always wars of expansion for more room. Thus there has been a regular and progressive evolution of religion going on side by side with the evolution of brain and civilization, and in a geometrical ratio like civilization, for at the present time the theology of our pulpits would have caused the burning at the stake of its believers only a few centuries ago. Even thirty years ago the clergy would have been scandalized by present sermons.

Instead of recognizing that brain, which had developed for the sole end of surviving natural adversities, had subsequently been devoted to another purpose —civilization — writers announce all sorts of causes of man's brain development. The long period of infancy is stated as a cause by John Fiske, but it is a result of an evolution having nothing to do with the brain. Mammals arose simply because by normal variations some animals were able to give a trifle of nourishment to their young, and this slight advantage was really a tremendous one in the end, for it was the determining cause for survival where others like the saurians, though highly specialized became extinct as soon as enemies increased. It followed that those giving nourishment and care longest were able to survive in spite of physical feebleness.

Hence the prolonging of infancy and pregnancy resulted ages before the brain developed to its maximum, and the earlier mammals were almost as brainless as the saurians. It is undoubtedly true that the more intelligent beings were able to look after their young the best and survived in larger numbers, but a long infancy by itself without other conditions of severity in the environment will not enlarge the brain any faster than it has done for the apes. Articulate speech has also been given as a cause of brain development, whereas we have shown that it is a very recent result of brain development. The erect posture freeing the anterior limbs for development into arms and hands, is very closely connected with brain development, for the two went on simultaneously, each the cause, as well as the effect, of the other, for one is impossible without the other. Brainier animals not having the best variations in arm and hand were not as favorably situated as those which happened to have both variations— slight increase of brain as well as slight increase of arm specialization.

Let us relegate to the scientific garret all those predictions of the future big-headed man with attenuated body and the wide hipped women with birth canals large enough for the children's heads. We need never be afraid of the narrow- hipped women dying out from inability to give birth to children. Future specialized brains will be small enough — they are small enough now, too small for their possessors' judgments to be trustworthy except in their narrow specialty and often not even in that. Nor need we be afraid of the future specialist being as limited as the idiot Blind Tom, such variations being always the result of degeneration and doomed to extinction. The fittest is and will be the specialist having sufficient intelligence besides to think over and utilize his special abilities to the greatest good. Such evolution cannot possibly be racial deterioration as Col. H. Elsdale asserts (*19th Cent.,* Aug.).

Far from deterioration, it is evidence of very high social evolution. Men who do not know that evolution means the survival of the fittest and not necessarily the survival of what they may consider the best, are apt to enlarge upon the forced survival, of the criminal, the feeble-minded and the specialist and claim that man upsets the laws of evolution. Man is unable to upset any law any more than he destroys the laws of gravitation by the invention of a balloon. He is just as much subject to evolution now as ever for "there is no truce to the struggle for existence." The evolution of the specialized small-brained man in civilization is never lawless but follows the law of the survival of the fittest—he is an item in that "change from a state of indefinite incoherent homogeneity to a state of definite heterogeneity" of the modern social body. He becomes an artist in the "harmonious orchestration of specialists."

Writers like John Fiske who think we have, through intelligence, escaped the influence of evolutionary laws, have wholly missed the essential idea of evolution. Instead of having escaped man seems now to be in a second stage of tremendously rapid evolution in the direction of specialization, an evolution more rapid even than that of the glacial times, for there is a marked change in the last 2000 years. It is another of Le Conte's "critical periods", separating eras. The glacial period separated long eras of anthropoids and man, and this new critical period separates Le Conte's "Psychozoic era" into two parts of era of savage man, and the future era of specialists. Civilization will change us but we will not be degenerated, anymore than frail hairless man is a degenerate gorilla.

In very many other respects man is now undergoing a most rapid evolution, but as it involves other characters than the brain we need only touch upon it. Men are always overcrowded for that is the basis of evolution, but the density of population is so great now that if we did not keep pace with it in our sanitary arrangements, to remove our own poisons, more than 9/1.0 of us would die. Thus in unsanitary 14th century England it is said that half of the four million people died of plague and one-fourth of the 100 millions in Europe. We are now eliminating those least immune to diseases of crowds such as consumption and typhoid, for these susceptibles are unfit for the environment. The most immune survive as the fittest, so that eventually all men will be immune to lung diseases like the Jews.

We will also be immune to typhoid, or the crowd diseases will no longer be fatal, just as mumps, measles, etc., have ceased to be fatal in infancy. W^Te need not follow it further, for it has been enlarged upon by Reid in "The Present Evolution of Man," it is only mentioned as further evidence that in other characteristics, as well as in brain, we are in a "critical period" of Le Conte, and undergoing a most tremendously rapid evolution. The cause of the last , "critical period," the glacial climate, is not a bit more powerful factor, than the changes in living brought about by the present critical period—recent civilization.

In a remarkable posthumous paper, Grant Allen rails against the British social system which preserves as parasites in the aristocracy, such inferior men and does its best to repress its best brains. He shows that there is great variation in all families and states that "all men are born free and unequal." This is a curious mixture of two axioms and is not true. It is an axiom of political life, that "all men are born free and equal"and this is true; but in their other relations it is only true of paleolithic savages, for it is a law that, *Civilized men are born dependent and unequal*

The Civilizing Mission

British Columbia may be said to have a standard comparable, at least in essential features, with the most highly developed social organization elsewhere. Its communal characteristics are not; it is needless to say, evolved from local and primitive conditions, but transplanted from the most highly civilized parts of the British Empire. . . With . . . churches, schools, lodges, social forms, old-time recreation - all re-established on former lines[—]it is often a surprise to newcomers, who have associated life in the "wild and woolly West" with bears, cowboys, Indians, bowie-knives and desparadoes [sic], to find that they are still far away from the danger of being eaten up by wild beasts, tomahawked and scalped, or shot at sight. They find a state of society almost identical with that which they left.

R. Edward Gosnell, Provincial Librarian and Archivist, and Secretary to the Premier of British Columbia, wrote the *Yearbook* as his part of the campaign to establish British Columbia as a place of note on the map of the still expanding British Empire. A well-known British Columbian, he was altogether a newspaperman, a civil servant, and founder of the Provincial Bureau of Information. He was also an historian, an ardent imperialist, and a founding member of Vancouver's premier amateur learned society, the Art, Historical and Scientific Association (AHSA). Like many others, he firmly believed that British Columbia's destiny lay as a greater Britain on the Pacific, where British arts and institutions will expand under fresh impetus, "where the British flag will forever fly".

This idea of a British destiny needs to be placed squarely into the geopolitical context of the 19th and early 20th centuries. For nearly four hundred years, Europeans had been colonizing huge parts of the world. By the mid 19th century, the British were pre-eminent among the imperia lists. British colonies were established in all regions, on all continents of the planet. British Columbia was one such colonial outpost. During this period, with its Manifest Destiny re- awakened, the United States also began to build its empire. By mid-century, it was expanding north and west. In 1846, the Americans annexed British territory to the south of modern British Columbia, down to the Columbia River in Oregon,

Later, in 1867, on the day after Canadian confederation, the United States purchased Alaska from the Russians. British Columbia found itself flanked by the United States on two sides. Moreover, in 1858 upwards of 20,000 prospectors had shipped out of San Francisco for the Cariboo gold fields, swamping the small non-aboriginal population of British settlers. Few of these prospectors were British. Aside from the colonial government, the Royal Navy in Victoria, the Royal Engineers in New Westminster, and a few British settlers, there was little to forestall eventual annexation. With British Columbia as the land bridge between the abundance of the new Alaskan frontier and a rapacious American empire to the south, the question at the time, in many minds, was, will - and can - British Columbia remain British?

Central to the imperialist project was the role of education, and particularly of adult education, in the process of colonization. Throughout the colonized world, a wonderful spectacle ... of learning, from arboretums to zoos ... were established under imperialism's patronage, it [being] not difficult to argue that the whole venture had about it something of a great public education project intent on bringing the world together under the roof of European learning. According to Willinsky, the intellectual interests of imperialism could be characterized as reflecting a particular 'will to know.' At its root was a desire to take hold of the world, and it was the equal, in its acquisitiveness, to any financial interest in empire.. .This will to know became an integral part of the economic and administrative apparatus of imperialism, and in the process I was too often dedicated to defining and extending the privileges of the West.

The imperialist agenda, according to Edward Said (1995), was about "power using knowledge to advance itself". Learning and education would serve in the Europeanization of the world.

Educated European and especially British immigrants, on foreign shores, would bring with them what Said (1978) has called their "imaginative geography" of the world. In that geography, Europe was the centre of civilization. The rest of the world, in contrast, was less civilized —or uncivilized; it was mysterious, barbarous and savage.

Arriving with their imaginative geography, and their dreams of economic gain, these immigrants came to civilize this alien world, this distant other. In the face of backwoods brutishness, despondency, and Canadian whisky, there was among them an educated contingent who came with their middle-class and upper-class tastes and sensibilities. They worked, often tirelessly, in the new colonial homes to reinstate the literary, athletic and scholarly pursuits of the "old country." In short, they tried to recreate best of "Home" in their new environment.

The competition between political, economic and cultural ideals has been captured by Cole (1996), Harris (1997), and MacDonald (1996) in their analyses of immigrant life in the early life of the province. British Columbia's rich yet rugged geography drew the vast majority of settlers, hell-bent on establishing themselves economically. Old world skills meant little; there was only limited agricultural land and there were few[r] factories. New yet more rudimentary skills were all that were necessary in the extraction and primary processing of timber, fish and ore. Home ties, including regional culture and class position, were difficult to maintain in a polyglot population. Capital was king, and labour was its consort.

Conflict - both labour and racial - was the norm. In contrast, in some special "Edenic" places in the province notably Victoria and the Saanich Peninsula, the Gulf Islands, and the Cowichan, Comox and Okanagan Valleys, British Columbia offered something akin to the setting and climate of Home, in the British Isles. Immigrants of more refined tastes and ideals found in these places, and in Vancouver, a more suitable environment in which to promote the high standards of British culture and civilization. Vancouver's place is especially important as it was here that capital and culture met.

My research focuses particularly on Vancouver. As the province's new metropolis, the situation in Vancouver echoed the competition of ideals found throughout the province. Born in the 1860s, of continental North American (as opposed to British) business interests, the nascent metropolis of the new Canadian province became the proving ground for the establishment of a civilization at the far edge of the British Empire. During the period until World War I, tens of thousands of newcomers streamed into the city, seeking adventure, prosperity, and new lives. The settlers were predominantly British (from the United Kingdom and from central and eastern Canada).

Many certainly came from the British middle classes that Gosnell had hoped to attract. The majority of residents, before the Great War, were male, although the numbers of women and families were increasing rapidly, pushing the demand for a more civilized environment. A few Americans also continued to migrate north into British Columbia, after the initial influx during the Cariboo gold rush. Several thousand Asians, particularly from China and Japan., added to the city's makeup, in addition to the aboriginal Coastal Salish inhabitants. In fact, the Asian and aboriginal inhabitants were set outside the city's social boundaries. For most European residents they were beyond the pale of civilization. They were "other."

Adult education in the early life of Vancouver and British Columbia took on a primary mission of cultivating British literary, aesthetic and scientific tastes and skills amongst the immigrant population. In the years before World War I, such adult education was primarily of the non formal variety, involving mutual learning in private associations and organizations. For example, in addition to the earliest literarv and mechanics' institutes, there were Gosnell's Art, Historical and Scientific Association (AHSA), the Burrard Literary Club, the Arts and Crafts Association, the Women's Musical Club, the Men's and the Women's Canadian Clubs, the Naturalists' Field Club, the British Columbia Mountaineering Club, and the YMCA and YWCA. With its lectures and conversaziones, and its public museum, the

AHSA was one of the earliest, and was the leading, of such organizations, in the development of Vancouver.

In the upheaval of transplanted lives, ideas were discussed, debated and tested in their new environment. Here, individuals in mutual association, worked to inform, indeed to form, the semblance of an aesthetic, historical, scientific, and civic culture in their new towns and cities. In some cases, "English for Foreigners" and job skills were taught as part of both cultural and Christian missionary work. Socially fragmented and isolated, far from home, these educational missionaries, these "devoted few" stood and advanced their beachhead of British civilization and culture. They worked together, through their intellectual, scientific and cultural organizations to make and to keep British Columbia British. This studv examines the values and interests that drove the formation of this variant of British civilization.

Culture, however valiant its mission, faced formidable foes. Indeed, as early as the beginnings of the City of Vancouver, after the arrival of the Canadian Pacific Railway in 1887, the missionaries of culture and civilization stated quite clearly who their foes were and what was needed. For Gertrude Mellon, prominent social activist and "mother" of the Art, Historical and Scientific Association, it was the "usual concomitants of all the nationalities." For Mellon, they were "all bent on one goal, the participation in the wealth and natural advantages of a glorious heritage not yet encroached upon by the hand of man." If not restrained, she said, "a harvest of corruption and unhealthy surroundings" would be the natural consequence. Restraint for Mellon, as for others, meant civilizing and refining, for inspiring taste and a spirit of inquiry, and for providing rational (i.e., healthy) forms of recreation. Restraint also meant consciously including as members both socially active women and the more prominent of one of the city's "barbarian" groups, the Japanese.

In recognition of the role of women in the formation and management of the association, the AHSA elected women to both the vice-presidency and presidency. And significantly, until the City built a public museum for the AHSA collection, in 1905, the association counted a few Japanese diplomats and clergymen among its executive membership. Among other such foes, targeted for the civilizing mission, were professionals, businessmen, and skilled workers - "all sorts and conditions of men and women who regard their daily vocations as something higher than mere wage earning drudgery".

At risk of the seamier parts of boomtown life, the YMCA and YWCA targeted those "Young men [and women]... way from home and moral restraint ... on the downward road to destruction" (Vigilant, author of a letter- to- the-editor in support of a YMCA, 1886). For young adults, a "social resort" was required for protection; rational recreation; moral, intellectual and vocational training; and spiritual uplifting. Businessmen and corporate leaders, so moved by "that American spirit which keeps us all moving under high pressure" were another object of attention. So were professionals whose tastes ought to be more refined- "a people apparently so devoid of excellence in the practice of the Art [Architecture]".

All were targets of the civilizing mission. Even the oft-feared "great masses of people" were to be included. For the "great masses," the AHSA created a public museum - a necessity of every highly civilized community," designed to provide them with a place for "recreation and happiness ... to think and study and from such casual visits [to] carry away a desire and intention to further investigate and receive educational benefits from". What sort of education depends on how one understands and values the artifacts and curios on display, the "spoils of the empire," as Willinsky (1998) would say. Finally there were those in the environment who as "savage and uncivilized peoples [local First Nations peoples]" were not to be included, except as objects of study. As Hill-Tout said, in his address to the AHSA, and particularly to the business community, these savages "reveal to us the steps and stages by which the advanced races of the world have reached their present intellectual position and attainments, and because they show us the origins and meaning of many of our own customs and beliefs."

Now it must be pointed out that these educational missionaries were nbt of a single group; they represented separate, though often overlapping constituencies and they conveyed somewhat different messages. The AHSA held the premier position in the local society, and its membership reflected that of the most educated and the most prestigious citizens, including executive members of the CPR. Similar memberships could be found in the Women's Musical Club, drawing especially from the new Tudor Revival mansions of Shaughnessy, and to a lesser extent, the Canadian Clubs with their businessmen and wives. The Arts and Crafts Association, on the other hand, incorporated the more Romantic and communitarian philosophies of John Ruskin and William Morris. It included as members anyone skilled in the arts and crafts, from architects and photographers to bakers and cabinet makers.

A contingent of women artists, supported by a constitutionally guaranteed vice-presidency, rounded out this daring group. The natural history associations also reflected more cosmopolitan memberships, including stenographers and school teachers. The membership of these clubs and societies generally reflected the dominant English and Anglican elements of the local population. Finally, and in contrast, an even more modest and inclusive membership filled the ranks of the YMC A and YWCA, as well as the Burrard Literary Club (BLC). While their leadership represented the business community, the Y's and the BLC general membership were more Canadian, Scottish, Irish and Welsh, and more middle-brow Protestant (Presbyterian, Methodist).

Their members included preponderance of skilled

tradesmen and apprentices, clerks, and in the case of the BLC, at least one Japanese diplomat. The popularity of the 'Y' idea is such that other 'YMCAs' also existed in Vancouver: the Chinese YMCA, the YMCA (Japanese Branch), and the Jewish Young Men's Christian Association [sic]. The leading clubs and societies, such as the AHSA, were quite English and Anglican. Regardless of social position and organizational goals and programs, the message of all the associations always pointed towards the value of mutual learning and enlightenment, art and nature, culture and civilization.

Hear, for example, the inspirational words of Reverend Norman Tucker, rector of Vancouver's Christ Church (Anglican) Cathedral. He is ad- dressing the Earl of Aberdeen, Governor-General of Canada, at the opening of the 1894 Exhibition of the Art, Historical and Scientific Association. Note his references to the issues of both race and greed. His words are Romantic and a touch Utilitarian. As Tucker tells his audience, the AHSA aims to cultivate a taste for the beauties and refinements of life; to pursue studies that raise the mind above the materializing struggle for existence; to surround our community with the works of taste and beauty; to inspire our minds with the great deeds of our fellow-men and especially of our Yellow-countrymen; to explore the mysterious treasure house of nature and to admire and to utilize the marvelous forces concealed in her bosom - In one word, to appeal to our higher instincts and to develop our higher powers.

As uplifting and inspiring as Tucker's words are, the link to the Empire is clear. He was speaking to the Governor-General of Canada, Queen Victoria's official representative. Thirteen years later (1907), in his inaugural address at the formation of Vancouver's Canadian Club, the next Governor-General, Earl Grey, directly links the ideals of Empire with the goals of learning and civic enlightenment. Earl Grey also points to the need for reorientation away from London, towards Canada: "Use your Club as a window through which the best and the purest light of the United States, of the Old World and of the New, can shine upon the life of your town, and by the warmth and brightness of their rays contribute to the enlightenment of your city." By 1913, however, President Elizabeth Rogers (Women's Canadian Club) strongly reasserts the link between learning, Empire and the highest of civilization:

The splendid vision grows and unfolds an ideal such as no people, from the earliest dawn of time have beheld, the ideal of a great and multiplied and extended British civilization, which we here, and men abroad may unite in declaring to be one of the most beneficent instrumentalities ever given to the world.

Behind these statements is the noteworthy fact of overlapping memberships between the AHSA and the two Canadian Clubs, and the struggle over patriotism and allegiance. The link between learning and Empire was not just at the most obvious geopolitical level. It was also apparent in the origins and actual programs of learning within the whole array of mutual enlightenment associations. All of the associations, except possibly the Canadian Clubs, exemplified British models. They were founded largely by British immigrants. And they concerned topics and issues in common with British and colonial needs and activities.

Willinsky (1998) points out the Imperial goals of collecting, classifying, displaying and educating others about the natural order of the world. In addition to the public exhibitions of the AHSA and the Arts & Crafts Association, it was also important to bring to Vancouver an understanding of the world. To wit, the AHSA program in 1909, for example, ranged widely, from "The Early Bibliography of the N.W. Coast," "Huxley's Life Work," "Ancient Cities of the Euphrates Valley," "Moral Significance of the Fine Arts," "A Trip through West Africa" and "Wireless Telegraphy." And at home, there was a need to acquire an Acknowledge...of the fauna, flora and geological formations of this neighborhood [sic]". Put more eloquently in his 1912 lecture before the B.C. Mountaineering Club, Provincial Biologist and member John Davidson intoned:

Keep on! And show us that your mental faculties are equal to your physical powers, that you are able to force your way through the dense bush of elementary botany, ascend to the summit and obtain the wider view which results from your overcoming obstacles, and rising to a higher level than that which you started.

Similarly, in a plea for literary societies, W. R. Dunlop in 1914 argues that:

The Literary Society . . . apart from the social function it may fulfill has too often been regarded with a passive complacency by the majority.... Yet it deserves practical recognition. If not a brilliant electric light it is at least a lamp; and its members, like [R. L. Stevenson's lamplighter, are helping to 'knock a luminous hole in the dusk.

In all the associations, questions arose over the utility of intellectual and aesthetic cultivation in the rugged, undeveloped, capitalistic West. Each association addressed the issue in its own way, with les- sons provided in arts and crafts, scientific research, historical study, music, and debate and public speaking. It was not an easy balance, but a necessary one, particularly if the more noble ideas were to survive rather lean support and to find expression. In the most practical and commercial of the mutual learning associations, the YMCA, with its emphases on sport and spiritual development, the question was answered this way: "The higher purpose of the work is to make possible a larger life, a broader mental horizon and the development of a manly, Christian character. It is at the same time specially adapted to increase the immediate efficiency and earning capacity of the students". Vancouver's YMCA started the city's first public program of adult vocational education in 1906. So successful was this experiment that, in 1910, the Vancouver Board of Education took it over.

Associations for adult education in British Columbia were formed and worked diligently to place their stamp on the formation of the new colonial civilization. While they could not fully recreate Gosnell's British life on Canada's North Pacific coast, they did play a prominent role in articulating and shaping the social actions of many elements of the city's population. And while the press always seemed to be towards utility and American-style "efficiency," there was modest success in creating local exemplars of what may be seen as the Tight' of British civilization, in the 'darkness' of rainforest and rough streets. Sadly, the boundaries of class and racial distinction were also re-asserted. Indeed, the cultivation of the higher elements of British civilization served to legitimate the link between cultural competence, status and social distinction, and to distance in the public's mind the links to business and power.

Bibliography

Ayyar, Vaidyanatha R.V., (1997), 'Educational Planning and Administration in India: Retrospect and Prospect', *Journal of Educational Planning and Administration*, Vol. XII, No.2, April 1997, pp.167-214.

Ayyar, Vaidyanatha R.V.,(1997), 'Basic Education and Human Rights', *Journal of Educational Planning and Administration*, Vol. XI, No. 1, January 1997, pp. 67-87.

Basu, A.N., (1947), *Education in Modern India*, Orient Book Co., Calcutta.

Bhola, H.S., *Campaigning for Literacy*, UNESCO, 1984.

Dayal, Bhagwan (1955), *The Development of Modern Indian Education*, Orient Longman, Bombay.

Department of School Education, Government of Madhya Pradesh, Bhopal, *Annual Administrative Report* (1998-99).

Education for All - The Indian Scene, Department of Education, Ministry of Human Resource Development, GOI, Dec., 1993.

Gore, M.S., (1995), *Indian Education: Structure and Process*, Rawat Publication, Jaipur.

Govinda, R., (1997), *Decentralisation of Education Management: Experiences from South Asia*, International Institute for Educational Planning, Paris.

Haq, Ehsanul., (1997), *Education, Polity and Society*, Shipra Publications, Delhi.

Jolly, K.G., (1992), *Literacy for All by 2001: Strategies at District Level*, D.K. Publishers, New Delhi.

Limaye, P.M., (1945), *Education in India Today,* Deccan Education Society, Poona.

Mahajan Baldev and Others, (1994), *Education Administration in Madhya Pradesh (NIEPA),* Vikas Publishing House, New Delhi.

Mehta, P.L. and Poonga, Rakhi (1997), *Free and Compulsory Education,* Deep and Deep Publications, New Delhi.

Naik, J.P., (1966), *Elementary Education in India - The 'Unfinished Business',* Asia Publishing House, New Delhi.

Premi, M.K., (1972), *Educational Planning in India,* Sterling Publishers, New Delhi.

Ramachandra, Vimala,(1996),*Women and Girls' Education in South Asia.* India Country Paper, (mimeo), 1996.

Rao, Digumarti Bhaskara (1997), *Success story of a Primary Education Project,* APH Publishing Corporation, New Delhi.

Sen, Amartya and Dreze, Jean, (1995), "Basic Education as a Political Issue', *journal of Educational Planning and Administration,* Vol- IX, No. 1, January 1995, pp. 1-26.

Sharma Amita & Gopal Krishnan R., (1996), *Bringing the People Back In: From LokSampark Abhiyan to Education Guarantee Scheme* (Document 3, Rajiv Gandhi Mission, October 1996).

Singh, U.K., and Sudarshan, K.N., (1996), *Primary Education,* Discovery Publishing House, New Delhi.

Sinha, Amarjeet (1998), *Primary Schooling in India,* Vikas Publishing House, New Delhi.

Tilak, J.B.G., (1992), *Educational Planning at Grassroots,* Ashish Publishing House, New Delhi.

Venkatesh, B. and Athreya, Sheela Rani Chunkath, (1996), *Literacy and Empowerment,* Sage Publishing.

Zellener, A. A. (1951), *Education in India,* Bookman Associates, New York.

Index

■■■